A LITTLE TALK WITH GOD

BY

I am mother – a black woman

Your child and daughter

Many days the tears come and I ask you why

Why am I the product of much hatred, abuse, human injustice – prejudice?

Is it the colour of my skin or is the fact that I am created by you – of you – the true daughter of God

In thee God do I put my trust and pray that one day the black man and woman will truly learn to respect themselves

I pray them truth, justice, strength, true love

I pray that they come to learn the significance of Mother and Child – them – the children of God

I pray that one day they will learn to respect the colour of beauty – their skin – the beauty of their hue – skin tone - hair

I pray that one day that each and every black man upon the face of the globe embrace the beauty of their black mother, their black child, their black wife – the black woman – the true Gods - Angels

I pray that one day the black man will come to respect their black woman and grow in beauty of All – all that you have given them in truth within the universe as well as of your garden. That which resides in them

God a nation without truth is like the walking dead

An ignorant fool that walks blindly into hell

God in order for us to know you we must know the truth

We must embrace our true heritage – our place in your universe

We must be unified in the cause of Life – Truth

We must respect Life - Self

We must know our true heritage because you did not make us as slaves you made us of you. You made us your children – the children of God. Therefore we are Gods because we are of you.

You created us out of your true love – a little like you but over time we've forgotten the truth that God is black and you made us black – like you.

Over time we've learnt to disrespect ourselves

We've learnt to disrespect you – cast you aside

We've listened to fools that have sold us out to the highest bidder tell us about you when you are in us all – we are like you

We've sat at the sidelines and watch as our black men and women disrespect us and abandon their children

We've sat at the sidelines and watch as our black men and women rape us of our dignity and brought us shame and disgrace in your sight

We've sat at the sidelines and watch as our black men and women disrespect our fertility by becoming whores and prostitute to an unknown system – the Babylonian system of lies and deceit

We've forgotten all hence we're become nations of fools acting as fools instead of acting and walking as kings and queens that know the truth

Yes we've lost our way because we let others rape us of our heritage and tell us we are slaves when we fully know that we are the original creations of You – God – the universe

We have forgotten that the universe revolves around us and without us the universe will die – become dead – barren

We've forgotten you God because if we had kept you we would've never been enslaved and deceived by nations that have no regard for life – truth

We've forgotten everything hence other nations hate us and tell us lies

We've forgotten everything – all, hence we praise and worship the gods of death – dead gods.

Instead of giving true thanks to you we give it to the dead hence we have become like unto the walking dead. We have no life hence we die.

We've forgotten that Life cannot die and truth can never die because it is what keeps us going

What keeps this universe revolving – birthing – giving birth to new life.

We've forgotten that we were the ones to give birth to good and evil

We've forgotten that all life came from us through the gift of Life – birth - truth

Now we have abandoned All and BLACK MOTHER PRAYS for all – Life once again

The tears flow God as my spirit weeps for children that have forgotten their own – Life.

MICHELLE J. LYONS

My peeps I don't know if the title of this book is appropriate because I had another title for it as outlined in my other books.

I started out with poems but have since changed this because somehow starting with poems/poetry did not feel right and I cannot wrestle with my spirit over this. Even with editing this book poems did not seem right and I have to do the right thing in the sight of God and me as well as you my readers.

I also have to do a better job of organizing my work and thoughts, meaning keep my poems in order.

I don't know what I was thinking and maybe you can help me because I am so out of sync.

I so need help and I hope and pray that God will send me that special and good person to help me organize my writing as well as help me to make you over stand or comprehend better. So pray good prayers for me that God does this. If you don't want this tell me and tell God. If I am confusing you tell God and tell me and we will work something out.

I am hoping for the day when God will say Michelle now you can go and talk to my people and show them, hey that will be great because my peeps and true loved ones we will be on fire. Not literal fire but God will be with us and we be praying and singing and having fun the way God wants it to be.

Okay okay I am just dreaming because you know me, miss shy and not as articulate vocally. I am boring and no I don't want to hire some one to teach me how to talk to you. That beautiful job of speech I am leaving to the God that I truly love and hold dear to me.

So with all that said, I do hope you enjoy this book and yes Sister Paulette I am going back to writing romance. I have some ideas but I want to collaborate with someone on my lingerie line. Have to get these ideas out and I see the person I want to collaborate with in my mind just not sure if God will allow it. This is up to him.

So sit back and enjoy the book.

Feedback welcomed but save the swearing and cussing for later when you see me. You can tell me I have no right, but please do not throw your Bibles, Qurans or Holy Books at me. Well ya go ahead but not physically though because I don't like pain.

Yes I am opening up the cans of worms now. Dear Lord from Africa to Europe, from Europe to Jamaica will be at me now.

Yes I know you church goers are saying serves you right and trust me I am coming after you. Yes some of you are calling me Bitch. Baby girl all you say I know it. Go ahead if it will make you feel better. Go right ahead and do it all.

Ban my books too but guess what YOU CANNOT AND WILL NEVER BAN GOD BECAUSE THIS EARTH AND UNIVERSE BELONGS TO HIM AND NONE OF YOU CAN TAKE IT. NOT EVEN THE DEVIL HIMSELF BECAUSE HE NEVER CREATED OR MADE IT. GOD DID.

NO LAND ON THE FACE OF THE PLANET EARTH BELONGS TO ANY HUMAN. THEY CAN'T PAY GOD FOR IT, NOR DO ANY OF YOU KNOW THE USE AND BEAUTY OF IT.

I PAY MY TAXES.

WELL GUESS WHAT BOO WHO TO YOU BECAUSE YOU ARE GOING TO DIE AND LEAVE IT AND SOMEONE ELSE WILL POSSESS IT SO IT IS NOT YOURS. NEVER WILL BE YOURS. IT WILL ALWAYS BE GOD'S AND WILL ALWAYS BELONG TO GOD. SO TELL ME NOW WHAT ARE YOU KILLING YOURSELF FOR? WHAT ARE YOU FIGHTING FOR?

Michelle

A LITTLE TALK WITH GOD

You know it is disheartening to see what is going on in the world today. Children no longer have respect for the family structure. There is an entitlement attitude amongst the black race and this is so infinitely wrong. This attitude must stop in order for us to move forward in a positive way. We can no longer sit and blame the different races for our backwards and wayward ways. In order for someone to respect you you have to respect yourself. A blind man cannot see where he is going unless he hath vision – truth and true guidance. I know this entitlement is also evident in other races but I cannot speak for other races I can only speak of what I see in my own society. And to be honest this great sin – racial rift and divide must stop or we will all end up in hell crying out to God for mercy.

On this note to all the single mothers out there and for all the children that are causing mothers and fathers pain I dedicate Black Mother Pray by Tarrus Riley ft. Jimmy Riley. This song reaches the heart soul of pain, compassion, truth and true love.

For those that are seeking the truth of life I give you and dedicate Marcus Garvey by Tarrus Riley. Hopefully this song will aid you in your journey or request for the truth of Life – God. Know that God is the truth and he is Life of all Life and this knowledge cannot change. As blacks we must know that God belongs to all because he created all out of true love. My readers that are Whites and Chinese know that when I say blacks you are infinitely included because in God's world and my world you are black. Meaning if you live for life and live a good life you are black and there is no distinction in colour or class. If you have read my other books you will have right knowledge. No one can fume and if you do then you are not children of God but children of evil – the dead – death. From you are good no one can tell you that you are not black. Send them to me and trust me I will school them – teach them.

No come on now. Listen it matters not what my race say or if someone say your skin tone is not black. Listen to me "RUN DEM" and you can tell my race to go find and learn their history because God's abode does not have black people alone and God infinitely do not deal in skin tone because it is not all blacks are black and not all whites white and not all Chinese Chinese.

Hear me now and listen keenly. Anyone that say their race alone is going to reside with God tell them TEK WEY YUSELF" the only place they are going to reside is in hell because God's people are not one race alone and God does not deal in racism or colorism – racial divide. Know God only deal with his people and no one else meaning God deals with and deal in good which is the truth and not lies.

Now listen to the song Marcus Garvey because this song was not written on one level. You have to open your eyes because we do not know where we are from nor do we know our history hence we have become like the walking dead – the dead. Yes this is why we worship and bow down to death in prayer – worship also.

Know that a person with vision – truth is lost and will never find their way.

Without truth we are doomed to death and this is why we commit sin and die – perish.

God where is the family today?

Where is the true love today?

God look at every nation upon this globe and tell me what you see?

What is happening to us?

Why can't we escape this great sin – judgment?

God look at the confusion and killings across the globe because of this great lie – sin?

Baby forgive me but today I am angry because it hurts me to see what is going on with humans within the Earth

We are not taking heed.

Father no one cares because the lie is so good that we all believe in it. My heart greaves for the people of this planet because I know what is headed there way but yet none can see it. They refuse to listen, refuse to see your way. They refuse to let go of sin.

My spirit cannot cry anymore. I can't do this alone and I must now free myself. I have to take heed to your word and step aside. You told me to step aside and free myself because you cannot trust them and I am to love myself because you do truly love me.

You are showing me things in songs and I have to listen now. I have to listen but the tears are there. Tears there for them because I know things will be no different from the time of Noah and if they don't listen now there will be no saving them.

I know time and time again you have shown them and none have clung to you. None have clung to your words and teachings because even when you take them out of their pit they fall back into it.

God I know you and I cannot let them take my soul from me. I cannot let them take my soul from you. I cannot let them rape me of my dignity; I cannot let wicked people break me because I know the goodness of you. I know the goodness and the beauty of your abode, the beauty and goodness in you.

I grieve for you, knowing that you have done so much good for humanity and they have turned from you – turned against you.

God they cannot see how perfect the lie was. They cannot see just how cunning this man is. He wants to get into paradise to cause more chaos but he cannot. He's married us, married your children because this is his hope to get to you but he does not know that even though he's married us he cannot get in because we will take his way and that was what we did. We took his language, his way of life, his way of doing things, greed, murder, rape, slavery, starvation, everything that is his we took but he does not know, we do not know that all that he does to rape us of our dignity he cannot enter the kingdom, your kingdom.

Father, look at us, truly look at the shame we have brought unto you. I too have brought you shame and disgrace and I do hope with all the love you have for me you will truly forgive me and accept my repentance. I don't want to sin no more father, I don't want to sin no more. This life of sin is too hard, I don't need it and I don't want it. It makes you ignorant and stupid, intellectually stupid and foolish.

It's caused me to hate, lust after vanity, it's costing me my home with you in paradise and I don't want or need sin anymore. I do not want or need to live like a fool anymore.

Father you took me out of my home and brought me into a place where you showed me just how truthful the devil can make his lies. Father I learned because after hearing just how perfect this man told his lie I told him thank you and until this day he does not know why I told him thank you. If he reads this book he will now know why I said thank you. I was there father, I was there and many evenings I cried, I begged you to take me out of there and you did. You took me out of hell because that was like hell unto me.

Now I am free but I am not truly free because I need lies out of my life. I do not need it coming from mouth because this I am guilty of.

I need to be free of it all. I need it to be free from my life, from the lips of my children, from the lips of my family, from the lips of my Peeps and True Loved Ones. Father all I have is words and I do all that I can to write truth, yes I write fiction, love stories but the truth is in these books. Father I need total honesty in my life now and this is why I am totally honest with you and my readers. I have suffered too much and I know the cost of lies. I know it leads to more lies and eventual death, death of mind body and soul-spirit.

Father I don't want to die amongst these people, I don't want my spirit to die amongst them because none truly love you. If we cared the earth would not be scheduled to die. Father we of ourselves can save us but all refuse to save themselves.

- Deception is real
- Lies are perfect
- Lies have become the truth to us because we want it to be and now it is
- Man will forever hide from the truth
- Will forever run from the truth
- Did Adam and Eve not run and hide from it when they did wrong
- This man's lies was so perfect and true that Eve believed him trusted him over you
- She deceived us

- She deceived you
- She deceived herself
- Today we are still believing him
- We are still trusting him
- We are still doing his bidding
- God we say we believe and refuse to know
- No one want to know
- Everyone want to be true but refuse to acknowledge that the truth is within them
- Refuse to acknowledge that the truth is you
- When the spirit hits us do we not cry out Allelujah
- Do we not cry out to you
- We cry out to you because the truth is now within us and we cannot hide from it but with all that man still shy away from it. Run from it – the truth.
- You are within us
- But after all that is done, you showing them how beautiful that spirit is we turn from you
- Do things to displease you instead of trying to harness that spirit
- Instead of truly loving you and letting you govern our lives and reside with us
- Time and time again we have turned from you

- We would rather listen to lies and let it rape us than listen to your true words
- None can see
- None want to know the truth
- None want to see the truth - you
- We would rather kill to know lies than stand steadfast in the truth which is you

Father they say they have books but yet with all the books and knowledge they have none can speak of the truth, tell of the truth. Instead they spread lies and say it is the truth. Now tell me how can anyone see you?

If we accept you say we know you how can we readily accept lies?

How can we say we are going to see you without knowing you?

How can we say we know you and praise you when we still worship lies?

How can we say we are going to heaven when blood is on our hands?

How can we say we are going to heaven when we drink blood baptize in blood

How can we say we are going to heaven when lies spew from our lips

Hatred is in our hearts

We live our lives in deception, lies, deceit and hate

Greed and vanity

I was once lost too but because I pleaded with you and told you I need total honest with you I changed my ways and you are leading me to the truth and this your people need to know.

They need to know that:

- When you are with them nothing can harm or touch them
- If harm or evil comes to them it is something that they have done
- They came off your path

They need to know that:

- Hell is real
- The devil cannot get into heaven no matter how much he tries, no matter how he marries into our fold, marries our brothers and sisters. He will never get in and this he knows. This people need to know
- Heaven is guarded and sealed and you will never let him in no matter the cost
- You will never let his people in no matter the cost
- People need to know that if we continue to intermarry with his people we will not be able to enter paradise because our nature will be of this man and as it is our nature is of this man because we are fighting amongst ourselves, killing each other without cause, raping each other spiritually, we bully and take what is not

ours and then turn around and say you told us to

- Check from the days of old until now. What are we doing
- Are we not going into other peoples land, homes and taking what is not ours
- We use war as a means to do so
- The interest of National Security to do so
- We need to know that this man and his race have been around from the beginning of time and if they fully comprehend the Ying and the Yang they will know but the Ying and the Yang is not all, it is just one piece and they will never piece it together because they don't know how to and they will never know how to
- People need to know that they cannot win the devil in the physical domain because this is his playing field
- His domain
- We made it so
- We gave the devil the power to use us and abuse us
- We gave him the power to this domain and now he has us living in fear and fearing you
- He is physical and he knows all the tricks and corners of this domain. We need to know the truth because we are not just physical beings but spiritual beings as well

- We originated from the spiritual world and we gave him a way in

- Eve did and we are still giving him a way into the spiritual world.

- We are giving his children a way into the spiritual world but into your abode he is totally and infinitely locked off

- His children is totally and infinitely locked off from your abode

- He is going to die in the spiritual world

- His children are going to die in the spiritual world and this your children need to know

- They need to cut all ties with him – evil and come to you lest they will die with him

- He wants to trap us in his world and right now he's doing a very good job of it and he will not let go so easily. He will not stop until every last child that belongs to you meaning every true Jews are bowing down to him and worshiping at his feet. His people have created lethal drugs and diseases to kill nations. Now Cancer, Drug abuse, all manner of diseases is on the rise and it will not stop until your people separate themselves from all evil. He is sending you a Message God but I will no longer bow down to him nor will I worship at his feet. He is dirty and filled with filth. He is not clean and will never be clean. That is why I cling to you and come to you with everything in truth and honesty. Something he cannot do because all he does is lie and deceive. He mimics the truth but no truth is within him. No truth comes from him.

- My forefathers new this

- We had it in Egypt so they enslaved us to get it

- You taught us how to build pyramids and shrines to keep the balance and tell the truth of our origins it was done not only in Egypt but in all of Africa – all your lands. They stole the art of making pyramids from us hence they brought it to the North, North America and South America and the Caribbean. They wanted what we had but it does not matter now because all that was done in the past we do not need. We do not need shrines anymore because the truth, your truth resides in me and is engraved on me and in me. The truth is engrained – etched and engraved in your people.

- Father we gave them the knowledge because they brought fear, hate and war to our people as well as into our lives. They brought their filth to our peaceful land. Many accepted their way, became a part of their domain, their clan. We fell from grace because we did not fully trust you. We listened to the lies of this man and we are still doing it until this day. They brought the filth of their religion and religious beliefs in our land and corrupted it – defiled it (the land). They did pollute us with their idolistic filth – the worship of man. Our souls and spirit did become polluted. They told us we had to die and we listened. We forgot truth cannot die. We forgot that true is Life and will forever live on. Truth is goodness – Life but lies are a sin – sinful – death hence we die because we live by their lies.

- Father your people need to know the truth and you have to open their eyes unto it before it is too late. I have told you that they need to know and once you tell them if they reject the truth this time around leave them to their fate because they are telling you that they don't respect you nor do they need you.

- They would rather go to hell with this man

- They rather his lies and not the truth

- They rather live his way and not your way

- They would rather stay ignorant, hate and kill each other because they are happy doing this, living this way, his way – the way of stress and hate – loneliness – death.

- They are telling you Fuck You

- ***They are saying you are the liar***

- They are telling you unconditionally that they do not truly love you or need you.

- They are telling you unconditionally that they love this man and his worship more than you and your truth.

- They are telling you unconditionally that they want to reside with him in his kingdom – they want to die.

- They are telling you Paradise, the kingdom of your abode means nothing to them and will continue to mean nothing to them because they made hell their home.

- They are telling you that they have chosen not just for them but for future generations to come – their children and grandchildren.

- They are telling you that the children they bare out of the womb they have dedicated them unto this man

- They are telling you to continue to go because you are not needed anymore, they are doing just fine without you.

Father just as he lied to Eve and gave her half truth he is doing it today. Giving half truth and this is why he has religion. Religion will never give the full truth and he knows this.

He uses this to trap – kill the soul and spirit

Father he took Eve out this is how good this man is

He took her out

He took the rest of our people out

Showed them how beautiful life is living his way but he never showed them their deaths and debts – their burdensome soul.

He showed us that we will not die because we lived but it is a pity that we believed him because we did die. We do die because life cannot die it is eternal – infinite. We can no longer communicate with you face to face, we can no longer walk freely from your abode to earth and from earth back to your abode, we can no longer walk naked without clothes, we could no longer live forever and be happy.

He knew he was not a spiritual being but physical in every aspect of life.

All he knows is the physical and this is why he created murder, showed his children how to murder and kill like him so that the earth will be dirty – filthy hence keeping you out of your own abode.

If he cannot get into Paradise he is going to do all that it takes to tell the truth about his abode and he did tell Eve but he did not tell her of her abode because he knew not of that abode. He lied to her, made his lies to look like the truth.

He knew not the joys of Your abode which is not heaven or Paradise as we know

He knew and will forever know that he will never get to your abode because the abode he reside in is made of darkness, pure evil, sin and whatever he gives darkness must surround it. Darkness must be in the background.

He knows his power is of the physical realm and not of the spiritual.

He knows he's death – Sin

He kills and all those that have died in death they give him the power to remain in the physical and do damage

Father you have to educate right. Your people must once again know that you are spiritual, pure energy and not because we cannot see you it does not mean that we cannot communicate with you. We can communicate with you but communicate how?

We know of vibrations but we cannot vibrate the body at will.

Father you have to communicate the truth to them, the full truth without a shadow of a doubt.

Father you cannot let negative energy and deceit blind the world to the atrocities of man anymore. If you continue to let this happen you will be as guilty as man. You cannot say you truly love and let evil continue to dominate when you of yourself can do something about it. There are children hurting; families hurting, people dying and starving and you cannot under any circumstances let this continue to happen. If it continues to happen you of yourself are giving man, humans all right to question your true love and integrity. Yes I know you cannot interfere with evil but you can redeem and reclaim your people.

God something must be done to clean the filth up on planet earth and despite what we have done in the past, despite what is happening you cannot turn a blind eye to it. Everything originated with you and despite giving us WILL, we are still making the wrong decisions. We need you to direct us.

We fight amongst each other, kill each other and not one of us knows what we are fighting for. Man cannot comprehend that the physical is just a state of Being and what we do here in the physical affect us in the spiritual and it has to stop.

You have to help to shut down spiritual and physical evil. You have to help us to close – shut all the backdoors to spiritual and physical evil. I know time because spiritual time and physical time existed as one; better put they were unified and were not out of sync. I know this and you cannot persist on separating the two. I know if you let them come together right away man will be doomed and you have to spread time out. You have to allot time for certain things to happen but you cannot anymore.

Have you not learnt from the past? If man refuse to listen this time around let their destruction take fold because we are telling you that we do not care and no matter how much you love us you have to do as the time of old. You have to truly leave us alone. You cannot warn anymore. You cannot save anymore because we are the ones that do not want saving. We are telling you we don't want saving so you have to let us be. You cannot let us as humans spit in your face anymore. You have to know when to walk away and not let us hurt you anymore because you cannot show and continuously show and no one is listening.

- ***Have we not lied on you enough?***

- ***Have we not turned from you enough?***

- ***So why are you being a sucker for punishment when it comes to us – humanity?***

If we are telling you we don't love you by our actions why the hell are you sticking around? Come on now don't let me truly get mad at you. Look at us, what the hell are we doing? We are fucking up the planet, we fucked it so bad that nature is trying to fix the damage that we have done and can't. Nature has been defeated by man why the hell are you letting man defeat you?

- ***Why the hell are you playing our games?***

- ***You are not like man***

- ***You are not like any of us so why are you letting man spit in your face when we know we can do better.***

- ***Baby if someone tells you time and time again they don't care, they don't love you why the hell are you hanging on and putting up with the pain and abuse?***

Come on now God truly love your damned self because we don't care. From the Garden of Eden until

<u>now what have we taught you and you are still not learning. Stop being a damn big head bud for humans and respect and truly love your damned self. Come on now. I know when to walk away why cant you?</u>

I love you dearly and you told me in Love is Calling I was foolish because you were always there for me. Now I am telling you not to be a fool to man. Turn from evil, the evil ones and look to the ones that truly love you and have been there for you. Those are the people that will not fail you because they aim on holding on steadfast to you. They are your roots and they truly love you. The ones that truly love you and do not base anything that they do on what you can do for them – material gain. They do because they truly love you and want what is best for you and in truth I am so tired of people using you for this and that.

I infinitely love and cherish you. If I had my way God, Lovey and Eternal Father I would do so much good unto you that you would cry tears of joy – true love. God if only if only my dear because you know me as well as the full truth, if only infinitely trust me I would more than show you.

God I too have sinned and I refuse to take myself out of the picture because I am guilty also.

Sweetie I love you wholeheartedly – unconditionally and the one thing I have told you is that I cannot be fake with you and people do not understand this. They will never comprehend this. Baby I can only tell you how I feel it is up to you to listen and truly learn from my truth – unconditional love..

- You are truth and love
- You are the light in the darkness
- Night and day – true goodness

- You are family
- Husband
- Wife
- Friend
- Confidant
- All to me

There are a lot of people that truly love you and would like to live and walk in your footsteps. It is up to you now to accept them and build your true kingdom with them. You cannot shut them out anymore. Do not disappoint us and do something about it because as ***it is man does not know that their time is almost up and that Wormwood is real. It is on the way to this planet and it will take shape. They do not know that Noah's Ark is now. Right now and the door is almost closed.***

They still cannot comprehend the scope of this meteor and many will be too late when they realize this. This is no joke. Billions of people will die and the oil, money and land that they are all fighting for will not save them.

Like I've said nature is trying and failing miserably at it. It cannot continue to try and fix our mistakes because it is too far gone.

The temperature at the Earth's core is rising and many will die of heat and starvation – man made diseases. Those that do not die of this will die from the meteor which Revelations call Wormwood.

Baby I don't know how much more warning these people need. I cannot help them only you can. ***I tried praying for my own people in Jamaica and I vomited big time.***

Their sins are too far gone and only they can help themselves – save themselves because you are not listening to me when it comes to them.

You are not hearing my prayer so I learned to stop. Father what else is there. I am tired baby tired of thinking about the people of this planet, knowing the faith that befalls them and no one is listening. I can't do it anymore because none is left to save them. ***I do not know who she is and if she does not live clean then yes none will be there to save them.*** I don't know if she's on this planet, where she resides, but man will have to wait and see. Only you know.

I cannot predict time, or tell the future all I can tell is what you have shown me and given me. Baby they are going to die and there will be no resting place in heaven for many of them. For us that have converted and since turn back to you all I can hope and pray for is for your true forgiveness and that you will wipe our slates clean on that true and dreadful day. I have to say dreadful because billions will not reside in paradise with you and none can blame you because they would have known the truth and turn from it yet again.

Right now billions are rejecting and it is a shame. My Love, True Love and Allelujah you have to lift the spell that is upon the people of the planet earth. You have to, baby you have to take the makeup off sin. Baby you have to take the makeup off sin and let your people see it for what it truly is. I cannot do it you have to do it. Baby you have to or we will all be lost, baby please you have to help, you have to do this. Your people cannot go down in Sin without knowing the truth about it. Religion is nothing but makeup and you have to take the mask off it. You have to let the full truth be known about religion because you did not give anyone of us religions of men to kill our spirits and soul.

Baby you cannot shield us anymore. You cannot hide us from the truth anymore. It is not working. We have to know because as it is everyone thinks they are going to reside with you in Paradise and this is not true. They need the truth, one last time Father one last time. Show them the truth and if they refuse to listen **LET THY WILL BE DONE FOREVERMORE.**

Father I know what I said earlier but open their eyes to know the truth. If we close it then we would not have truly loved and cared about you. We would not have loved or cared about ourselves. This you will know to be infinitely true. Then you can truly say you have done all that you can do for man because you gave us another chance and we did not heed your calling, we choose to die by our faith, that which we choose in the physical. **WE CHOSE EVIL OVER YOU.**

Father there is so much more that I want to discuss with you and as I humble myself to you I reach out to you for Sudan. Father as I pray for the people of Sudan and the Mother Land. Africa, which we call Nubia I pray that you truly bless the land of Africa and let your people open their eyes to the truth and come home to you. Father, from Kenya to Mozambique; from Ethiopia to Somalia, from South Africa to Ivory Coast; from Ghana to Jamaica; from Jamaica to North America everywhere that your true people reside. Those that truly love you and are keeping your faith no matter color or creed as man would categorize us I ask that you open our eyes and do not let OIL be our domain or factor for a peaceful and beautiful way of life – a good life. Let us not fight anymore for what our brothers and sisters have but know that what you have given us is well received and blessed and no one can take it from us if we do not give it to them. Father let's not give what you have given us to evil anymore. Let us truly keep what you have given us and cherish it. God let us pass this beauty on to our children and grandchildren from everlasting to everlasting.

A LITTLE TALK WITH GOD

Father what you have given us man is trying to take, and they pit each one against the other and we don't know because we have lost our way. My Love, hear me today and answer my prayer. Take the enemies both physical and spiritual out of the Mother Land – the lands of your true people and let true peace and harmony, your peace and harmony reign in our home, the home that you have given us to keep until we finally return to you. Come home.

Michelle

God what is the trend of man that we are sealed by our faith, our own destruction. Saving grace does not reside with man but resides with you. I have taken them from the Jr. Kinder Garden state to the Sr. Kinder Garden state but many will turn from this and continue to do their own thing. They will not see what you are trying to tell them because they have been so brainwashed by religion that they will refuse you once again.

God how do I bring them to stage one?

If they cannot accept the Jr. & Sr. Kinder Garden stage they will not accept this stage because now they will be moving onwards to fully comprehending you. Father they will have to comprehend the Void which they call Nothing but in truth that Nothing or Void is Something because you cannot have Nothing but Something. It is confusing for the mind to grasp this because it is so complex but yet so simple once you comprehend it.

They will not comprehend the concept of two because they were taught the concept of one, and this oneness will be apart of their own destruction because life cannot be one but two. They still do not comprehend the soul which is the spirit and it would be nice to put it simply without confusing them. They still cannot comprehend that everything is in their genes. Everything was in the beginning and you cannot will anything into being. This is impossible on a molecular and organic scale – structure.

Father I took them back to the beginning but that is not the true beginning and I do not know if they can comprehend this. I don't know if they will accept this stage which is the truth.

The dilemma and confusion starts, but yet there is no confusion but knowledge. I will try to break it down for them so that they can move forward. I hope you help me not to confuse them because all that they have learnt they will have to throw it out because that was the start of knowledge and in this chapter the previous does not relate in all degrees.

So Father, My Peeps and True Loved Ones here we go. Jamaicans here we go because this relates to you as well.

Revelations did say the Angel told John to eat the book up and he did eat it. The book went down but as soon as it got to the belly it was not sweet neither was my first book because many of you are reeling and condemning.

I know the book (Blind Obsession Rebuttal-The Truth is Now or Never) has not hit the global market as yet and when it does shit will hit the fan. Nations will be in an uproar. Some countries will want to ban the book saying it is blasphemy, racist, it spreads hate, I will be the cause of the great divide, people will try to kill me, many things will come my way and happen to me but I know God will defend me because the truth cannot divide. The truth is freedom, it is strength, it is the truth, it is honest. The truth can never be false it can only be infinitely true.

See many people will refuse to accept the truth and scientist, the clergy; my family will denounce it saying it is utter nonsense. So be it because what we do not comprehend we hate and cast it to the side.

In life everyone is looking for something or someone to save them while they go on sinning and doing the things they are not to do and yes we would rather accept lies and cast the truth to one side.

How many of you will say the bible is full or errors, some will hold true that there are books missing from the bible, some will refuse to read it, blacks and whites alike will try to lynch me, try to rock my faith, many will try to do all to break me, slander me but that is life. Everyone wants the truth to be from their own race. Whites want God and

Jesus to be White, Blacks want God and Jesus to be Black but yet none know the truth within them, that God is Energy for which we say a spiritual being and the darkness that surround us – within this universe is also him because that darkness is light but we cannot comprehend it.

Every nation upon the face of the planet want God to come from them because we put physical attributes to God and cannot comprehend that God is Energy. Our minds refuse to let us concede to the truth because once we concede and can think for ourselves the mind becomes useless. There is no longer that void within us - darkness. We are free because we know the truth and the truth have set us free.

Every race on the face of the planet is trying to disprove and no matter how God show you and prove to you you will not listen. We look at spooks and the supernatural but cannot comprehend that all is Natural. We cannot comprehend that there is nothing supernatural about life on earth. We cannot comprehend that there is no supernatural birth, supernatural death, supernatural anything. All is Natural. We as humans add supernatural attributes to man to convince us that this is true without looking into it.

We say supernatural birth when in actuality there is only natural birth, a man and a woman having sex and conceiving a child.

For all of you, who have the book Blind Obsession; see how I used the analogy of love. In one instance I said "his voodoo love" it does not mean he bewitched her or use Voodoo, or Obeah as we Jamaican's would say. It just means his love is strong, intoxicating – powerful. It is so strong that she could not pull herself away from him but in some places people will think he used Voodoo or Black Magic because our thoughts are conditioned this way.

Now with all that said and I have burst the bubble for a lot of people and make you come back to reality, come back to normal here we go. Sorry My Peeps and True Loved Ones but I had to go there for you to go on.

Some of you may not want to go on because I have just taken the fun out of writing, the mystery out of romance.

Yes it's gone for me now too. That spark is gone but I know it will come back later if not tomorrow.

Also in this stage of education there will be no music.

No songs because this stage is the serious stage.

This is life and it is up to you to accept it or reject it.

Many mistakes will be made but I will try my best to correct all. I do not have an editor or anyone to proof read my books so I am depending on all of you to correct my mistakes and trust me there will be a few until God sends me the right person to help me. Not to change his words but to correct my spelling mistakes and verb confusions. Sometimes clarity is hard because I write as the information flows and it hard at times to find the correct words in English for you to comprehend or understand. Sometimes I write in Patois but that's for the days when information flows in Patois and yes for the days when I need to vent. Onwards I go.

Sister Pat I do not have the bible in front of me and I will not be using it with this lesson because it is self explanatory. Meaning you can open it and read it and I will not be telling you which verse to go to because you would already know.

Now forget about what I told you previously – not literally. Keep that knowledge in the back of your mind because like

A LITTLE TALK WITH GOD

I've said I am moving on to another level and trust me there will be a lot of chatter.

Yes I know I have rambled on without telling you anything thus far.

"You figure," some of you are saying.

Some are saying, "Get on with it already I am tried of the chatter."

Here we go. I am hoping the lot of you have seen 10 000BC and have absorbed what the movie is trying to tell you, the trap, the slavery, the people, which race was deceiving whom by making them believe in a false God. They enslaved the people and got them to work for them. Look back at Egypt, the slavery that happened there and how God sent Moses to rescue the people but more importantly to take Life out of Egypt. This we call the Ying and Yang. 10 000BC correlates to this but this movie goes deeper and I will try my best to explain why because it deals with Blue Eyes. The girl that was saved had blue eyes.

Remember the earth was one mass of Land with the exception of four (4) rivers which you can correlate to the four different races Whites, Blacks, Indians, and Chinese. You can also correlate this to the four continents but today we have added more due to the separation of the land during the great flood. Yes we can correlate this to North, South, East and West. There are many factors you can correlate this to because the mind will make you correlate it. See it but these are minor and not major and you will see why over time or by the end of this book. The square some people say is the perfect containment unit but this is incorrect. The square could never be the perfect containment unit because it is put together – hath four equal sides and can be pulled apart to make smaller equal squares. You can add to it but the triangle and circle is different and over time you will know why. Just keep in mind that they correlate to life – true life.

I will toggle, meaning jump from here to there but I will try not to confuse.

Egypt, I would like to begin here but my mind is saying no go back to the beginning of Genesis.

In the beginning God created the heavens and the earth and the earth was without form or void. Read it clearly for yourself. I do not have my bible with me and I do not want to confuse so read it. That void we say is **_nothing_** correct?

"Yes because there was nothing there. It was dark, pitch black." This is what some are saying and some are saying God was there because when you read further down it said and God moved upon the face of deep.

Is this correct?

"Not word for word but yes you are correct."

Can you see this void?

No

So therefore there was nothing there?

Yes

Wrong

There was something there. That something was the Void, that blackness but what we do not know or what we cannot correlate was that within that darkness people resided. People lived in that darkness.

No

Yes

No

Yes

Shut the hell up

Bullshit

No

Yes

People there cannot be Nothing there, there have to be Something. That void is something therefore, the void cannot be Nothing. That darkness can be seen so to say you cannot see it is an infinite lie. This Nothing and Something your mind cannot correlate or comprehend. Nothing is Something and Something is Nothing.

Confused?

Yes

Welcome to my world. Just kidding and please do not rack your brain over this because if you do you will get a headache, and it will make you go literally loco, crazy. When you introduce this concept to the mind you are putting it in overdrive because the mind cannot conceive the concept of Nothing and Something. It's confused because it was conditioned to think within the box, and accept certain logic that we deem as illogical when in fact it is logical. Also to say Zero is nothing is wrong because that Zero is something but we say it's nothing.

So now you know we cannot have nothing we must have something.

That nothing is something and that something is nothing.

This does not make any sense to some and some are saying no but in fact it makes perfect sense because it is your mind that is telling you that this does not make any sense.

Are you with me so far?

No

Look at the Ying and the Yang

It doesn't help

Can you see God in his full likeness?

No

Now you fully comprehend the concept of void. We the children of God cannot comprehend God nor can we comprehend the scope of God and this is why there is a void there. That void we call darkness – nothing. Know that God never created a void but because we sinned and became sinful therefore we live in the dark – created that void. God never left us we left God. Yes this is why Genesis talks about a void. This void evil cannot comprehend – they are confused by it hence man cannot explain the void nor can they comprehend it. We see darkness but if you look closely you will see the light in the darkness. A perfect way to explain this is if your room is pitch dark and you wait a few seconds your eyes will adjust to the darkness. Another example is when you close your eyes your eyes will adjust to the darkness and you begin to see light. Hopefully you get it because this is the best way for me to explain it.

But Genesis says and said.

Yes it did now look at the Ying and Yang. Do you see the darkness and the light?

Yes

Is there not light in the darkness and darkness in the light?

Yes

Get it now?

Oh

Got it

I think so

Let's move on because I don't want to confuse myself trying to explain because it can get confusing. Maybe one day I will show you on a chalkboard if you still do not comprehend.

Onwards we go. God created everything in Genesis chapter one including Male and Female correct.

Yes

So we know for a fact that God did not create the things by himself he had help.

Somewhat

Come on people I do not want to get my bible but I have to. Hold on.

(

Time to get my bible

)

I'm back. A bit slow but I am back. Read Genesis chapter 1. God created everything good and blessed it. He created all the beast of the fields, divided the firmament but when it came to creating man he said, "Let us."

Do what?

"Make man in our own image." Keep reading.

My question now is who are these people, what happened to them. God created them and blessed them and told them to be fruitful and multiply and replenish the earth.

What happened to these people?

Why would God tell them to replenish the earth and subdue it and have dominion over the animals and fishes?

Remember when you get to Chapter two (2) man was formed from the dust of the earth and he did not have a wife and God gave him a help mate.

Now if any of you believe that God literally took a rib one of Adam's ribs and made Eve slap yourself and call yourself stupid.

Need I go any further, can you decipher the bible now because I am getting bored. You can figure it out right?

No

Come on people energy has always been there, people have always been there, that energy is the air we breathe, the water we drink which is God. It's on other planets, within the universe it's just that man have adapted to the environment that we are in. Not because we don't see it, it does not mean it is not there. The one thing that is true for everything is air the air we breathe and this we cannot see nor touch. We feel it on our body, physical body and soul is dependent upon it.

Everything have to or has to breathe. This planet breathes. It must expel bad air – fart – gas.

Confused?

Yes

Then I am doing a poor job of it and this is better left to a classroom where we can talk face to face because I cannot explain it in the terms that would not confuse you. I know what I need to say but to formulate it in book form is impossible because I am so going to confuse the hell out of you.

"Okay you are weird, you just peaked my interest then to shatter it."

I am not shattering it but just don't know how to put it so that it makes sense to you.

Try

Hard

Try

It's hard but here we go

- Adam and Eve was not the first set of people on the land

- The first creation is not the first creation but it is the first known creation to man or that we know of

- God told those people to replenish the land and this is disputed by some saying it is a contradiction but it isn't, there were people here before that creation and man cannot comprehend this.

- ***Those that God created were good as well as blessed and could do nothing wrong***

- Eve came though sperm, the use of egg and sperm and not a rib as the bible will have it. Look into it. I have yet to see Scientists take the rib of a man and form woman. If they have slap me and call me stupid because I have never heard of this.

- Look at the male chromosome XY, one female and one male. Get it and forget Genesis Chapter 5 where it said this is generations when Adam was created because you know **Adam was never created. He was formed meaning every make up the earth has, he has it too**. Iron, Water, Potassium, Dirt, you name it we have it. Also know that the genes go a lot deeper. The genes also refer to and represent God. How we perceive him in the spiritual and physical.

Bullshit you say

Read Genesis chapter 1 verse 26 again. "Let us make man"

It took two, a male and a female. Got it?

No because what you are saying does not make sense.

Look at life itself is there anything supernatural about it. For you to have a child what do you need? Do you not need a sperm and an egg, a male and female?

Yes we can talk about asexual reproduction or imorphaditeism but please people do no bring me there it's already complicated as it is trying to get you to think logically and not illogically. Yes think of the original Star Trek with Mr. Spock. Everything with him was based on Logic and when it did not make sense he would tell you it is illogical. Meaning it does not make sense. In Mr. Spock's world everything had its place, an origin and that had to do with the mind and how we think. Humans are conditioned to think inside the box. We seldom see outside of it and this is where logic comes in.

Why would God create using the power of two and form using the power of one. Does that make any sense?

Stop it this is not the mystery of God, and stop saying God is God, he's the miracle worker, he performs wonders and we do not know the power that he has.

That's a load of crap. Why would God do things to confuse you and bring about confusion?

Why would God take a rib from Adam and create Eve when there were people outside of the Garden of Eden and Eve was not the only person in the Garden of Eden. Eve was never the mother of civilization. If she was how do you account for the other races on the planet?

How did the White race came into being?

How did the Chinese race come into being?

The simple fact is that we do not know but in fact we do know and because of ignorance and prejudice we keep hiding the truth.

Before I go further I am going to tell you and know the truth. Now I am going to go to Egypt and tell all of you Egyptians that no matter how you try to hide the truth and cheat the black people out of their rightful land and heritage you will infinitely never ever win because the lots of you are Babylonians that go around and steal. You are all fucking thieves hence you're all the fucking princes of Persia. A band of motherfucking

thieves that rape, rob and destroy. This is all you know hence you conquered Egypt but like I've said in my other books God will never give you life because you are not truthful to life you are all truthful to death because you're all death's children. None of you can dispute this. So matter how you say that the great Kings and Queens of Egypt where white it matters to me not because guess what the white race came from the black race. It is in our genes hence you have the Ying and Yang. Look at it carefully and eat the shit of your deceit. Every life on the face of this planet came from the black race and because you cannot comprehend this you hate our ass and spread lies about us.

Stop riding off the black man's coat tail and get your own damned history because you are not our people. You are true Nodites because just as God has his own race of people evil hath his and you're all Evil's children – the clan of Satan.

Oh yes you can come to me with the White and Blue Nile and trust me I will put your asses in your places because none of you know the significance of the White and Blue Nile. You know not the significance of Light Blue and White. Know that you were never the original inhabitants of Egypt so go fuck off. You are not blacks and could never be blacks. You are all a bunch of fucking racist bastards that want to feel important but you're not important and it's time we as black people wake the fuck up and respect our heritage and place in this universe. I am fucking tired of wannabees stealing our fucking history and giving us shit to eat and say it's our history.

No fucking baddy must tell us about our history when it is in us. Stop fucking wannabee and respect your fucking selves and heritage man come on.

God did not make us slaves we made ourselves slaves because we gave up God for Babylonian shit – filth.

Look at us today. We are fucking disgraces trying to salvage and build nations that are not ours while our own countries beg bread like dogs because of these Babylonian assholes that care not for us.

We fight along them for a place in hell. Wake up and build your own black nations. Stop letting these people live off your coattail. Who the fuck are they that you have to fight for their men, religion, money, women and land. Stop it. Stop disrespecting yourself because they are the same one that class your asses as monkeys and dogs but yet you kiss their asses and rape yourself of your dignity and pride.

We are acting like fucking scavengers while they eat our bread and throw us the what lef off a dem table. Wi a dog? Come on now. God no mek wi like him so why the fuck would you want to be like someone else?

Respect your damn self and stop bringing God shame and disgrace. When we stop all of this God will reside once again with us.

Fuck we take up filth and say it is God. If religion could save anyone would not the world be better?

LISTEN TO THE SONG MARCUS GARVEY BY TARRUS RILEY.

It's time you wake the fuck up or I swear by my word and truth that I will petition God and if I have to cry I will fucking cry and let him infinitely leave your asses to walla in shit with the Babylonians because you are not learning. How much more should come and try to wake the lots of you up. Come on now. Stop balling to

God bout unnu pain because unnu want di pain. Unnu want the Babylonian system hence unnu read dem nassi book and sey a God book. The bible is the fucking book of the dead – the book of sin. When unnu falla it unnu dead – unnu die.

Can God die. Damn fool fool no wonder unnu live in sin and shape inna iniquity. Unna a iniquity because unnu deal inna iniquity an go a iniquity place go worship dem God.

The lot of unnu fi bun out lacka Satan. Fiya fi unnu – damn fool. Respect yourself and life.

Anyone that is White and Chinese that laugh and say I am racist can kiss my ass because the rant above does not go for blacks alone it goes for you because when I am cussing I do not see the different races. You are all banded under the Jamaican banner so take your punishment.

Say it so I can put your asses in your place because I've told you. God's children are black and in the eyes of God. if you are good you fall under the black banner baby and no one can change this or take it away from you because you have the full truth and I will once again remind you of the Ying and Yang and more importantly the Blue and White Nile.

No matter how you dominate Egypt and steal the books of the ancients – my forefathers and change them you cannot change history – our truth and true history because our history not only started with the genes it started with God and this universe.

Sorry people but I have to rant because no matter how much God has tried to save his people and in this case I am saying the black race we ignore him. No we are like unto Eve when it comes to God. We would rather accept sin and lies – deceit – death rather than live life and chose God,

Eve did this shit and we are still doing the same shit Eve did. Come on now. All of us are Eve – the children of sin because we cannot live right or do right. Everyone of us know the story of Eve but yet none of us know that we are Eve – the mothers and children of sin. Come on now man we need to wake up and do better. Put down the ropes and chains of sin. Let it the hell go and let sin die with sin. Stop killing yourself for sin because you are going to die and I am fed up of telling you all this. I am fed up of God trying to show us and teach us and we are not learning so now I am telling God to leave us.

God is gone from us read your book of sin. The more we sin is the more God leaves us but yet we want to continue to consume the poisonous shit they are giving us to read and sing. Wake up man come on now.

We have the knowledge of God and this universe but refuse to accept the truth. We want to forever live as the blind.

We want to forever teach our children to be blind then turn around and complain.

If you know not the truth will your children know the truth?

If you continue to teach lies will your children not learn lies and tell lies – grow up in lies?

If you know not your history will your children know theirs? Come on now.

If you don't know where you are coming from how the hell do you expect your children to know?

We know not God and what he can do. Look at it if God wanted to kill you and me, he would not use water, flood, guns, cross bows you name it he would not use it. All he would do is leave. Take away the air that we breathe and we know this because we have his life, his breath within us. When we die is it not the breath of life that leaves us. Our bodies cannot breathe in air anymore so everything collapse.

So why make us die, why do we have to die?

Because we became so evil, and wicked, lusting and killing each other God gave us all an allotted time on the face of the planet which is 120 years this according to your book of sin. Know that life hath no time limit. Death and sin hath a time limit. True and Good Life cannot die but sin dies hence you infinitely know that the "wages of sin is death" meaning sins pay is death.

Get it now.

NON

Sorry but I am going to go on it's all in Genesis and now that your eyes are open you can comprehend it or have full comprehension or understanding which ever you prefer.

- Eve did not eat a fruit, no apple, or poppy seed she had sex with a man

- She let the man inside her garden – the vagina people, damn people. Jamaicans also call the vagina the garden, your oasis, your cherry, your fruit. Get it.

No

She went buck wild with one of the men outside the garden of God and that man was Adam if you truly want to know.

Adam was not a child of God and this is where full knowledge comes in. God specifically told her, even showed her Adam was not the right person for her and she did not listen. At times my mind tells me she did not comprehend God's words like I did. I am speaking from experience because God showed me my life and course of action if a got involved with this man and because I did not comprehend I went full speed ahead in the relationship and trust me it was hell on wheels. I would never wish that relationship on anyone hence I have since learnt and learned about colours and this is why I teach them to you. You must know your colours and what God is trying to tell you because spiritual evil comes to earth dressed in full black clothing. Yes this is death how death takes life. Death must wear black. So because Eve did not listen – she allowed sin in. Because she did this sin was able to gain full access to all the lands on earth. Hence sin is in the four corners of the globe and this is why you have the square, the cross, North, West, East and South. Each side of the 4 is equal 6666 which equal 24. The 24 hour day and clock all of these represent 4 which is the beginning of evil. Meaning when evil came into existence – being. Yes the bible fiddles with the story to give sin significance but sin is not significant when it comes to Good because Good have and has nothing to do with Sin. Sin is the one to seek importance when it has none. The same thing Eve did we are doing. We are giving evil life – power and this is infinitely wrong. Life and Death have absolutely nothing to do with each other. Death is death and life is life. We are the ones to give death life by sinning. If we were to cut back on our sins sin would gradually die a painful death. Eve did get pregnant and brought forth an evil child Cain according to your bible – book of sin. She let evil into her garden and got caught. The Devil or Satan as you call him tapped that bootie, tapped that ass and after he was done tapping it she laid with her husband afterwards this according to your bible but your book of sin – bible told it in a different context – it lied. Adam was Sin the sinful one hence sin rules and have dominion over the land. Now you will have full comprehension of Genesis or beginning to have comprehension of your book of sin – lies and deceit.

- Her first child Cain belongs to her lover and this is why when God was dishing out punishment he said he was going to put "Enmity between his seed and Adams seed" Read the story of Cain and Abel if you do not know it. (this according to your book of sin and lies.)

- Infinitely know that God never, infinitely never ever put enmity between his children – the children of God and the children of Nod. Yes the children of good and evil.

Get it now. The bible is like dreams people you got to figure it out and use your own common sense. Church does not tell you this because some pastors want to keep you ignorant believing Eve ate an apple, or a fruit off a tree. Some pastors don't even know. The fact is none want to know that Eve sinned. She cheated on her husband if you read the bible – your book of sin. The infinite truth is Eve never fornicated. She fell inlove with a Nodite. A child of the dead – sin for which you call Adam who is actually Satan. These people (the people of Nod) were not good hence good and evil lived side by side. By marrying evil she caused sin to pollute the earth and this is what's happening until this day.

Evil puts strife between you and others. The true and living God can infinitely never put enmity and strife between anyone because God is good all the time. Know that if God put enmity between you and anyone he would be breaking his own law – the Ying and Yang. Yes the laws of creation.

I've told you time and time again that God does not deal in stink – dirty – filth – nastiness – sin – evil. God is infinitely clean and not one thing must be out of place or unclean with God.

Know what your book of sin is trying to do because your bible is the true book of sin. It deals in filth and nastiness so it could never be from God or of God. Know this. If you were to look at the story of Adam and Eve at face value you would see the nastiness in it and God is infinitely not nasty. If God took a rib from Adam to make Eve that would make Adam Eve's father. Eve would have slept and procreated with her own father. This story is no different from Abraham and Lot. This was the Nodite way. Every aspect of sin they did hence you have it in the bible. The bible condones incest in inbreeding and this is an infinite sin and not of God. Many of us were brought up thinking this is okay but it is not okay. All that we read in the bible is a sin. It's all a lie to keep you sinning so that you can go to hell and in all honesty these preachers do not care if you sin – believe in sin because they are getting paid. This is disheartening because hell has and have them and this is why "in my father's house there are many mansions." None of them know that death has a special place reserved for them because none of them will see God not even their children and children's children because death does not play. Everything that sin and death do they do for keeps. Sin goes from generation to generation hence we have generational curses that can never be broken. Your family is eternally indebted to sin – death. This is why I keep telling you that God has and have nothing to do with evil. Once you have made that choice you are indebted to that choice. Eve got killed out and she could never go back in so what say you that have done worse than Eve. Do not get me wrong because God refuses no one from his abode. You have to be good not evil. You have to put forth a honest and good effort meaning you have to show God that you are truthful and honest to him. You are one of his roots.

People this is not a game this is reality and this is why I pester God to reveal the true truth of creation to people. None of us can go to God believing in lies.

Look at you do you not have life?

Yes you answer

Look at death does it have life?

No you answer

Now tell me why would you want death?

Why do you choose death when you can have eternal life with the True and Living God?

God has given you life keep it and don't give it to death. Your life is important because you need it. It's not fair to let other's take it from you. Listen it's better to know the truth in the living rather than in death because what you can change in the living you cannot change it in death. Know this.

God as for you I truly love you infinitely and you cannot allow humanity to continue to tell lies on you and use you as a scapegoat. No one can bargain with you for life because life is freely given we as humans are the ones to take it and value it not.

You cannot continue to give of you and humanity keeps destroying it. From the diseases go right down to weapons of death and pollution we are showing you that we value nothing of yours and its time for you to truly walk away from humanity.

If they do not take heed truly leave because you can't be giving good food and we are wasting it. Casting it aside like it is worthless. Come on now. Do better. How many times have I cried for you and feel your pain?

You of yourself have told me to step aside and let you handle my situation when I kept bugging you. Now I am telling you the same thing. Truly step aside and let sin have humanity because I know hell is full of people. I've seen hell, been there. God I know the chains of hell because it held me for a time and not even Satan I said I want to go there but this is the choice he made. Everyone thinks the flesh is it but it is not the flesh that feels pain it is the spirit that feels the pain. The pain we feel is the spirits way of saying it gets worse than this in hell so think before you act. You don't want to go there because the pain you feel will be 10 000 times worse.

God what more can you do to show humanity the truth?

Lovey you have done enough but I am telling you to truly walk away now. You cannot protect those that do not want your protection. Those that need you truly need you be there for them but for those that continue to refuse you leave them the hell alone to face their own hell and when they call to you plug up your ears meaning close them off. Lovey the truth and love of you is precious to me. Your happiness is infinitely important to me but you cannot continue to uphold of slackness and nastiness. You are not slack and nasty you are infinitely clean and we as your children have to redeem ourselves and become clean. Truly separate your true people from that of sins people. If your children say no they want to say amongst evil leave them alone because the pathway of evil is death.

They know sin is a lie and it deceives and if they want to continue to buy into the lies of sin let them be. Let them go down with evil. All they are saying to you and me is that they respect sin and death more than you.

God, Lovey and Eternal Father there is no sugar coating anything anymore because the sugar coating method does not work.

Now my Peeps and True Loved Ones you know the truth the full truth.

Now do you know that Adam and Eve were not the only people on the face of the planet?

No

Okay when Cain left his parents abode he went into Nod, where did these people come from and why would he tell God that if he went into Nod someone would kill him. He had to have known about these people in Nod. Tell me why would God set a mark on him so that whoever saw him would not kill him?

Know this also God did not give Cain a mark. God did not set a mark on Cain. This is a lie being told on God. Cain was born with his father's birthmark. I repeat he was born with his father's birthmark much like some of us have. This mark is your mark to identify you with the family you were born in. You already know about the three (3) daughters of sin. Each having a 6 in their foreheads so I will not repeat myself and yes this is why certain race of Hindu or Indian decent mark their foreheads with the red dot. This represents the mark of the beast – the mark of sin – their father's birthmark. This mark is not to be confused with the dot that some people get naturally in their foreheads. One is the birthmark of sin while the other is naturally given due to wisdom and this in some way explains the eye in the triangle – the third eye.

Read it for yourself. Do not take my word for it.

So what you are saying is that God is not one

That their was other beings prior to the first creation that man know of

You are saying the creation in Genesis 1 was spiritual beings in human form and this is why John in Revelations and Daniel gave the description of a man, a black man.

You are saying Satan as we call this man had sex with Eve and produced Cain and he Satan is actually Adam. He was the God of sin and this is why Muslims say it is Adam's remains that are in the Kaaba. Adam is there God. And he is dead – death.

You are saying Eve could not have been the mother of all living beings because there were people outside the garden and there were people, creations prior to Adam and Eve being formed

You are confirming this by saying Cain went into Nod the land of the dead – his forefathers where there were other people lived plus he told God they would kill him because he knew just how dangerous and wicked these people were. (this is also in genesis people)

You are saying they had nothing to do with the two hundred fallen angels because all that God created was good and cannot turn bad. So there could never ever be bad angels. Angels cannot turn they have to be good because they were created good.

You are also saying angels cannot re-incarnate or procreate in humans or with humans because they are clean and void of all sins. Humans are sinful and do commit sin so because of this angels cannot re-incarnate or incarnate anyone.

Yes, by George I think you've got it.

Now my question to you is how did these people get here?

Why were they so evil? If they are not fallen angels who were they?

Look at the Ying and the Yang it also represents two different races in the spiritual world – good and evil.

But you said the Ying and the Yang is God in the truest form that the eyes can perceive meaning see him in.

Yes and there is so much more but I have to teach you on the level that you know before I can give you the full comprehension. This is the beginning of your journey but you have to comprehend creation on your level first before you can move on. Creation is not complicated but it becomes complicated when the mind – brain cannot comprehend it.

And

God cannot be both

But he is. Go back to Genesis where it said and low man has become like one of us knowing good and evil.

Now I am messed up because I am no further ahead than I was before. I need to talk to you face to face for you to explain because you are not doing a very good job of it.

How are you messed up?

It is simple but yet complicated because neither one of you can comprehend the spiritual and the physical. Bring science into this. Think of the North and South poles. The push pull effect. In science you need negative and positive energy on a molecular level but on a spiritual level you do not need negative energy. In the spiritual life is not dependent on negative energy and you cannot find negative energy in the spiritual realm just positive energy.

It is not to say there is no negative energy in the spiritual realm there is but this is the in-between stage. This is what you call the stage of flux - fluxuation. The limbo stage – the stage of death then for better comprehension. Christians

A LITTLE TALK WITH GOD

call this the resurrection stage. The stage where you are at rest and awaiting the day of resurrection.

Were the spiritual and physical on one accord back then?

Yes

Why did God create one and formed the other?

Angels which are spiritual beings are created and these angels or spiritual beings were humans but in the physical form. They could not die and they did not die. They were and still are spiritual beings. Remember earth was pure and there was no evil in the light prior to Adam and Eve and with Adam and Eve. Meaning the earth was fairly young and not all the land was in the light meaning half was in darkness and half was in the light much like it is today. It was going to take time for the light to fully engulf the planet but because the people of the dark could not wait one had a brilliant scheme and he used this scheme to his advantage. Listen the man was a hustler and he hustled Eve. After the split or rift in time because of what Eve did meaning joining light with darkness – negative energy. Good had to leave because the earth was now dirty and I've told you God and his angels cannot go into a dirty land nor can he stay in it. It is not clean. Eve chose this man so therefore she lost her spirituality meaning she accepted blood and became fully human. She was no longer pure because she accepted death and this is why everyone has to die. She made the choice for us by letting evil in. This act affected the 2 races that were in the light. Know that God did not say "and low man had become like one of us knowing good and evil." Evil said this and not God. After she defiled herself she became evil like one of them. She brought forth evil from her loins and this is why she must receive her children when they die. See evil needs her because she was the one to release evil into the world. She gave evil the key to the back door – meaning she released evil from its prison. I am trying not to confuse you but I think this book is confusing because it in some way takes away from what I have thought you so far. I've given you different scenarios not to confuse you but to help you on your journey. Know infinitely that Eve was the mother of evil and she still is this cannot change and no matter how people want to take their place they cannot. Eve gave up life for death – evil and she did become evil – like evil hence we are married to evil and have children for evil. This can change in the living but it cannot change in death. Remember there are good and evil children but you can break the cycle of death by asking God for good and children before you have them. You cannot teach your children lies and expect them to change in the future. They will come to teach lies and keep the cycle of death going so it is imperative you teach them the truth.

Listen it does not matter what you think of me because I've told you hell is not nice. We complain about the heat on earth but this heat is nothing compared to spiritual heat. Know that the flesh means nothing because it is not the flesh that feels pain but the spirit. This pain is deadly because it (the spirit) is trying to show you that this pain is nothing compared to the spiritual pain you will feel if you let death take your life.

I cannot take you further back just yet. I cannot tell you of the beginnings of God and Good because God have yet to reveal this to me. I need to be purified – totally clean for God to show me the inside of his abode.

I cannot tell you of the beginnings of Nod and Evil because that aspect of evil meaning the true beginnings of evil I cannot tell you because that has not been revealed to me.

I have seen heaven and Hell and I will tell you to strive to get to God's abode because it is that peaceful, beautiful and serene.

Hell on the other hand is not serene meaning you will never be at rest in hell.

Know that we are made of energy and energy hath life and it can take on any shape and size, any form of life – good life because it is not all life that is good and not all energy that is good. If you know about electricity and water you will have full understanding. If I explain it I will utterly confuse you further.

How does water relate to this?

Water is the true energy source for all not just in the physical but in the spiritual as well. Water is like a curse unto evil but a blessing unto good in the spiritual world. This is why it is imperative that you keep your waterways clean and void of harsh chemicals. It is also imperative that we stop dumping all manner and matter of waste in our waterways. This is a sin. Water is a pure source and this is why evil cause us to destroy it.

Because Eve accepted death good became truly earthly. We now had flesh meaning we have all the makeup of the physical earth, water – blood, flesh that houses bacteria, dirt, minerals etc. Earth was a paradise for all good life and evil was kept at bay.

Oh God this book is confusing because I want to bring you on another level and I am doing a poor job of it because there are spiritual evil and this is the deadliest form of evil there is. Spiritual evil is true evil because it affects both worlds but yet I cannot tell you about it without confusing the heck out of you hence I am going around in a circle.

Angels are living but we cannot see them even though they are in the form of men and women. The reason why we cannot see them is because we accepted sin and was cast out of the Garden of Eden and this is why our physical eyes cannot see them. It is not to say that people cannot some people can see angels and spirits. These people we say have the Gift of God. Don't even look in my direction because I do not have the Gift of God to behold his angels face to face in the physical. I have seen them in dreams but not face to face in the physical. To be fully honest no one can see angels they can only see spirits and there is a big difference between angels and spirits. Remember prior to the fall of man humanity – good life had an all access path to God. Evil did not because like I've said God hath nothing to do with evil. God's children were kept at bay, protected from evil. The circle could not be broken but evil found a way to break it. Evil which is man used woman to do so and if you read your book of sin it tells you evil has always enlisted woman to bring down nations including God's people. Know that no one can bring down God's people because we are the root of God and the roots of God cannot fail him. They infinitely cannot turn to evil because to a large degree evil is taken from you. Evil is something the children of God walk away from and try to separate themselves from. Good cannot integrate with evil this is a grave sin. Anyone that is of God refuse evil this I infinitely know. Eve broke the circle because like I said this is how evil got dominion of the earth and this is why in your book of sin it said God said "to have dominion over the land and subdue it". This is not of God and the True and Living God did not say this. Evil said this and yes this is why the earth is dominated by evil and wicked people. Evil must subdue the land and control it. Earth does not belong to evil but because of what Eve did evil took control.

Know that the True and Living God controls and dominate no one. He lets you live in peace as well as lets you live free – stress free. Remember the circle had no beginning or ending. This is life – God. Life hath no beginning or ending in its truest from and this is why we as humans cannot comprehend the scope of life. We can comprehend death because we give ourselves to death. Death has a beginning and an ending but Life does not like I've said.

If we can or could comprehend the scope of life, death would not be on earth and all of you would live and not die.

There are so many in-betweens that it does get confusing and contradictory at times but this cannot be helped. Once you have sound knowledge of life and death or good and evil you will fully comprehend because everything will fall perfectly into place.

Onwards I go.

If you read your book of sin which is the bible this is why John in Revelations described these beings, angels as humans, looking like a human being, the Angel looked like the son of man. The original beings were black and for anyone to say otherwise is wrong. Even if you were to read Daniel on a same context or human level Daniel described these beings as black but there is a greater meaning and overstanding to Daniel that humanity – man cannot comprehend. Yes I am reverting to colour but in this context and content it cannot be helped.

The origin of the white race is not known nor is it known in the bible and one cannot say look at the Italians or the Greeks because white civilization started in these lands.

Your book of sin is not based on white history because according to it whites has no origin nor do they have a history and this is wrong.

Listen a man without a history is like the leaves that blow in the wind. He will forever be lost trying to find himself because he or she does not know where to begin and this is sad.

No race upon the face of this planet can take another man's history and say that it is his. Yes this is what's happening today. We all hate each other, hate the black race but yet live by the black race's culture. Live by the black standard because in truth if you read Revelations of your bible it tells you specifically that Jesus was black a black man even though Jesus did not exist. So why hate the black race if it is a black man that you are bowing down to and worshipping. What sense does it make to hate when you know not what you are hating?

You cannot hate Blacks and expect to see God

You cannot hate Whites and expect to see God

You cannot hate Chinese and expect to see God

You cannot hate Jews and expect to see God

You cannot hate Muslims and expect to see God

You cannot hate your fellowman and expect to see God

You cannot hate your parents and expect to see God

All these things you must know because God is void of hate and hates no one. God is clean and he requires good and clean people to represent him. Hence when God show you his children he shows you them as Black and this no one can dispute because black is the colour of God if you want to give God a colour.

No one, absolutely no one can dispute God not even evil because God's records are right and exact. The content of his character is right and exact. Everything about God is right and exact.

Know that God's people are Black and Evil's people are White. This is the Ying and Yang and it cannot be disputed. To dispute this means you are disputing God and his creation and this is why I tell you to infinitely know your colours. Know the energy of colours because we are all beings of energy whether you are good or bad.

You must know where you stand with God.

Now for anyone to say evil is white is disputing God and saying God is a liar because you know not of the spiritual realm. Look at the Ying and Yang for clarification. So for anyone to hate another race based on colour of skin is wrong. We the children of God know that when we see a white god or white Jesus on the wall we know that that person acknowledges death. That person or church is saying their God is death and it is death that they are living for. Hence their mansion will be found in hell and not with the True and Living God.

Yes for anyone to put a picture of a black god on their wall is infinitely committing sin because no human on the face of this planet or within the earth can depict the true image of God.

Know that when I say God is black I am speaking about the energy and signature of God. But because I am human I use black in human context to represent Good.

Know that you will have some people that will use this (the black analogy) as a bargaining tool to hate. For those that use this and say see all whites are evil I infinitely leave them to God and their judgment. Anyone that is Good fall under the category of Black and it does not matter the colour or creed. So for me to say all whites are evil and are going to burn in hell I would be condemning my soul to hell. I would also be condemning my families as well as children's soul to hell and this is wrong.

Know the category you belong to. If you are good stay good and do not stray.

If you are evil stay evil and do not stray. If evil want or wants to leave the fold of evil they can do so and walk on the true road of God but I cannot encourage anyone to do so because like I've told you God does not deal in nastiness – evil.

If you are evil and want to live for God have a life you have to prove to God that you are truthful and honest because the path to truth is not an easy one. It is paved with pitfalls.

No I am not discouraging you. You have to know that what evil has because he will not willingly give up so easily and this is why I tell you there are many pitfalls. Yes God makes your way clear for you and alleviate the stresses and pain but it does not mean the stresses of life does not creep in sometimes because it does. Trust me infinitely on this because I am speaking from experience.

Are there White Angels, Chinese Angels?

I have yet to see one but the guides that deliver the message to you are White and Chinese.

Has God ever used Middle Eastern people to give the message?

Yes, she looked more Afghani

You said you saw the Crystal City

Yes but I did not see inside of it. I saw a black lady, clothed in white around it with a diamond in her navel outside of it, meaning guarding it from what I gather.

So there are no White Angels then?

To say that you are blaspheming because when I was walking on the wrong pathway God told me I was doing something that was wrong and I did not listen. It was a White lady clothed in white with a red band around her waist that first appeared to me in my dream – vision and man did I blast her. I kept doing what I was doing and the same White lady appeared to me again and I still did not listen. It was when I was led to a black woman saw a black lady I changed my tune and trust me I learnt to behave myself eventually. So to say there are no White Angels or guides I would be incorrect and I would be lying.

Remember I told you within the garden when I went back in time in my dream I saw Whites and Blacks living in peace. When I saw the Jewish man he was white and the lady was white but the children were black with the exception of his daughter who was of mixed lineage. All the rest of the children were pure black. I did not see one White child nor did I see any Chinese. The two adults were the protector of the children and this is how it must be in the end. The Jewish nation cannot say God's children are white, all white because this is false. The Jews have the key to life this is a fact but not all White Jews are Jews because if they were they would not spread hate nor would they hate the black race. They would know the significance of the Blue and White Nile. Yes the colour. They would not write books of lies against God because they know the importance of the true Lion of Judah – the true lineage of God – God's children.

The language that was given to me, the language of God I call it, was given to me by an Afghani looking woman so I do not know what key Afghanistan hold. I cannot say this lady was of Afghani decent she just looked like them and no she was definitely, infinitely not of Indian origin.

Now we have reverted back to colour people.

Now back on board because we have a long way to go and you are still sitting on the Sr. Kinder garden stage as well as toggling back on forth like on a teeter totter.

Are you saying Whites and Chinese cannot get to Paradise only blacks can?

A LITTLE TALK WITH GOD

No I am not and for anyone to say this is a damned liar.

Infinitely know that God locks no one from his abode if you are good. Evil is infinitely locked out from his abode but good – good people are not. God's door is never closed to his people. God's people are the ones to close all doors to him.

Infinitely know if we continue to sin and do wrongs God will infinitely leave because he cannot keep on giving us his life line and we continue to ignore him and spit in his face.

Blacks and Whites reside with God and yes Chinese so get off the colour trip and let's move forward because once you get to the next level you will see that colour becomes irrelevant and only Energy or the Spirit matters. This you cannot see in the full or true state. This is because we are in a physical state and that is all we can see. We use colours to depict life, light and vibration in human form but not everything is in human form.

The life in the darkness blends into the darkness so you cannot see them – see this life. This life has a pulling effect. It is so strong that you have to be careful of this life form – spiritual life. Yes for some this is why in your sleep you feel like someone is holding you down.

This score of this life force or spiritual being is scary because we cannot comprehend the scope of this power. I do not fully comprehend it and hopefully one day God will let me comprehend the scope of it.

If man could fully comprehend energy we would learn to respect it and not waste it. Try looking directly into the sun. You can't can you because it will blind you. This heat, energy is apart of you. The Ying and Yang so keep the Ying and Yang in mind and stop being hung up over colour because when you get to heaven you will not see colour as you know it. Everything must be different, it is changed and you are changed in order to get to the realm of God.

Remember as children we use to sing in church, "We shall be changed, changed from mortal to immortality in a twinkling of an eye."

Know that this song is infinitely true but not in the physical realm but infinitely true in the spiritual realm. This is where God well no his Angels change you. Not on earth but in the spiritual realm. You have to change, there is no and ifs or buts about this. **_You infinitely must change and will be changed._** Hence I will forever tell you the life you live in the physical determines where you go in the spiritual. God cannot interfere with life in the physical and if he did he would go against the laws of creation – the Ying and Yang like I've told you. And no the blue and white does not come into play here. Like I've said because we have chosen death God cannot interfere in the choice we have made. If we are good it is different. God will guide you on the right path but he will never interfere. He cannot do this so don't say I am good and God is going to interfere. This is wishful thinking on your part and it will never happen.

You said God does not change anyone.

Yes I did.

God does not change anyone in the physical because he is not physical. The laws of creation is the laws of creation because this is where physics comes into play in regards to motion, vibrations, space and time – sound. The physical is not God's abode and never was or will be. Remember there was a connection between the spiritual and the physical and when you read Genesis you see this connection and once again I am going to tell you to look at the Ying and the Yang.

Do you have it?

A LITTLE TALK WITH GOD

No

Okay back to the beginning.

People of the Garden, White and Black and I am going to include Chinese here because this race has mixed with the black race and have kept the ARK OF GOD for centuries, whether they know it or not they kept it and whether they want to accept it, it is up to them. The ark of the Covenant – Life is the Ying and Yang.

Now here we go. You can use the 3X to one analogy here.

Get it now.

Yes my brother you can say there is three times more female to one male and to use this analogy to represent races is false. In the spiritual realm there are two (2) males to every one female. To fully explain it to you will confuse you so I am going to leave it at that. Just know this okay.

Thank you my brother but oblige me.

No because you are wrong do not give us ¼ of God's food but give us the full amount.

Alright here we go

There are two sets of people that were formed

The people of light

The people of dark

Both races know about each other

Children of light called children of God- Jews by man's account

Children of dark called Lucifer's children or Children of Man – Devil, Evil – Children of Darkness – the children of Nod by man's account

One race good

One race bad

One Ying

One Yang

Children of light were good and had direct contact with God and did things that was good and pleasing to God

Children of the dark had no direct contact with God because they walked in to darkness and did everything that was bad – committed sins in the dark – at night.

Hence you have the children of God and the children of Nod.

The Garden of Eden and Nod but this analogy is incorrect. The correct analogy is the land of God and the land of Nod. This is right knowledge. The Blue and White Nile has nothing to do with analogy either so do not correlate the Blue and White Nile here. Right knowledge this have and has to do with the Poles. The North and South Pole – Polaris. Yes people this is why they say Santa resides in the south pole because Santa represents evil – the devil. Just move the "N" from between the A and the T to the end of the A and you get Satan. Santa – Satan. The north have a greater pull whereas the south does not. One good one evil get it now.

Hell and Heaven

Heaven and Hell

Equal balance was upon the land but because the children of darkness could never be like the children of light a perfect plan was devised to throw off the children of light and it worked flawlessly. It was so perfect and true that we are falling for it today.

Are you with me so far?

No

Man. People everything that I have said can be broken down in simpler terms. Use your knowledge to figure it out

Two races

Good and Evil

Light and Dark

Life and Death

Good is life

Bad is death

There is more light than there is darkness

When you have the light of God you will live forever and this was what the children of darkness wanted. They wanted to live forever because they knew eventually they were going to die.

The children of light which was of the garden could not die. God told them this and we know this to be true when God said the day you eat of the tree you will surely die. What God was saying or meaning the day you leave me God – leave my abode you will die.

You will no longer have my protection

You will no longer see me

You will no longer be able to communicate face to face with me

You will no longer be a part of me and you will be kicked out of my abode permanently because you are now defiled – dirty – sinful.

You will have to leave my side and live in stress and heartache for the rest of your life

You will become slaves – beggars to sin because sin now owns you – control you

You would have accepted death, which is evil and this was what happened. Eve accepted death when she laid with sin. She died immediately spiritually but God left the light within her. She accepted the physical world and all its offerings and was now closed off from the spiritual realm. She no longer had direct access. She was now like the children of darkness – the living dead because she became like them. She had to toil in sin. Life was no longer easy for her it was hard.

In order for her to get back to the spiritual level she had to die in the physical because this is the only way for evil to get in. BUT go where, hell or heaven? She died and went directly to hell hence when evil dies they go back to her. Eve is the mother of sin hence the book of sin – the bible included her and tells you about her. The mother of evil is Eve and this is where the mother and child comes in. Eve was never the mother of Good and could never be.

She could never reside in heaven because she did accept the offerings of sin. She did not repent of this sin by saying God I am sorry. This is us today. We do wrong but refuse to GO TO GOD IN TRUTH AND ASK FOR FORGIVENESS.

And no God does not reside in heaven his abode is very different like I have stated before and this is where you should strive to be – in the abode of God

Everyone got punished including Lucifer or Satan or this man – Adam because he did wrong. He interfered and should have never done that. So because of this sin Man, Lucifer or Satan – Adam will never be able to enter Paradise. Hell is his domain and this pissed him off. He did not realize that once the course of his time lapsed – he could have entered God's abode but he did not want to wait. He wanted to cheat his way in and he got caught. He did wrong and until this day he is still doing wrong. He lied and know infinitely that God does not like lies. Trust me God will infinitely walk away from you if you lie to him so always strive to tell God the truth. No half truths because half truths are a lie. You must tell God the full truth at all times. Listen to me now. If God say Kenny you talk too much and you are a person that love to talk tell God you love to talk. Talking is your passion and this is what you love to do but before you do this look into yourself and see what God is trying to tell you. If you are one to gossip and carry news this is what God is trying to tell you. He's telling you to stop because he sees where you are going to get yourself in serious trouble. So stop what you are doing. Your chatty chatty mouth is going to get you into trouble if not killed so turn away from your gossip and live. If your passion is to talk then become a telesales person or a professor – a lecturer and turn your passion into something positive. Tell God this is what you need and trust me he will open positive doors for you. Never use your talking to spread evil or gossip because then you are not true to your passion. If you love Mix up and Blender just turn to the Jamaican Star every Tuesday and Thursday and you will get nuff mix up and blen blen. Laade di bunna oman and man dem keep you on your toes truss me.

Yes this is why darkness cannot comprehend the light because darkness wants what God have. **_He wants life. Know the darkness in the light because there is life in the darkness. Darkness have life and the darkness is life that void we cannot comprehend. It is confusing because I am speaking from a physical context. Know that not all in the darkness is bad. In the physical darkness is bad but in the spiritual it is different hence I cannot explain the darkness properly to you. Hopefully I have not confused you because like I said this book is confusing._**

Are you still with me?

Yes

Evil must never overcome good and right now we are maintaining and sustaining evil both in the spiritual and physical. Once evil attain the breath of life that's it for good evil cannot die and good would have to go elsewhere.

Have I lost you?

No

So when we accept darkness in the physical we're accepting evil which is death.

We are accepting the abode which evil resides in which is physical darkness and spiritual death.

Know that when you have accepted life meaning when you are walking on the pathway of God the first thing you are offered is a septre with darkness around it. If you accept this septre you accept evil. You must mislead and deceive because you have accepted the offerings of sin – death. After a time you will be offered another septre if you did not accept the first one. This septre has light around it and this is the correct septre. With this septre you cannot deceive or spread lies and no it is not everyone that is offered this septre this septre is for God's chosen only. The ones he has chosen to lead his people. Know that many will say they have this septre but do not be deceived because this gift is not a physical gift but a spiritual one. Many people want to be but not many can be because before you get this gift you have to literally live in hell meaning be bound in hell for a time. This is a test and trust me this test is deadly to you in the physical. You can literally lose your mind – go insane because no one on earth can take you out or save you. No amount of prayer can help you you have to go through it. This is why I tell you do not jerk or screw around with your life because you need it. The spiritual realm is not a joke and I wish these clergy people would start preaching and teaching right. None of them know the scope of hell or the degree of the spiritual fire and wickedness in hell. Spiritual death is the wickedest death a man or woman can face so stop dicking around with your lives. Evil knows how deadly hell is and it is trying to escape it so why the hell would you want to go there and die a miserable death.

Truly take a look at the globe today and see the mess we are creating and the shit we are doing to self. Now think of hell because all we do on earth to each other is nothing compared to the torture – pain of hell. The pain of hell is infinitely worse because you will want water to quench your thirst and none will be offered to you.

You will want to sleep but cannot sleep – rest

You will cry out for help and none will come

You will cry out for your mother but no mother will be there to help you

You will cry out to God for help and he will not hear you because he cannot interfere with the children of hell - death. God has nothing to do with hell and death and you will learn this the hard way. Listen people I refuse to sugar coat anything for you. You need to know the truth of good and evil.

Your children will cry out for help and no help will come because you have given them over to hell – evil and no one can blame evil for this because we all know "THE WAGES OF SIN IS DEATH" meaning the pay of sin is death.

The book of Genesis told you this because this was what Eve did and she died. This is what we still do today and we die. Some die horrible deaths and this does not have to be this way.

This plain (the physical) dominates who we are and who you will become in the afterlife

Can we go back to the way it was?

In our present state of mind, NO but perfection and truth is attainable. This can be accomplished over time if you have given up your evil ways and start walking on the pathway of God.

Right now in our present physical state we cannot become fully spiritual because we have accepted sin - death. We are surrounded by evil and evil affects our state of mind as well as the way we live.

It is not to say that it cannot happen, meaning humans attaining full spirituality in the physical.

It can happen if we turn from evil and teach our children to accept God – Life and all the goodness life has to over. In order to do this we have to keep our children clean as well as separate them from evil.

You have to teach them to walk in God's integrity

Live for God and not man

A LITTLE TALK WITH GOD

Teach them to live by the honesty and truth of God

Before we have children we are to ask God for this everything that is good we must ask God for because if we don't we are allowing evil to take charge of their lives as well as allowing evil to distort and teach them – kill them.

Even if we don't I mean we forget to ask we are to pray for everything good once the baby is lodged in the cradle of life which is the womb

Tell God you want, clean children that will abide by his rules and regulations. Truly loving, caring and obedient children that will cling to life – good life meaning the goodness of God.

Children that will cleave to God and never ever leave his fold to walk in the footsteps of sin or death

Tell God to show them the way clearly so that they can communicate, truthfully, harmoniously, peacefully and lovingly with him

This we must do and we must teach our children to ask God for these things before we consummate the union between man and woman. Yes there is more but you have the concept and truth of what you must do. Everything that is good and holy, pleasing to God ask him for it for that child and teach that child to carry on this tradition, **not the tradition of man but the tradition of God** by teaching their children and so forth.

Okay so far

No

What about me?

I want to live forever, live with God.

<u>You cannot, not in this polluted state. Once we die we are changed so that we can live with God. This stage is not for evil and wicked people but for good people. God cannot change evil to cleanliness because before that person died they lived the ways of evil so no matter the confessions on the death bed that person will infinitely not walk with God because he or she is the son or daughter of evil.</u>

In the physical we live for hate, lust, greed, murder, rape and vanity and it is because of this we cannot live a pure state in the physical. Know that my sins affect you and all around me. You've heard one bad apple spoils the whole or entire bunch well this is infinitely true.

So you are saying I cannot and will never see God?

<u>No, infinitely no If I said you cannot reside with God, or see him I would be lying to you and taking away your glory and soul and that would be infinitely wrong of me.</u>

Once we accept God, and not Man, meaning teachings of men and prophets – liars (prophets to me are liars – deceivers hence I call the profits money makers that hath nothing to do with God.) God gives us messengers not prophets because none of them profit from your soul. Prophets profit because they lead your soul to hell with the lies and deceit they spread. Once you accept God you will be underway. It does not mean you will not die a physical death, you will but your children will not taste death. Well no, yes. Some of our kids including mine will taste death because I did not ask God for the things I have listed above. Now that I know I am trying to teach them but I cannot force it upon them, it is up to them to accept this and live by it. It is up to them to choose life and not death. It is up to them to choose God – the True and Living God. It is also up to them to live for life and not death.

So you are saying if we ask God for everything that is good and we start walking right and living right we can bring back the balance between the spiritual and physical realm and eventually over time man will not die.

Yes because now we are bringing back God's Kingdom and you are living for God and not Man.

So why make us die then or give us an allotted amount of time on the face of the planet?

Because we accepted what man had to offer, the lust, the greed, the whoredom, the killing, the fighting against each other, the pitting of one race against the other and more importantly we have accepted RELIGION and the lies religion spread. We baptize ourselves in sin each and every day and think this is good when it is not good.

We accepted sin and now we are bowing down to sin and saying sin is our God. Death is our God when we know otherwise. RELIGION is one of the greatest and biggest lie to ever been told and the sad part of it is, it brings your soul to hell and take away your life but yet we cannot get enough of it. God has given us life and we have to stay with life no matter how hard it gets because the pain you feel God is not doing it but negative forces and people around you that are doing it.

It's not to say you don't want to give up on life and not care you will but those are the days when evil has taken hold of us. Evil isn't necessarily you it can be your children's friend that don't think. It could be your children that are insensitive. Your children that is vain and bothersome – troublesome. There are many forces out there so learn and know them. You could be trying but others around you are not and at times it gets frustrating – makes you angry. This is why I await and cherish the day when good is fully and infinitely separated from evil. Trust me if I could separate good from evil right now I would infinitely do it no questions asked. If God was to say Michelle reside here away from evil I would say take me there now. Not tomorrow, not the next day but now. God don't have to tell me twice. Trust me I would be like transport me there now in less than a nanosecond. Honey child I want nothing to do with evil because evil angers my spirit – soul. Evil is crosses and damned curse and thorn in my life. If only God would listen to me and hear me on this I would be so happy. Girlfriend and Boyfriend do you know the joy it would give me not walking in nasty places that is owned by evil? Do you know the joy and pleasure it would give me not buying anything from them? Do you know the pleasure and joy it gives me not to listen to their music? Do you know the pleasure and Joy that it would give me not to live amongst them? Woo Nelly the peace and tranquility, the harmony, the balance and union I would have with nature and the animals. This is why sometimes I quarrel and argue with God because he sees and knows my needs but slow to act. Evil is bothersome and stressful. Evil causes you pain so why would I want to live amongst wicked and evil people. I'm trying to escape them right this minute but God seems like he is not listening to me, he's taking his time in aiding me.

Does God want his people to lay with wicked and evil people?

No he does not. None of God's children must associate or marry sinful people. When we marry and even lay with wicked and sinful people we are turning from God. We are telling God that we don't care about him or appreciate him.

But sometimes you don't know these people are wicked and evil.

True but God does show you them and this is why I tell you about colours because God does and do use colours to represent Good and Evil.

So no race is excluded from God's abode?

No. Evil and wicked people are excluded from God's abode. So if you are Chinese and wicked you are excluded.

If you are Black and wicked you are excluded

If you are White and wicked you are excluded

If you are Indian and wicked you are excluded

Infinitely know that God does not exclude anyone from his abode based on skin colour. God exclude us based on our sins, the evils and wickedness that we do, the lies we tell, the deceit that we do, the whoring and blasphemy that we do.

The biggest no one of the biggest flaw of humanity today is beauty – vanity. Sin is vain but yet beautiful to the eye and because of this sin uses beauty in his regime of deceit. Oh man is sin ever narcissistical and vain. This is and was one of the reasons why the children of God came out of the garden. We could not see our own beauty and how divine we were. We were not fleshy in the physical sense. Our beauty was not in skin or skin colour but in the light and goodness of God. We were not vain but trust me we were infinitely gorgeous and pure – true. But because this man was that beautiful Eve fell for him and he used his beauty to his advantage and until this day he is using it. Their complexion was darker, cool and beautiful and they were a beautiful set of people. I told you what Satan looked like. The man is hot, cute, and fine, he is that expensive purse, or wallet you carry around, as well as show off on. The man is sexy, more than 3 hotties.

We saw the beauty of skin and appearance but we do not see the heart or the sins that lies within the heart which is the brain. This is why we need to rely on God to show us evil in it's true and pure state because we do not know.

If God say Ken this woman is not the right one for you and show her in black clothing listen. Infinitely listen because she is your physical death – meaning your life will be a living nightmare and she will leave you with nothing. She will take your life in the end so infinitely know what God is telling you and listen. I didn't and it cost me so I am telling you and teaching you.

So the heart that we have it is not a heart?

No baby that is just a muscle, the brain is the heart but I don't want to confuse you because what you have been taught is about the heart. So let's leave it at that without me confusing you. We will keep the heart the heart and the brain the brain okay.

So you are not taking that away from me?

No baby because you know the brain is the heart, there is two parts to it, a good and a bad, (will), everything we do is controlled by the brain which is the heart not your heart, heart as you know it but the heart of everything known to man which is Good and Evil, Negative and Positive, the Ying and the Yang.

Got it

Yes

Good

Man I have so gone so off track because I have yet to move forward.

Moving forward I do hope I have cleared up some things. It is better to talk face to face then we can read together to get full comprehension but since I am not face to face with you I have to write and hope that I have clarified a lot of things that you do not know.

Yes I know many of you still cannot comprehend what I am trying to say because you are still hung up on the physical because that is all you know. The physical is all that you can comprehend because a lot of you think once you are dead you are dead and life does not carry on. But life does carry on for good but not for evil. Evil must die in the spiritual and this cannot change to please anyone. The skin is just a shell for the bones and your bones are the true you. It houses everything about you and can tell all about you. The bone for those who know and do not know is a prison. It is the prison for the soul meaning spirit and as you move along in your spirituality you will know and see what I am talking about.

But we die

No we don't, the shell that houses you shuts down well die then in your terminology but the true you cannot die just like that. Man hath not the authority to command the spirit unless he or she is given authority to do so. Meaning man cannot kill the spirit just like that in the living or in the spiritual realm. In the spiritual evil dies and must die like I have said. You must pay your dues for the injustice and sins you have committed in the physical realm then you die. If you are good you are changed and you move on to a higher life.

You cannot kill electricity or energy in its true form. You can kill the body but the soul or spirit which ever you prefer cannot die. Man cannot kill this energy, because this source comes from God and it is with God that this energy must go back to meaning good life must go. Energy is divided into two parts negative and positive – north and south. Negative energy dies in the spiritual it cannot live but good or positive energy moves on to the realm of God. Yes you can call this the stage of life and death or the stage of death and change. Good must change to move forward in life hence the use of the word change.

But we die.

Eventually in the spiritual you will die and this depends on the life you live on the earth like I've said before. If you are evil you die and if you are good you live. Move on to eternal life – peace – good.

Why though couldn't God just change this, change the future?

Go back on his word?

Yes

No

Remember he gave us everlasting life in the beginning but we chose to listen to the darkness-that man that came out of the dark. We accepted death and not life. Our ancestors gave up life for death and we are still doing it today. With life – true life there is no death. We deem God – The True and Living God to be a liar and deem sin as the truthful one. Eve did this and we are still doing this. Again I will state "THE WAGES OF SIN IS DEATH BUT TRUTH IS LIFE EVERLASTING". God cannot interfere with the choice we have made as stated before. Because we chose death sin has an all access pass to earth. Evil spirits are left to roam and wreak havoc in our lives. We are the ones to make the choice to commit sins and refuse to relinquish this act. We refuse to accept life hence we kill each other, hate each other, murder each other, rape each other and so forth. We chose the realm of darkness and eventually everyone followed suit. If you continue to read Genesis it told you man became evil, followed evil to our own damnation and death. Read it yourself. Man became so evil that it repented God that he had made us from the dust of the earth. Genesis said he was going to kill us but he God allotted us with time on earth which is 120 years. (Genesis chapter 6) for those who are still looking.

I know the bible said God is going to kill everyone but he didn't he left us to our own doom. God does not kill know this. Death/Sin kills and God is not sin nor is he death. God is life and he cannot die. Noah's family was not clean. God found favour in Noah and this is why his family was saved not because of their good deeds but because of Noah. The people could have prevented their own doom but because their heart was corrupt, yes baby the mind for those who know. Everyone died except for Noah and his family because Noah listened to God, trusted God and God saved him.

Now think people if God wanted to kill everyone why would God tell Noah to build an ark, gather animals clean and unclean.

For you church going black people stop saying because he is God. Man I am so sick of hearing that. I told you and you are still not listening. If God killed he would not use water to kill, he would take away the breath of life, air. Understand now.

Oh please stop and do not let me go postal on your backside. No no not postal, do not get me upset. I told you pastors have no part in this because they are corrupt. They walk in corruption, talk in corruption, make you pray in corruption, drink the filth of yours as well as their corruption, and no matter how much I show you this you still want to defend them and accept them and not accept

God. God told Noah what to do. If the people of that day and time were not corrupt, if they wanted to be saved they would have listened but God knew that they wouldn't so he went to the one person that still held him dear. He was not as corrupt as the people; he still kept the faith to the best of his ability.

Are you corrupt?

I am because I am not doing all that God has told me to do meaning I still eat meat on a daily basis. And people it is not wrong to eat meat but what kind of meat. It is not all meat or plant that is good to eat. You have to know your body and what it can tolerate. Certain meats you must stay away from and not consume it and you already know this. I have not turned to a true vegetarian way of life and not everyone can be a true vegetarian because God did not make us all Vegans. We are to consume more vegetables and fruits meaning if you consume meat seven (7) days per week cut back and eat a vegan diet twice per week. No meat just vegetables and fruits. Make a special day when you consume vegetables and fruit. You have to listen to your body because your body does talk to you and not because you jog or exercise does it make you fully healthy. If your spirit is not healthy then your body is not healthy. If your spirit is not clean then your body will not be clean and this you need to know.

But but

But but nothing

Go back to Genesis chapter one and see what God gave the people he created to eat. Know that spiritual beings do not eat meat or vegetables they are pure energy and requires no physical food to sustain them. Water is one of their sources and I've told you we must infinitely keep our waterways clean and pure because water is one of the God's true blessings. Water cleans and purify everything.

Go further in Genesis and see what God told Noah to eat

But but

No but but nothing we are not listening to God but listening to man. Know that man wrote this into the bible. God did not tell us to be purely Vegans because we cannot be. I told you we accepted blood and it does not mean if you eat meat you are going to die. Further, it does not mean God is going to punish you for eating meat either because the choice of meat in the spiritual realm is Chicken. Both good and evil use chicken as their choice of meat. Cheese Pizza with tomato sauce I have yet to find out the meaning for but I have an idea as to what it means. Please note there is a difference between spirits and angels and it is spirits that use chicken and not God's angels. You need to know the difference and the further you go on towards the spiritual realm the more you learn and you will know the difference between the two.

I told you God cannot change his laws nor can he change them to suit man

So God hates me for eating meat

No he does not. He knew from the day we left the garden we would not stay true to him so he has allotted for our misgivings. Do not think that we do not have to account for it in the spiritual because we have to. Like I have said chicken is the choice of food in the spirit world. Both sides bake chicken or have it on a stove cooking. No you do not see fire because spiritual fire is different from physical fire. Angels do not eat meat nor do they use it or refer it to you. I have yet to see this with God's Angels – Spiritual Beings.

So you are saying there were rings around the Earth just like the rings of Saturn?

Yes

You are saying these rings had water?

Yes

Read Genesis chapter 7 verse 11

Yes it is called the fountain of the great deep

Huh huh forget it don't even think about it

Now if God said he was going to kill everything why did he save Noah and the animals?

Think why would he use water and remember earth is a young planet, well more developed than the other planets.

Yeah because it sustains life

What kind of life though?

Organic and inorganic life

Does that mean other planets cannot sustain life?

No because if I say yes you are going to tell me no.

You are right about that

Other planets house different life forms because matter, yes energy is everywhere, it cannot die.

Well what about anti-matter?

Ask a scientist I am so not one.

Okay go back on board because I still say we die.

We do not die. Our shell dies. When the spirit which is energy leaves us the journey continues

Can you get it back? Bring that spirit back into the body and make it walk again in the living

No, if your time has expired it has expired.

Doctors have brought people back to life

True but was there time up?

Okay.

But Jesus

Don't even go there because you know better.

But

Think, how the hell can a decaying person come back to life? Worms was eating the carcass of that body and someone just came along and says rise and the body just stood up and rise.

Damn I think we believe in too many Mummy and Zombie stories, or the writers were having a field day when they were translating the bible.

Absolutely no one can bring the dead back to life. Well no I shouldn't say that because the dead comes back to life in the movies. So throw that one out.

<u>Come on please, not even the Pharaohs could bring the dead back to life. These people would like for you to think they can raise the dead but they can't. They need the secret to death that is why they invaded Egypt and that is why they are still in the land raping the dead. Stealing the jewels of the death, raping the dead of whatever dignity they have left.</u>

They want to get to Paradise but they cannot. Raping the dead will not help you. Yes we built the pyramids but the pyramids are so much more. Ah the beauty of home, our birthplace of light, education, everything holy came out of this land. We know about the dead but is the dead truly dead?

Ethiopia you know this. A great man once resided in your land. A great man that knew about the elements, thunder, lightening. He knew about nature, everything that were once holy including the temple of God resided in you but you turned your backs on God and this is why the bible say that your land will be desolate. You had the power of life but you gave it away.

Do not think that God has forgotten what you did because your land is hated by God and hate is the wrong choice of word. Displeased is a better word. Now Jamaica and Jamaicans posing you up and following after you. Trust me they are following after your condemnation. Nothing that you do will be loved or favoured by God because you were the first nation to turn your backs on God. You accepted the Babylonians even intermarried them and then turn around and say you are pure. Pure evil is what suits you because you trampled down God and brought shame and disgrace to him. Some of you have the nerve to say you have the ark of the convenient. Where is it then? If you still have it why is your land still desolate – barren? Why are your people starving and begging bred? Do not tell me about the Italians and other races because every nation have to account for their sins. You do not have the ark of the convenient because God took it from you. God left you to your will.

You trampled God down with your shoes. God's holy land you walked on it with your shoes and this is why God is displeased with you. You did God wrong but refuse to admit the truth. You did not keep God's land holy, but defiled the land and for that you will have more than have hell to pay because God has not forgotten the way you hurt him and what you did to him.

Say what you want but remember I have told you that God has not forgotten and that pain sits right there in the cradle which is in the womb. Do you not know how much God loved you and you turned on him by defiling him. Trust me it hurt him so much that it is still hurting him. Wisdom was in your land. Everything Holy and Pure was in your land, the joys and beauty of him resided in your land but you took his happiness from him and he has not forgotten will never forget.

You don't have the Ark of the Covenant because God took it and brought it into Egypt and because of the iniquities of the Amorites God took it from Egypt and brought it into a foreign land. Made it rest with a people that did not care for idols or man and there it resides until this day.

You knew the significance of death, so did the people of Egypt and this is what they are searching for until this day. The key to get into Paradise but they cannot have the key to death. Never will get the key to death. This is why they rape the land until this day and claiming it is theirs when they know the land is not theirs.

But it is only a matter of time before God and the dead evicts them and all that is wicked from his kingdom.

God will separate the good from the bad and WOE be unto man when he does. No money, no prayer, no nothing will save you because good will not hear, nor will they be able to assist the wicked, give them bread. God will not hear and he will seal his people with his true language so that when you all speak it is not comprehended so no matter how you marry your tongue with others you can and will never marry God's tongue, because you can't speak it, write it, do nothing with it. So keep marrying your language. It means nothing to God because your language is not his and will never be and no matter what you do. No matter the invoking of the dead, the trying to bring the dead back to life, raping of the dead it will not work because there will come a time when the dead will turn back on you. None of you know how to turn back the dead. Trust me it won't be long before the dead rise and walk side by side with you. Oh wait we are the living dead so the dead walk side by side with us. Soon the dead will feast more on our flesh. Cannibalism will become the new norm of society real soon. Man will eat man more and more because soon there will be scarcity of food on a global scale given our current environmental trend.

Like I said the choice you make today will determine the life you live in the spiritual realm. If you are wicked in the physical you cannot be good in the spiritual. No one, not even Jesus can save you because Revelations told you that everyone will have to give account for their sins.

By now you know that Jesus did not exist.

No one, absolutely no one can speak for you in the grave.

Once you are dead you are dead. There are no ands ifs or buts about this. Once you have made the choice to die you will die and God cannot do anything about this because this is your choice. You made the decision to follow death to your graves.

You can dispute me and call me all manner of names even throw you bibles at me and rebuke me but know for a fact you will die because death was your choice in the living.

God cannot bend his rules for anyone not even me. Yes it would be nice if he could but he cannot. He must adhere to the truth.

Death must adhere to his truth as well and that is death.

We know the great lie and lies of deceit by the Babylonians and we must break away from them. Why the hell should I die or you die for a race of liars, vipers and deceivers that hath not your best interest at heart. This is why they are known as the snake because they are cold blooded murders that value not life. They caused us to die because of their lies and deceit but yet we have compassion for them.

We lie on God and say God loves everybody. God do not truly love or love everybody. The reason why the sun and moon still shine is because of his good people. Come on now. When you tell people God loves everybody we are saying God loves Satan. He loves evil. This is bullshit because God don't deal in stink and nastiness so stop telling people that God loves everyone when you know infinitely that this is a lie. Stop telling lies on God because you don't know him. If we knew God none of us would make this statement. We would all be ashamed and confounded where we sit or lay.

When did God ever tell you he likes unclean people and things come on now?

God cannot stand stink. I can't stand it because it's a nasty and disgusting person that likes stink – filth.

I can't stand the smell of shit much less. I can't even stand the smell of death. Death stinks. I told you when a wicked person is going to die a horrible death they emit the smell of shit – filth – kaka – tubaris – feces. If you are walking on the pathway of God you smell this before the person dies. You don't have to know the person. You can see death before it happens because death does not come just like that. Physical time have to catch up to spiritual time. I've told you this so know and stop being ignorant because ignorance is a sin. It is a deadly sin that can and will cause you to lose it all including your place with God.

You cannot take ignorance to God and say I do not know because we all know. I will repeat it yet again "THE WAGES OF SIN IS DEATH". We know sin is death so we cannot say God I do not know. Trust me he will say did you not know that the wages of sin is death?

Your answer will be yes and if you lie to God trust me you will be a goner. You will be stopped in your tracks because your sentence will be infinite death – hell.

No one can say no because we know. We even tell our children lies are sins – sinful.

No man or spirit can go before God with lies. None. So if you think someone is going to stand up for you and say God I plea his or her case you had better think again because no one can get to God in an unclean state and trust me none of God's children, guides and angels will stand up for any of you because they know better. A clean person cannot represent an unclean one. If a clean person represents the unclean then that clean person becomes unclean meaning he or she is taking on your sins. Oh Nelly trust me he or she will lose their soul because they will never see God's abode so know who you represent and pray for.

I will repeat know who you represent and who you pray for. Someone may ask you for prayer but before you do go to God first. I am warning you. Go to God first because it's not everyone that can pray for others. Some people that pray for you are unclean. They are wolves in sheep's clothing.

I infinitely care about you and God and I refuse to turn against God. Yes I get mad at him and cuss him out like I've said but this is our relationship. This is me with God. I don't want or need your soul – spirit. You need it and I will forever tell you it is not fair for anyone to rob you of it. God does not rob you of it so why are you purposely letting others rob you of it. I've told you God does not deal in stink and will never deal in stink so you had better know the truth. Lies cannot and will never get you in the abode of

God so know where you stand with God because time is winding down. Do not be like the children of old and wait until the last minute. You all know the story of Noah and Noah's time is now. It's either you are onboard with God or stay the hell off. Evil is not dicking around anymore. So if you want to dick around with your life go right ahead but none of us can say God did not try to save us yet again. I am going to say this if we let evil win it will be purposely done. Meaning knowing all that we know and we do not smarten up and live for life then all that happens to us would be our fault. Our actions would be done on purpose because we now know the truth.

Know that death does not give back the life he has taken. Death plays for keeps.

Evil plays for keeps so good luck thinking that someone is going to save you in the grave.

What belongs to death is deaths and what belongs to God is God's. This cannot be changed to accommodate any one in any given religion because God is not a religion he is Life.

Death in the physical is very important and that is why you have to bury your dead accordingly and people do not say bury me any and anyway because that is plain out disrespectful. Do not disrespect the dead. Do you hear me, do not disrespect the dead and bury yourself accordingly.

So are you going to tell us about the dead?

No, not in the way you want me to tell you. Just listen to me, respect the dead and bury them accordingly, with dignity and pride. I don't care is he's a mass murderer, respect the dead, do you hear me. I am telling you to respect the dead. I will drill it in your head. Respect the dead and bury your dead accordingly.

A LITTLE TALK WITH GOD

Now that I have repeated myself however many times I am going to say it one last time. Respect your dead and bury the dead accordingly.

Yes mam but I just want to be thrown into a box.

You are not listening. If you want to be buried in a gold casket that is fine, if you want to be buried in a casket that is all white that is fine, if you want to be buried in a casket that looks like a Mercedes Benz that is fine but make that final resting place beautiful and peaceful do you hear me. If you want flowers around your grave go ahead. This is your final resting place. Do not say throw me in a box trust me you will regret it.

But I am dead

Your body is dead but your spirit is still alive

But but

No buts.

No one should rape your grave – rape the dead

I know what I said about my mother and yes I can do that. No, I will not be raping her but I will be taking her from hell and putting her in paradise.

Chose a proper resting place for your body and respect where you are put to rest. No one has the right to disrespect you or rape your abode thousands of years down the line. That is just plain out sick and disrespectful. It is disgraceful and a huge dishonour unto the dead – death.

Do not think that the dead does not have a voice. They do and once it is heard there will be hell to pay. Whether you believe me on this it is up to you but trust me on the dead, respect it, know the truth.

But your body is gone?

Is your bones gone?

Are your bones still not there?

So how can you say your body is gone?

Think.

But we do not have peace when we die?

Who the hell told you that?

Well I was told you are going to be tormented when you die.

Are you a bad person, are you not trying to live by God's standards, do you not love God, truly love God and doing your best to live for him despite your setbacks and drawbacks?

Do you covet your neighbour because of what he or she has?

NO

Do you willingly hurt people?

No

Do you visit the obeah man, voodoo priest, shaman, whomever you go to to hurt your brothers and sisters?

NO

Do you set up your neighbour to kill them or for them to fall?

NO

Do you hate your neighbour and their children?

NO

Do you look over your neighbour's children when they are not there and ensure that everything is alright with them?

NO, well, no because people are funny and you don't want any problems.

Fine but if you see your neighbours children playing in the streets do you not tell them to stop, it is dangerous and they could get hurt?

NO

Why?

Have you seen some of the neighbourhoods we live in?

Some of these kids carry guns and knives you don't talk to them.

Some are gang members

And

I don't want to get killed no way

If you pray and talk to God, talk to these kids gently and show them would they see you as a threat? Would they not see you as someone who cared, wanted better for them?

Not all because some of the ones you help turn against you, want to even kill you

AAAAHH WELCOME TO GOD'S WORLD

Not so pretty is it?

God has been doing this for centuries but we are still turning him away. He's not knocking anymore. He's tired and he has stopped knocking, we have to kick his door down now. No baby knocking does not work you have to pound on his door because we made it this way.

Now back to the dead, if you do all that you can and it is good why would you have to worry about your soul in the grave?

You will not be tormented so you have nothing to worry about honey.

What if I do all that is evil?

Then you can't live in peace with the ones that have done good you will be separated.

Honey you will be tormented and your soul or spirit will live in hell.

Can the dead torment the living?

Yes but which one of the dead?

Good does not torment the living but evil does.

I don't believe that

Like I've told you belief or to believe is like the branches and limbs of a tree but knowledge is key.

Should you worry about death?

No but it is hard not to because none of us want to leave what we have here on earth.

Ya I hear you.

But it does not mean that what we have here on earth we can't have it there. We cannot take our homes, money, land, cars, boats, yacht, whatever we have with us, but it does not mean you are not rich in the afterlife.

What?

Take the physical out of it people because eyes are lighting up and dancing, some of you are smiling from ear to ear.

There is nothing physical in the afterlife. It is a different state.

So can the dead be happy?

Are you happy?

Well I could do with some money to pay my bills, get a little something something.

But are you happy?

That will make me happy

But are you happy?

For that moment in time yes

But are you happy?

No

So why not make yourself happy?

How?

Go for a coffee with a friend every now and then

Go to the movies to see your favorite show

Buy your favourite songs on ITunes

Take your children for an ice cream

A LITTLE TALK WITH GOD

They are grown

Take them to dinner

Funds limited

Save $5 or $10 from each paycheque until you have the desired amount you want to spend and take them to dinner

It will take two months

So

Okay I get you

Do those things, little things you want to do, little things that bring you joy and happiness, little things that make your family smile, including you and yes these things make God happy. Trust me on that one I know.

You have not answered my question, can the dead be happy?

You tell me

I am not dead

Well if you pass off twenty years from now let me know

How?

That's the beauty of being dead

You are weird

True

You are evading my question

How?

You have not given me an answer

I did

No you did not

I did

No

Oh man do I have to spell it out for you?

Yes because you brought up the subject

Are you going to do all I tell you to do?

What did you tell me to do?

Occasionally take your children out for an ice cream, go to the movies, have coffee with friends, take your family to dinner, maybe take that vacation a couple of years down the line with your family if I can afford it.

Ya but does money have to be involved because I am not working and I have limited funds.

Can you make dinner every now and then for them?

Yes

Help your wife or girlfriend with laundry when she is too tired?

Now you are pushing it

Come on she needs a break too. Instead of hanging out with the boys and going to the club hang out with your kids for the day and give her a break

I have teenage kids going out with mommy and daddy is weird

A LITTLE TALK WITH GOD

Dinner is not weird. Invite a couple of their friends for those of you that can afford it and let them choose 1 friend

Hey you have forgotten Mr. Financially strapped over here

No I have not

Pop open a box of popcorn let the kids choose a movie they want to watch and watch it with them without complaint, just enjoy it

No I will not suggest any movies this is your time with your children

The ice cream truck comes around in the summer

And the ice cream is a dollar fifty isn't it

More

You can afford two fifty

Sometimes

Make a frozen treat and let them help you

But

Stop because all you are telling me is that you don't want to do it

Ya

Ya

Ya

Going to do it?

I will try but I am not promising

Then you might be happy when you are laid to rest

A LITTLE TALK WITH GOD

Come on

Am I telling you anything that is bad?

No

So

Okay

Then yes you can, indefinitely yes you can be happy when you die

You need a good life though

Good life according to whose standards, God or Man?

Well man, the bible

Ah boy come here let me knock you in the head with my index finger.

Your good life is according to God's standards, not the bible, not mans

But the bible was written for a purpose

And I have told you to keep you enslaved and ignorant - stupid

I can't break from the bible though

I am not saying break from it because it shows you our beginning meaning the beginning of humans or organic life as well as the eventual end. It does not give you the true beginning but shows you some of it. The bible is known as the book of sin in the spiritual world because the bible does lie and deceive. You have to be careful and if you truly love God trust me you will eventually walk away from it. The bible tell lies on God and because of this God's children must now follow it. The bible is not the book of

God but the book of Sin. It is sins book that is used to deceive and rob you of your soul – spirit. You have to infinitely respect God no matter how much you quarrel with him. You cannot let books of lies and people that tell lies come between you and God. That is wrong. I will infinitely tell you this if you feel deeply and truthfully that I am wrong and I'm deceiving you then I am not the right person for you and God is not the right God for you. Life is not for you. I refuse to deceive anyone. I would say fuck it all before I deceive anyone. Life is too precious and the abundance of truth and love I get from God is too precious for me to let go. Please deceive you fuck that shit. I am plain and straight. I will make mistakes because I am human just like you and I do have flaws. If you are looking for someone that is perfect and without sin to teach you then honey you've come to the wrong place. This lioness don't play when it comes to my honey. Naha no way God is my honey and sugar dumpling and I will defend him but I refuse to take weapons of mass destruction to do it. Hell no that's evil's baby and mi no mingle inna dutty bungle. Evil can kiss my ass for all I care. No for real people. Take a look at the beauty of life. Forget the stress for a minute and take 15 minutes and sit there in utter silence and tell me how it feels. No for real go into your bedroom and just lay there and think of God. Turn off the noise, the radio and television, the laptops whatever. Yes the children and husbands too. Feel the serenity then tell me what's not to love when it comes to life.

Look at the lives of everyone in the bible how they lived a doomed way of life.

Are we not doing the same today?

Does the bible not tell you how cunning evil is?

Does the bible not tell you if you walk in the pathway of evil you will die?

Did God not tell you the same thing?

But God does not kill

No he doesn't, evil kills and this is what you fail to realize and know.

Death killed his people but God saved his own.

What

Did Noah die?

No

Did the people that lived for wickedness and evil die?

Yes

Who killed them?

Death

Yes

When you follow the pathway of death you will die and there is no ands ifs or buts about this.

But I am going to die

How are you going to die?

I am not pure

None of us baby are pure. I'm not but it does not mean I don't truly love God and want what is best for him. I need and want everything that is good for him and this is why I am talking to you.

Your body dies here but your soul or spirit lives on. If you live right in this realm you will not die in the next. If you live badly you will die in the next. You cannot reside in God's abode if you are unclean or dirty. Evil makes you unclean and dirty hindering you from getting to God's abode.

You need to over stand death. We could not die, we weren't suppose to die but because of deceit and lies we accepted sin, thinking that sin was good and we learnt the hard way that it was a carefully plotted lie and until this day we are accepting this lie because it was designed and made to look like the full truth but it wasn't.

So back to you, live by God's standards and not the standards of the bible or man. Also remember you have to live in the confines of man's laws so no breaking the law. Living by God's standard does not give you any authority or right to break the laws outlined in society. You are to respect them.

But

When you are living for God and walking with God over tIme you will not hate. You will want to separate from evil because evil becomes vile to you. It becomes an abomination unto you.

You will not desire what others have

You will not have any desire to have affairs

You will not fornicate

You will see God and only God

You will want him to come and clean up the mess of the earth right away

You will not want to live near wicked and evil people

Your family will become important

You will do more with them

Spend more time with them

You will be satisfied with what you have

You will not overspend

You will not show off

No you will

You will show off because God is with you and you will hold your head up and be proud and sometimes you will want to say "hey world look at me,' and point to yourself and say 'I have God in me. I have him and he is mine mine mine and you can't have him." So yes you will show off in this sense.

You see it is important to know God and have that relationship with God so that we don't stray again.

I am no different from you. Although I am writing this book I am not rich or can afford it all. Honey problems have hit me hard financially and they keep coming but I am not giving up on God because I know he is working everything out for me. He told me to step aside and I am. Yes it's a song and I am. I was stressed but I can't be anymore. Sometimes you have to fall all the way down, lose it all before God picks you up. I have lost it all and I am still standing. I still have life, hope, and more importantly I still have God and he is helping me.

I am down and facing hardships and don't think that the devil won't come to you and offer it all to you. Trust me he will and this is why I wrote this to God and I am sharing it with you.

Here is what I told God

A LITTLE TALK WITH GOD

Day to day the hardships grow

No one in life but you

Family not there

There is only you

You feeling the pain

Wondering why God is letting this happen to you

Wondering why he can only love you

But not truly love you

In truth there is no pain

No sorrow

Just laughter

A passion for all the good that you do

No one sees you because you don't want to be seen

You don't want praise but better

You want good for all humanity

You wonder

Ponder

Even question faith itself

Yes even God too

The mind kicks in with everything negative

Yes it tries to sell you its truth

A LITTLE TALK WITH GOD

Tells you if God truly loved you why are you suffering

Why is it that he has left you homeless?

Penniless

Your bills piled high

You've just been evicted in the dead of winter

What are you to do?

It's cold, you have four kids

He's left you to live in the streets

You prayed to him

He knew this was coming and in all that you have done he's still not provided for you

He still did not provide you with a stable home

You have no home

Kill yourself

End it all

Go ahead and end it all because God don't love you

If he did he wouldn't be giving you negative thoughts such as this

He wouldn't want you to kill yourself

Come on does he truly love you

Does he even exist?

Shit the other side is better

A LITTLE TALK WITH GOD

There's no suffering

All you desire will be yours

Look at you struggling

Furniture mashed up

Kid's hungry sometimes

You're trapped in an apartment that has brought you nothing but sorrow – pain

Where's the love

You've been sick

You've asked God for help but has he truly helped you

Your sickness still fails you

Ails you

Look at the stress in your life

Your prayers are not being answered

Come on listen to me

Come to me and forget about your God

He can't help you because if he could you wouldn't be in the situation that you are in

You know that true love does not hurt so if your God truly, truly, truly loved you would he be letting all this happen to you.

You're smart

Come on think

A LITTLE TALK WITH GOD

Let me in and I will help you

You've written books of love and devotion unto him

Where are they now

Are they not still in limbo?

No one knows about them

He doesn't care to see you succeed

He's like that abusive husband

He's controlling, he doesn't want you to be loved or have anything in life

Everything you have tried in life to make yourself successful you have failed

So tell me who's hurting you

Who's the evil one in your life?

You've been abused so much in life

You know this

I know this

He knows this

I don't have to go into details

If your God, God was truly there for you why would he permit all these things to happen to you

He would have truly protected you

Shielded you

Shown you the truth

A LITTLE TALK WITH GOD

God isn't love

He's a fake

A murderer

A liar

Look at the world today

If he could have saved it wouldn't he have saved it?

Wouldn't he have done something about it?

Truly save it and not let the atrocities continue

Stop letting him use you

Stop letting God lie to you

He's not there for anyone

Come on your life is worse than Job

Worse than anyone I've ever known

You've been tested and tried

Wanted to die

Turn from him

You have children

Would you want them to suffer as you did?

No right

"No I wouldn't want them to suffer as I did."

So then why is this suffering being permitted?

A LITTLE TALK WITH GOD

I'm not testing you

Take my hand and let's go home

Go to my place where all will be right with you

I will feed you

Clothe you

Shelter you

Give you all your hearts desire

Just come with me to our home

A home of happiness and love

She sleeps on it

I sleep on all he has said to me

Everything is so perfect

The words are there and it sounds so sweet

I will have a home

My bills will be paid

I'll have money in the bank

My children won't have to go hungry anymore

God is this true

What this man said

Is it true?

All that my mind is telling me

Is it true?

All that I have done means nothing to you

My words of true love and devotion means nothing to you

My suffering you don't care

My homelessness

My financial woes

Tears

Pain

Is this all your doing

You are God

You are suppose to protect me

Shield me from all these things

How can you say you love me?

How can you say you are love and let this continue to happen to me?

How can you say you love me knowing my family, me, my children will be homeless soon

My bills I cannot pay

My rent I cannot pay

And instead of leading me perfectly you are destroying me

Do you not see my tears?

How is this love on your part?

He's offering more

He sounds right

It's hard on me because I want to give up on life

I want to end it all

I want to give up on you

It's too hard trying to live your way

No friends, parties

I don't even go out

Well I can't blame you for the not going out it's a choice I made

But you know what God

Because I truly

Truly

Infinitely truly love you more than you love me

Because you have taken me out of so much

Shown me so much and despite my setbacks you've stuck with me. You've never failed me but I have failed you

No you can give up on me but I will never give up on you nor go on the other side because I know the truth and goodness I have in you.

I know the love you have for me

I know the true love of you

So no, I will never turn from you or give up on you because this is what true love, true friendship, true bond is all about.

I do truly love you and I will not give in to him. I will not return to the days of old or be like my ancestors of the days of old.

God I know the deceit of sin and I choose good life over sin. I choose you. I have made my choice and now sin and his band of evil spirits and humans must respect my choice and leave me and my family infinitely alone. I choose good over evil and my choice is final and cannot change because my choice is written in God's book of life. My name is no longer in sins book but in the book of truth and no one can change this choice not even you God because my decision is binding and infinite with you.

Michelle

See my Peeps and True Loved Ones in life we are tested and tried by evil forces not just in the spiritual but also in the physical and it is so not easy to be strong. Sometimes you have to bare it alone but you are not alone. God is always there with you. Sometimes the help that we seek is not enough but you have to make due with what you have. God has not forsaken you he's just giving you what you need to help you get by for that day.

I know tomorrow is there but what you get today let it last you for tomorrow and the next day if you can. God is opening a positive door for you. You cannot see it and at times I wish he would teach clearly but our comprehension is not on his scope so the mind tries to decipher it the best way that it knows how to. Yes it's confusing but don't give up. I can't and I so can't turn from God.

Yes I would love to at times but that would mean I never truly loved God. Yes the grass is greener on the other side but guess what none of us sees the shit in it.

We know better now. The bible is there as a testament. Meaning it shows us how our forefathers failed. We should be learning but instead of learning we are still deceiving - failing. What good is that when our souls are at stake?

What good are we when we can't even trust God with our lives?

What good are we if we can't be truthful to God?

Yes I can say God screw you, hell this man is offering me so much more. Shit you're not offering me anything but pain and suffering. I can't pay my bills, I am being evicted, and I'm on my face. You are not giving me anything. Come on up the ante and do something. I can say all these things to God but what would it profit me. I am getting a quick fix now but what about my soul, my future, my children's future. What about the life time that I need and want with God?

I know the reason for my homelessness. God has already told me he cannot come into a messy home. He told me I have to live a clean life, live right. Once I am doing these things then he can come in and do all he needs to do. He's told me step aside and let him handle it and I am doing just that. I have to be patient because spiritual time and physical time is not the same. Spiritual time is further ahead. Physical time must catch up to spiritual time hence we say time and time again that God is slow but he is sure. Spiritual time can take years. Meaning the goodness that God has given you can take years before it comes to light.

All that the devil offers is a quick fix. He does these things to trap you and once he has you you cannot get out. His hold is so strong that you become indebted to him for all eternity.

You cannot repay your debt unto him. Eve found out the hard way. She died. An entire nation followed suit unto their death. Genesis told you this. The water's came and no one was saved except for a few animals, Noah and his family.

Today we are no different. Wormwood is coming. Revelations told you about wormwood. It is real and no one is taking heed so tell me how much will be saved this time around? How many people will get into God's Ark this time around?

We cannot turn a blind eye and say Jesus or the prophets are going to save me. They are dead. Yes the dead can protect you but who will give that authority for them do to so?

Who has the key to hell?

Many of you say Jesus but Jesus does not have the key. Jesus never existed and it's high time the churches start preaching and teaching right because as it is now they are held accountable for the lies that they preach and teach. Each member of the clergy will be held accountable for your sins. No, death cannot be held accountable nor can Sin be held accountable for your sins because we were told "the wages of sin is death". We are held accountable for our sins and we all know this. Revelations also told you the angel of God holds the key to death. The angel told John he had the key to hell. The angel told John that he is the Alpha and the Omega. He was in the beginning not Jesus. Read it in Revelations for yourself people. So if the angels have the key and was around from the beginning how can Jesus be the Saviour for all mankind and human kind?

Why do you go around and tell people that Jesus was in the beginning with God when Revelations tells you otherwise?

We can no longer continue on with the lies and deceit of sin and we can no longer deceive ourselves come on now.

We need to think and put things in perspective. We have to stop letting people give us quarter truths. We need the full truth.

We need to stop the lies we are telling on God.

It's about time we look into ourselves and see where we need to be because as it is we are the ones living a lie and deceiving ourselves. We are the ones to not listen. We are the ones to follow after lies because we love to be misled.

We love lies and all that lies have to offer.

We don't care about our fellow man

We don't care who we hurt

Who we kill

We are going to die soon so why care many of you are saying

We teach our children to accept lies and carry on the lies.

We teach our children to believe these lies and if God sends someone to say hey wait a minute you can't believe you must know you say the person is false, spreading lies and you try to kill them because it goes against the teachings of men – your bible.

So tell me how can God – the true and living God come into your life if you are not willing to listen?

A LITTLE TALK WITH GOD

How can God come into your life if you don't know him?

Yes there are false prophets but God does not send prophets to anyone he sends messengers. Know this and live.

There are false gods but life cannot be false it can only be good. And stop saying speak for yourself. Well I am speaking because God did not tell us to live above your means. God did not tell you to choose mister wrong. He showed you who to marry but you could not comprehend the scope of his language. God would infinitely never give you anyone or anything that is false. Here I will stress know your colours and the person God has given you to marry.

Well my children are lazy, nasty, unruly and I blame God for giving me them.

No you cannot. Go back to Genesis all that God created was good. We were the neglectful ones because we did not ask God for good and clean children.

Like you I have woes with my children but I cannot blame God for my woes because he did try to warn me but I did not listen. I could not comprehend the scope of his language hence I went full speed ahead in a relationship that cost me dearly. Yes God intervened and saved me but many are not that lucky – blessed – truly loved. I cannot leave the fold of God because I have seen his goodness first hand. I am a living testament of God's true love hence I made the statement above.

I made it out of hell why the hell would I want to go back there and disrespect and disgrace God. Evil offers me nothing but lies and deceit. God is not deceiving me evil is so for my sanity I chose and choose to walk away from evil. I have to live for truth – true love and that is God. The greatest asset anyone can have is true love because true love cannot deceive anyone. True love is the knowledge of God and the foundation of this universe. It is the foundation of God's children. So no I cannot give up God nor can I give up on him. I refuse to. I refuse to turn my back on goodness and I refuse to be ungrateful. I have to show God gratitude because he kept me sane throughout my pain and ordeals. When I needed him he stood up for me. He's been a father to my children, a protector to them and am to give that up for crap. I'm to give up God for someone that don't care about me and my family; someone that wants my life and the life of my family – children, hell no I don't love death so death can infinitely be gone from me. God is king and he will forever be mine, mine, mine; infinitely mine.

From the beginning until now we've had false everything but God, the true and living God will never send someone to deceive you and this is what you need to know. The Jews know this and this is why Jesus was never accepted and I've told you this. This man that claimed to be the son of God would never be accepted and could never be accepted because Jesus never existed. This man that you claim is the son of God is the son of death because he is depicted as white. We have black Jesus and there was and is no black Jesus. Impossible. There was never a black Jesus but there is a white Jesus. The God of Death or the son of death if you prefer is your Jesus. Jesus is death because I told you when evil dies they die clothed in full white and as a white person so your white Jesus represent death. And he is death because he is the one you believe that is going to save you. You say in order to go to heaven you have to be washed in the blood, saved and sanctified. You believe in nastiness and practice nastiness so because of this you are going to go to hell. God does not wash anyone in blood let me just clarify that. God's blessings come down in the form of water not blood. Woman pass

blood each month and for some it's painful so all of you are telling me you drink the blood of a woman's nana – nastiness. Come on now you are all that nasty. No wonder Jesus said according to your bible in my father's house there are many mansions and if it was not so I would not say so. Damn hell is full with nasty people. Nope don't want to go there it is too nasty and filthy for me. Don't need nastiness in my life. I am going to get vulgar here but can you imagine blood clots that some of you are drinking? Nasty. Gross and you say you are of God. God the true and living God told you to do this? Well I go on record as saying if God – my true love – the true and living God told you and humanity to do this then I say he's fucking nasty and he's not for me. No come on why the hell would anyone want to drink blood? Do you know how raw blood is? The true and living God would infinitely never tell anyone to do this. This goes to show you how fucking nasty and disgusting your Jesus is. He stinks because he's fucking nasty. This is what you believe in and practice so tell me how can God – the true and living God come back to earth and reside with any of us when we're so fucking nasty? You vehemently swear up and down that Jesus died on the cross to save your sins but yet the people of the earth are still sinful. If we are still sinful then his death was in vain?

If he died for our sins why are we still sinning?

Should we not show him respect and put away all sins? Come on now.

Tell me why the hell would God let his own son if God had a son die for the sins of evil? Come on now. God loves evil that much that he would sacrifice his own son for evil? Come on now people. Really, this is what we think of God. We've come thus far to class God this low then turn around and say we're going to die and see God. Trust me it's the god of truth – life you'll be seeing and begging for mercy.

Why would God sacrifice his own for sin – wicked people?

And don't tell me so that all would be saved.

Did sin tell you he wanted to be saved?

Let me tell you this, if sin wanted to be saved, all sin would have to do is truly repent and ask God truthfully for forgiveness.

If sin truly wanted to be saved sin would stop sinning and start living a clean and truthful life.

God would never infinitely never ever let his children be a sacrifice unto evil and his people know that.

Let me clarify why some messengers die. Some come with religion when God never gave anyone religion. Some fornicate like Solomon and lose their crown meaning they lose the protection of God.

When God give you an order you have to do it for life because it is a lifetime order. You cannot stray from the truth God has given you.

Yes there is a bigger temptation but you cannot give into it. You have to stay true to God.

Many of our people died in Egypt

John the Baptist died, they had to kill him and we know why they killed him. There are places as children of God that we cannot go no matter the temptation. Don't think that God do not show you where to go because he does show you it is up to you to listen.

You cannot baptise with the Father, Son and Holy Ghost

You cannot baptise with water or be baptised period. If you are baptized you can repent of this but you must go to God with truth. If you do you will be forgiven. You can say God I truly did not know that baptism was wrong a sin and because I now know the truth I truly repent of this sin. God will forgive you of this because you did not know. If you've baptized your children you can go to God for forgiveness and repent. Know that when you baptize your children you are baptizing them unto death. Death has them.

No he doesn't you're saying

Yes he does

Stop crying now come on now because all is not lost. If you want your child to live for God and walk with God tell God you are dedicating your child in his good service and good care.

Infinitely never say God I am dedicating my child unto you. Make sure you tell God you dedicate your child in his good care. The key word is good. You have to be specific with God. This can be done before the child is born or after the child is born.

Why after?

Sometimes we forget to ask beforehand.

If I forget beforehand when do I ask God for this?

In the delivery room right when the baby is born. You do it because this is your bond between you and God for your child. If you don't want to do it that's fine but I refuse to tell you to ask a clergy. I refuse to do this.

Baptismal certificates are legal you are saying. It is legal in the sight of man and death but with God a CERTIFICATE

OF DEDICATION UNTO GOD OR a DEDICATION CERTIFICATE UNTO GOD is infinitely binding and legal in his sight. If you are to get a certificate let it be a dedication one. This is more legal because it is a lifetime commitment unto God. This is your truth.

Can this certificate be broken by me?

Yes because God does not hold you hostage like sin.

So I can break this dedication certificate if I want to?

Yes but I would not advise it because once you hit rock bottom the climb back up will not be pretty. Trust me some people never get back up from the fall so I would be careful if I were you. If God is protecting you say being protected by God. Don't give up on God please. I am begging you because hell's pain infinitely hurt and you cannot blame God for your loss because you were the one to leave the nest.

Listen all that I am telling you I did not know to do and this is why I beg God to not let my children walk in sin or do sinful things.

Is it easy?

No and this is because we have children with wicked and evil people meaning wicked and evil men and women.

This is not true some of you are saying.

Go back to Genesis and see what Cain did to Abel and then come back and talk to me.

Don't let me begin to tell you the stresses that some of these kids put you through. Oh Nelly – God have mercy because you see and know and that's all I got to say.

You cannot accept the Trinity and say it is of God because God is not a Trinity. And to say God is a trinity is an abomination unto him

How can he be three (3) when he is All - Allelujah?

He never was and never will me 3 in 1

There is no such thing as three in one

Yes water purifies and cleans the inside but God is PURE LOVE

You need to purify yourself with the Pure Love of God

No one can do this for you

You are the only one that can

No man can tell you how to love God

No one can tell you of the true Love of God but God himself

I can't do it

I can show you and teach you but I cannot tell you

God is the only one that can tell you

Guide you perfectly to him once you have accepted the truth

Know God to be the truth

Have a true and honest relationship with God and all evil becomes irrelevant meaning you don't want to do anything evil

Everything you need and desire you will want God to provide it and if God doesn't provide it you feel hurt and yes you will chew him out

You will want nothing from this evil system of things

All you will see is God because you are living for him

Lies that people tell will not matter because you are not in their way

You won't care what they do as long as they don't come to your doorway and do it

You won't want to hang out with them

You will want to stay true to your God

It's not to say you won't go to the movies

You will

You will want to go to dinner and you will

Everything that is clean and make you happy you will desire and do

Cheating on your wife will stop because you will not want to displease God or show him disrespect.

Listen God loathes a cheating husband and a cheating wife. God loathes whoredom and you all know this. Whoredom is a grave sin as well as an abomination unto God. If you are living the life of whoredom you need to stop and repent of your sins. You truly need to repent meaning stop your act and truly ask God to forgive you. Cheating which is whoredom is wrong and you know it so stop it. It is not right.

I've told you when the relationship seem to be getting stale be ingenious, do things to make it fun but do not bring another male or female in it for your enjoyment.

Lay and cuddle

Play with his pudgy

Play with him

Cuddle and watch a movie

Rub his head

Rub her head

Do things together that you like

If you like your space have it so long as he knows this is your space and he or she should respect that.

There is no boredom in true love

Read together

Do you see where I am going with this?

Go for long walks

Go bird watching

Ask God truthfully not to let your romance go stale

Plan for that romantic vacation or that romantic dinner

But let God show you what to do

Let God help you to live with your mate for a lifetime. If you have an evil mate then no at least he will not get to God's abode because he will be cut off and he is cut off. Trust me on this if you are living right with God God will move him out of the way. If you need evil out of your life you need to pray sincerely, truthfully and honestly. Talk to God and tell him your troubles, your pitfalls with him or her and he will show you what to do. If this person is hurting you ask God to return the blows to sender. Ask him to shield you so that evil does not take control of your life or befall you. **_And no God will never tell you to use evil. God does not tell anyone to kill so don't even go there._** God will show you what to do it is up to you to listen. If you have a controlling or abusive wife or husband it will be hard because you are scared. You fear what they will do to you trust me it is so not easy. Evil do all it can to keep you from God. Trust me it's not easy living with evil but you can win. You have victory over evil because no matter what evil and wicked people do to you know that they will never enter the abode of God. This is your victory so hold on to it. Evil cannot win and will never win no matter how hard evil and wicked people try.

Know that there is no goodness in evil and wicked people.

Know that evil must use evil to maintain and sustain him or herself. Meaning evil use evil to attain jobs and they must continue to go to these evil places because they are now indebted to evil. There is no little way out. There is no higher order in evil. Evil is evil and there are no greater or lesser evil they are all on one accord. This is why I will tell you about Life in drill life in your head because with evil there is only death and once you are in you are in for life. Don't even think your children will be immune to this. They are not because the children you have also belong to evil. There is no escape for them so truly think. The Jesus will save me syndrome does not apply because Jesus is a lie you know that. So tell me now can a liar save another liar without losing his soul?

Know that evil use evil to sell its product

Evil use evil to destroy humanity

Evil must and let no one tell you otherwise. Evil must perform animal and blood sacrifices unto evil. Evil must drink blood and have you basking in blood because evil is a parasite that infest the body – kills the body, mind and soul.

Some of the things I say to you may sound corny and hard but nothing is corny or hard in the sight of God

True Love is that beautiful because all you see is that person

All you see is God

Yes you will have bumps because jealous and envious people will want to separate you but you know what God will protect you from them. As long as you are true to God and your mate, wife or husband that's all that matters. It does not matter if you live in a cardboard box.

I always said I don't care if I live in a cardboard box with the man I truly loved. As long as we truly love each other we will make it. Meaning we work at doing better together, we are truthful to each other, we don't cheat each other and true love is not about that.

It's amazing I have yet to see anyone that truly loves. It's always about something but never about true love, living for God and staying faithful and true for all eternity.

Some may say this is a fairy tale. These are not attainable and all there is is love but you know what when you have truth, live for truth and give God your truth then you will know what I am talking about. Everything that you do is not all about you but for God. Doing the best you can for yourself and others. You think about others with love, true love. You wonder what you can do to help that person. Sometimes all you can do is pray for them.

Sometimes you can't because prayer can be interrupted by the spiritual wicked so you talk to God silently and let him know your intentions. Let him see your intentions and in his own time and way he will fix it.

You cannot lie to God. No one knows how important it is to have that truthful relationship with him. All that we do is centered around and on self and self gratification and this is wrong. I am not staying the devil cannot mend his ways and eventually get back in but mend his ways how. Is he willing to accept guilt? Is he willing to say I was wrong and you were right? Is he willing to repent and do that which is right and good in the sight of God? Is he willing to accept God and change his evil ways. With all that we know can the devil be trusted and I say no. He has proven time and time again that he cannot be trusted. There is not one jot of good in him but isn't this a lie on my part. For me to say that the devil cannot be trusted and that he has proven time and time again that he cannot be trusted is that not a lie on my part?

No

How is it not a lie?

He deceived Eve and he is causing this, causing us to sin. He's causing us to go against our will so you are correct. Plus when you go to church this is preached all the time. The devil is a liar, Encourage Yourself you told us to listen to it especially when Donald Lawrence said everything that the devil told me about myself is a lie, it's a lie.

True

But can the devil tell you about you?

Yes

No, the devil can only tell you what you want to hear so if you believe what he says about you to be the truth how is it a lie?

Are you not the one believing in his words – lies.

Do you not accept his book of lies – sin and say it is divinely inspired and of God?

Do you not say this book is factual and if you change one word of it God will take away the lot from your life?

Now tell me how can God take away from your life when God did not give you books of lies?

How can God take away from your life when God hath nothing to do with sin?

Tell me something can Sin tell you about God – The True and Living God?

No come on now. Can Sin tell you about God's abode?

No right. So if you know this why do you believe in sin and read the book and books of sin and say it is from God? Does that make any sense?

Life is life it is clean and no one can corrupt God or put stains on his record because God's records cannot be stained. As humans our records have stains and blemishes on it because we allow ourselves to be sucked in by sin. We listen to sin and neglect God and when sin put the pressure on us we cry to God. Come on now. Who are we to tell lies on God? Know the truth because there are two gods, the god of Death and the God of Life. Good and Evil. Sin can never be good because the choice that sin made is death. The choice that Eve made is death. The choice we are making today is death. So if we made and make the choice to die how can God save us? How can God truly help us and take us to his abode when we of ourselves did not choose him. Come on now.

Know that religion is not about choice it's about control and domination – death. Every facet of religion leads you to death because we made the choice to follow death.

And no one absolutely no one can say if your child do not go to church they will turn out bad. That is a load of crap to keep you ignorant and stupid. And yes it is an ignorant fool that speaks this way.

Let me tell you this every child need a mother and father. Just take a look at the ratio of single mothers and fathers household compared to the traditional family household that have or has a mother and father.

We've eroded the family structure to say its okay for a child to be raised in a single family household and this is wrong. It is a sin because that child was not produced by one parent it took two – a sperm and an egg.

When you teach a child good values at home they carry those values for lifetimes to come.

One parent cannot raise a child and it's time some of these dead beat dads and sperm donors realize this because trust me they will have hell to pay. Allelujah hell will have no fury when it comes to them.

As a parent or parents we cannot teach our children wrong and expect them to do right they will forever do wrong and to say you are going to look to the church for good values makes you sinful – wrong because the church teach lies and deceit. They teach how to sin thus making you and your child sinful. Nothing that the church do and does respect God. All that the church do and does is praise evil and worship evil. They rob you of your soul and place with God.

Can a dirty system teach you how to be clean?

Can Stan or evil teach you how to be holy? Come on now

Can a sinful man teach you about God? All they can teach you about is sin.

Can a dirty system teach you how to find God and truly know and love God? Come on now. Yes you may say I am casting stones and lots and in a way I am but I make no apologies to man for his or her sinful way. I too have sinned and it is God – The True and Living God that I look to for forgiveness and life not man. We are corrupt and have become corrupted hence we cannot find God nor know God.

Tell me with all the prayers the churches offer up to God why can't changes come?

With all the prayers offered up why hasn't sin fled from earth? Why hasn't sin been destroyed? Answer me and tell me if a dirty man can offer up prayers unto God and his prayer become clean?

Not even I can pray for you clean prayers if I am dirty. No one that is dirty can offer up clean prayers unto God. Come on now.

But but but. There are no buts because as God helps his own evil helps his own too so do not get it twisted.

Yes but the words are so strong – powerful that you do not know who to trust.

Yes it is because the lie becomes the truth in your eyes so therefore you believe. You do not know. But all that you say is bullshit. If God was your stay you would not say that "you do not know who to trust". If you truly trust God you would not say that. Know the truth because if you truly trust God and have faith in him you would know. Not even I can rock you with all that I write. You would tell me to fuck off and go to someone else with my crap. Come on now. You cannot fool God's children because when you don't know God show you no matter how evil mask the truth.

If you know the truth the devil cannot change you

Remember four quarters make one but is it one?

No because now you have four pieces.

A whole is a whole and it cannot be divided

So why are we listening to the devil?

Why are we letting evil divide and separate us? Come on now

If God is giving you everything whole why would you need four pieces to get one? It does not make any sense and this is what we need to look into. Four pieces cannot give you one it can only give you four.

But

There is no ands ifs or buts about God. If you are on God's path stay on it. Remember my poem on the previous pages. Know that the devil made everything sweet for me. He was telling me how wonderful and good he is. He told me what he could offer me. This did happen to me in my dream. All I had to do was hold his hand and everything would be fine in my life. But you cannot accept the devil's offering you have to stay true to God. Yes the devil will come and make everything look sweet and nice but it isn't. Yes he's going to give you the fancy car, the fancy house, the abundance of money and drugs, the abundance of sex, the glory but guess what he's not telling you about the consequences. He told Eve she would not die and she believed him and although she did not die in the physical right away, she did die in the spiritual right away. She could no longer see God. They also died in the physical eventually. Remember there was no pain in Eden, once they were kicked out did they not have to work, suffer, toil, feel pain, Cain their son killed Abel. She had goodness and the protection of God and gave it up for naught – nothing – garbage – filth. Yes the devil gives you all but no one has taken the time to read the fine print that says if you accept me you will:

- Die physically and spiritually
- You will feel eternal pain
- You will no longer be able to communicate with the true and living God face to face
- You will no longer be able to talk to God
- God will not protect you once you accept me
- Hell will be your everlasting home
- Paradise will not be attainable
- You will be my slave and you will serve me
- I will not let you loose
- Your children will serve me
- They will become mine to do with as I see fit
- They will obey me just as you will obey me
- They will fornicate, kill and do all that is evil
- I will be their God the one they have to listen to
- My debt you can infinitely never repay because this is our bond – pact

- An eternal and everlasting bond – pact that can never be broken by man, spirit or the true and living God.

- No one takes the time to read and know that any pact made with evil – the devil is absolute and can never be broken. It is an everlasting pact that is infinitely legal and binding. Your pact with sin is a binding contract that impacts your family and future generations because they too are a part of that contract with death – sin – the devil as you call him.

We don't take the time to know and this is sad. No one wants hardship but remember the song "weeping comes for a time but joy cometh in the morning." This is life for many of us. Staying strong is not easy when you are living in the devil's or evil's system of things. As a person that is trying to walk on the pathway of God – the true and living God know that you are not doing this for yourself you are doing this for your children, you are doing it for God and for future generations to come.

Yes I get negative thoughts at times but I cannot live my life by the negative. I know what people are saying. Some may say give up now but I can't. Once upon a time I did. I wanted to give up but I have come thus far to want and need to carry on. There is no fancy story here. Wickedness do exist and it is deadly. Wickedness is death. It rapes you of everything and the ones that are doing it to you don't care. This is their job because they have sold their souls to the devil. Their life is miserable so they want and need your life to be miserable also.

So why doesn't God protect you?

Trust me he does and he will do the same for you. You have to know that there is no life in death but there is life in life. Once again take a look at a dead body. There is no life in it so why strive to be like this. Now look at life – nature and see the beauty of it. This – Life is what you need to strive for.

You will be tested but it is up to you to pass those test and trust me evil will pull out all the stops for you to fail but you cannot give up. I know it is hard especially when you do not have anyone to share your views or help you go through your pain. God is there I know but sometimes you need a little human comfort.

Sometimes we fail but you know what pick yourself up and get back on track. I am rocked but I am determined to hold on to God.

What man can do to the flesh they cannot do to spirit trust me on this because you need to know this. Once your spirit leaves your body if you are good evil cannot touch it nor can evil harm you. (The spirit).

This is life and it is God. You have to live for God as well as live for yourself.

Whether you believe me or not it is up to you but you need to know the truth. You are the only one that can make the choice. No one can choose for you. Yes some of our parents choose for us but is that fair to you? Know that you can change this choice when you get older and wiser. Once you leave your parents the decision now becomes yours and it is up to you to choose good or evil. If you have a binding contract with death – evil this contract can never change because you are owned by evil. You are evil's slave and you must do the bidding of evil no matter the cost. I will not give you false hope. I refuse to.

There are two Paradises and how you choose to get there is up to you. You cannot wilfully hurt people in the physical and think you are going to reside with God. It is not going to happen. Never going to happen because you know what you are doing. You cannot

use religion to hurt others; you cannot use it to tell lies on God. You cannot use it as a by to get into heaven, you will not see heaven. No I cannot say that you will see heaven. Which heaven is the key? Trust me the heaven you see will be hell. There is no ands ifs or buts about it.

- It's amazing how we live our lives and think hate can get us an audience with God.

- Religion can get us an audience with God

- Selfishness can get us an audience with God

- We murder and think we can automatically go to Paradise with God. Certainly not mine. Your God but not the True and Living God.

Listen now and listen good and hear what I am going to tell you. Death is ugly – infinitely ugly in its true state of sin and filth. This hath nothing to do with physical beauty but sin – evil. Now take a good look at a dead body and see what I am talking about. Is there any smile on the face of death – that dead body?

Know that that dead body is us today. Sin makes us ugly and wrinkly because sin is death – lifeless – void of life and this is what the spirit is trying to show you when the flesh dies.

Yes there is so much more and I have gotten off topic again but that's me always off topic.

It's amazing how we say God is coming back and the question I ask you is "To where?

WHERE IS GOD COMING BACK TO?

To earth

A LITTLE TALK WITH GOD

To reside with us his people

And if you honestly believe this slap yourself twice. This time take your left hand and slap yourself on it twice with your right hand. Not hard but lightly.

Stop laughing some of you. You lying on the bed stop it. Come on this is so not funny because religion has nothing to do with this.

Listen and know that all facets of religion is dirty. If it was clean and the prayers offered up were clean evil would have fled from earth long ago. Evil could not stay nor would evil be controlling the political institutions, your church, your life, banking and education system, health system, military infrastructures and so forth. Trust me infinitely evil would not be able to stay but because religion is evil it continues to give evil a home. It continues to tell lies – deceive. Religion has nothing to do with God's people it has to do with evil's people because evil must tell lies to feed its people and continue the trend going. Evil must go into temples to pay homage to Satan – their God. God's people do not need temples because we know God is all around us meaning nature and all his goodness is free and freely given and we cannot find nature in temples, we cannot find him in temples, we cannot find his air and good food in temples.

I told God I wanted him to come into my home. Be there for me and with me but you know what he told me. He told me he could not come into a dirty home. We as humans cannot expect God to reside with us when our temple which is the spirit is dirty. He cannot come into our home if it is a mess. We cannot be pack rats and trust me I have since learnt to start throwing out things that were broken and not necessary. Man I should have been on Hoarders.

Man I never realized that I was such a hoarder and when I looked around me it was messy. My home was messy and still is because you know kids. They just throw things anywhere and it is such a chore trying to get them to clean up after themselves. They have a nasty habit of disorganizing when you have organized so hence I tell all of you when you are praying for children ask God for clean children. Children that will take pride in keeping their surroundings clean and organized because God cannot come into disorganization. He is clean and not dirty. So in order for God to reside with us we need to clean up ourselves, clean up our homes and clean up this planet. I am not saying God will not come back he will but our surroundings must be infinitely clean.

We can't keep doing what we are doing and think it is going to get us to Paradise, or the abode where God resides.

You cannot take filth to an abode that is perfect and clean and this is why when the flesh dies or we die in the flesh we must die clean – be clean.

But when you die are you not changed, you said we are changed.

Yes but how many of us die with a clean spirit? How many of us die living a clean life. ***If you are dirty here on earth you will be dirty in the spirit and you will not be changed in the spirit.*** A dirty person cannot be changed in the spiritual. Know also that a dirty preacher or pastor should infinitely never marry you or commit your body to the ground – earth. If there are no clean pastors and your children are of the age and they are clean let them preside over your body and commit it to the ground – earth. They must say good things about you and ask God to take your body to his abode of truth and righteousness – goodness.

You are destined for one place and one place only. A person that tries to live a clean life, do not hurt others; try to live according to God they will change and they are the ones that will reside with God - see God.

This is why I keep pounding it in your heads and tell you the life you live in the physical determines the life you live in the spiritual.

Yes those that are converted, the clean souls that have been converted will be tested in the grave because they did not know that being converted was wrong. TO BE CONVERTED IS AN ABOMINATION – A GRAVE SIN UNTO GOD. LET NO ONE CONVERT YOU BECAUSE NO ONE CAN CONVERT TO GOD. DO YOU HEAR ME NO ONE CAN CONVERT TO GOD SO LET NO ONE CONVERT YOU. ***CONVERSION IS A SIN BECAUSE GOD CANNOT BE CONVERTED*** BUT SIN CAN.

YOU WILL BE TESTED IN THE GRAVE IF YOU ARE GOOD AND HAVE BEEN CONVERTED AND IF YOU CAN'T ANSWER CORRECTLY MEANING IF YOU DON'T KNOW THE ANSWER AND DEPENDING ON YOUR GOODNESS ON EARTH YOU WILL GET A LIFE LINE TO REACH OUT TO THE LIVING FOR HELP AND IF THAT PERSON CANNOT GIVE YOU THE CORRECT ANSWER YOU WILL BE DOOMED. YOU WILL GO TO HELL. THERE IS NO SECOND OR THIRD RESURRECTION FOR THE WICKED. ONCE YOU DIE IN THE PHYSICAL YOU WILL DIE IN THE SPIRITUAL. THOSE THAT ANSWER THE QUESTIONS CORRECTLY IN THE GRAVE WILL BE CHANGED AND MOVE ON TO A BETTER AND HIGHER LIFE. THEREFORE YOU NEED TO KNOW AND NOT BELIEVE BECAUSE BELIEF WITH NEVER GET YOU INTO GOD'S ABODE. BELIEF IS NOT KNOWLEDGE. BELIEF IS DEATH.

This state meaning the state of being questioned and changed does not go for Christians it is for Muslims that were converted only. Those that tried to live a clean life because they did not know that living the life of a Muslim leads them to spiritual prison – not death but prison. Once they accepted Islam they will go to hell meaning they are locked up. They are the ones that we can go into hell and take out of prison. I repeat this is just for those that were converted and no one else. Christians will not go to heaven because they believe in death and accepted death so they will not change in the spiritual realm they will automatically go to hell. They die it's as plain as that.

Some of you will want to dispute this go ahead but going to church and paying tides don't make you holy it makes you sinful because the lot of you know neighbours and family members that require financial help and instead of helping them you would rather give your pastor your hard earned money. And do not bring up render onto Caesar that which is Caesar's and render onto God's that which is God bullshit.

This has to do with your taxes the churches robbing the government and people of their money. God have no use for money but the country that you live in does so pay your taxes. God requires clean souls – people to live for him. You cannot live for God according to what man tells you because man knows not God and you have to know God it's that simple.

I've told you God cannot interfere with the children of Death. What is for death belongs to death and that which is for life belongs to God. Evil deals in dirt and God deals in clean – cleanliness. So to drink blood whether physical or spiritual, to wash in blood whether physical or spiritual, to participate in animal sacrifices, human sacrifices and so forth is not of God it is of the devil – evil.

Many of you Christians say you have to be washed in the blood of the lamb. Tell me something would any of you wash yourself – your body in human and sheep's blood or blood of any kind? Come on now. You would not do this well some of you would not do this so why are we believing in nonsense – pagan and Babylonian worship – evil worship. Come on now. When did God tell you Joe I am nasty so therefore I need you to do nasty things? God is clean so why do we associate him with all kinds of nastiness?

If you find washing in blood is nasty and filthy how can washing in blood be clean?

How can you accept the washing in blood and say it is of God – clean? Come on now think and do better. Like I've said you cannot let people that have nothing to do with God tell you about God because all they will tell you are lies and this is what's happening.

Yes you can say that I am a lie because this is the way you feel. I will not change you and I refuse to change you are anyone. My job as asked by God was to write him a book and I am doing so. I told him I refuse to lie for him or tell lies and I refuse to hate or spread hate. God never told me to change anyone or interfere with evil and his people and I refuse to do so meaning interfere with evil and his people. All I write is to get God's people back on track and to prepare them for what is to come in the next 19 years and this 19 years depends on how we live our lives if it is clean or not. Know that if we continue on the pathway of destruction before 3032 humanity will be infinitely destroyed. This is not scare tactic it is real.

For those that say this is good I will die and see God or that a great god is going to come from the sky and rescue them better think again. You will die and you cannot change this. I have seen much destruction in my visions that have come to pass but was helpless to help these people. Destruction is hard to pinpoint and it is that confusing.

Yes you can interfere with death and the course of death if you have the authority to but this is a deadly road you are travelling. I know I said no one can command the death but death's authority is not absolute for those that know death – have the power over death. How do I explain this for you to comprehend? Here we go. Revelations told us and I reminded you that Revelations said the angel of God has the key to hell – death and he is the alpha and omega. This is infinitely true. God's angel or chosen hold the key to death and she can use it at will not he.

Know that death before it comes drains the life out of you any true child of God knows this because they can feel the life draining out of them. It is not necessarily them that is dying they are feeling the death of others. This feel is that taxing and draining on the body.

No this is not farfetched this is reality.

There are many mansions in hell but very little in heaven and you need to know this as well. God isn't messing around anymore. This is your final calling. I can't get you into heaven or Paradise to see God. I have to account for my own sins. I have to tell God why I did this this and this.

God told me to do something. He didn't tell me how to do it. That choice he left to me. I cannot wilfully spread hate and lies. It's not right and it is not fair. I cannot tell you you are going to go to heaven. If I said you are going to go I would be lying to you and telling a grave lie on God. I am shown certain things and I have to relay them to you. It is up to you to reject them or accept them. You need clean people presiding over your body in marriage and in death. If a dirty pastor or clergy marries you your marriage is not clean. If he or she buries you your body and spirit is not clean you will take on his dirt and become dirty and you will never get into heaven or God's abode. Yes your goodness is there but you are taking on his sins and if his sins are plenty and those sins outweigh your goodness then there is no way that you can get in. We Jamaicans have a saying that says what drop off a head must drop pan shoulder. Another saying we have is what noa ketch quakoo must ketch shirt. So know what you are doing and who is representing you because your pastor's dirty deeds do fall on you and I am going to repeat myself yet again IF THE HEAD IS DIRTY HOW CAN THE BODY BE CLEAN. You will never be clean. To put it clearly if you have one more good on your record or slate than bad and your pastor or clergy have nine faults – bad you will not get into heaven because that nine faults – bad is on your plate too. That person made you become dirty. You have to get rid of evil by separating yourself from evil. Do not let my sins or faults affect you. Each one of us can clean ourselves up and it is only by living a clean, truthful and honest life can we do this. We have to live clean and I cannot stress this enough.

We cannot continue to live our lives in sin anymore because sin leads to physical and spiritual death. It is not to say you cannot be happy in life. You can be.

If you love music continue to listen to music. I infinitely love music but music with messages. Music that is truthful to life. I infinitely will never endorse an artist because I do not know them nor do I know how clean they are. No that's not true I do hence I will only endorse the songs because of the message that they give. Know that it is not all the time I will give songs that have a definite message.

These are some of the songs I like just to give you an example. The beat is great and it gets my body going.

Elephant Man and Lady Saw – Si Dung Pon It

Elephant Man ft. Khargo – Slap Weh

Fiji ft J. Boog – Every Little Thing

Fiji ft Singa and J. Boog – Special Girl

J. Boog – See Her Again

A LITTLE TALK WITH GOD

Fiji – Naughty Girl

Mr. Vegas ft Shaggy, Josey Wales – Sweet Jamaica

Mr. Vegas – Rise Again, She's a Ho, Taxi Fare, Daggering+

Lady Saw – Party Till December

Lloyd – Lay it Down

J. Holiday – It's Yours

Milli Jackson – Misty Blue

Milli Jackson – If loving you is wrong

Prince – Purple Rain, Diamonds and Pearls

You have oldies group like Air supply, Duran Duran

There is Percy Sledge, Barry White – Oh Nelly Barry White with that thick, soulful and romantic voice of his that can get you in the mood at any time of the day or night.

Shirley Brown – Woman to Woman

Otis Redding – I've Got Dreams, Change is Gonna Come

Yellowman – the king of slackness in the early eighties when it came to reggae dance hall. People check out his music because they are timeless.

Peter Tosh

Bob Marley

Damian Marley – Man people do not know this man's hidden talents. If only he can break away and truly bruk out musically trust me none of his brothers would be able to touch him musically in my book. He is that good on another scale.

Tarrus Riley – All his music is worth listening to because he is that talented musically.

Do you see where I am going with the music. With God nothing changes and if you are x-rated with your wife it does not change. Honesty and truth is the key because sex can be that beautiful.

Play your music

Write your music

If you love sex continue to have sex but have it with one partner, your lifetime partner. Do not leave her and go elsewhere because God will cause you to lose it all. Eve lost it all, so did Solomon and David. When I said David he could not build the temple of God because of what he did to Uriah.

Write your stories, love stories, horror stories but let them be about honest life and not deceit. Yes you can show people how deceit and lies hurt in these stories, use them to teach honestly. Do you see where I am going with this?

If you love to design clothes do it. Do not stop

If you want to become a doctor do it

Nothing stops just because you have accepted God. Life continues. It's just mean you are living a clean and honest life.

Sin does not stop. It will be there but just not in you. You will strive to separate totally from sin not just in the physical but in the spiritual also.

People that have accepted evil will still exist even though you want God to make them disappear permanently

If you enjoy going to the movies go

All you are doing now is trying to live a clean life for God and not man

You are doing things to make you and God happy as well as debt and stress free.

You will change but change how?

People will still get under your nerve

You can still go for a drink to the pub with your friends but you won't desire to get drunk and carry on anymore

You will become more mature

More responsible because you are putting God first

God is becoming important to you now

Drugs you will conquer because you are no longer trapped in that state of mind

Yes you will have withdrawals at first and it will take time but over time a year or two you will conquer it.

You won't desire it anymore

You won't want to do drugs anymore

Infinitely trust me on this God will heal you this you have to know

Sometimes the stresses will get to you and your mind will kick in and say kill yourself but its chatter means nothing you will laugh. You will tell your mind to get behind you and don't come around here with your negative thoughts no more

You will hold the pill bottle and look at it and it does not phase you

You put the bottle down and see the meaningless of it meaning the meaningless of taking your own life.

Controlling the mind you cannot do by yourself

God is the control and if you call on God everyday

Just say hey God how ya doing

Or just think of God for no reason at all you will be fine, you will be controlling the mind and this is what WILL does not like. It likes to be in control at all times. It lies, gives you negative thoughts because negative thoughts have power. Dark power and this power kills. It will kill you because once it has you it will not let go. It will have you at its mercy.

- It is self absorbed
- Always wanting
- Can't be satisfied
- Manipulative
- Cunning
- Deceitful
- It lies
- It thinks nothing and no one is better than it
- It has to have control at all times

- It has to be in the drivers seat
- It cannot accept anyone else but himself
- It is vain
- It is vanity
- It is money
- The wife that always want and can't be satisfied no matter how much you do for her and give to her
- The husband that want sex every night and when he can't get it he goes elsewhere.

This is will for which we call the mind and we say it is the heart of the soul but it isn't. True love is the heart of the soul because true love cannot and will never hurt and it is very few that can truly love trust me on this infinitely.

With true love all that is evil is irrelevant. It matters not to you. This is the state where you need to be. This is the state of God. This is a clean state, a pure state. True love does not try to outdo. It shares.

True love does not cheat nor does it divide. It is honest and pure and it grows and blooms into all things that are beautiful. Yes true love can be naïve know this and when I say naïve at times we do not see the ills of the world. We lock it out and these ills or sins are not in our world. It is not to say you will not have problems you will but it is not so much the problems of the world but the problems with your children. In this world of God, the truthful world we strive to lock away evil but strive to have positive and good people around you.

True love does not fight for what another man has. True love does not want dirty money. It is fair and just in a divorce meaning if one is clean and the other is dirty good always strives for fairness and goodness. Sometimes we walk away without wanting anything from that dirty person.

True love is a true family that always put God first meaning we think of God and if our actions are going to hurt him. If we know it will hurt God and cause the devil to laugh and point at God we will not do it. Yes sometimes we fall because we do do things in anger. I am a living testament of this. Trust me evil will try every angle to get to you and don't think he won't use your children to get to you. Trust me he uses them.

True love does not have to work hard because it is the truth and it grows. Lies and evil have to work hard. Lies have to stay ahead of the game whereas truth just lay back and enjoy life.

True love work together with his or her partner whether the problem be health issues, financial woes and trust me once you start living a clean, truthful and honest life you will see and know what I mean about financial and health issues. Trust me when you least expect it you will have it because God does provide for you in a positive way. Yes it takes time but remember God does everything in Time because God is Time.

True love knows when to let go of love because there is no truth in love because love is evil it evolves.

Now with all that said KNOW AND NOT JUST BELIEVE

If God is giving you knowledge hold on to that knowledge and do not let someone come and take that knowledge from you. This is your knowledge. All that God gives to you is blessed and it is truthful and factual. Accept God and the knowledge he is giving to you and you can never go wrong. God is not wrong he is truthful. The devil is wrong and he is the one to spread lies – negative energy. The devil is the one to have you believing in lies knowing full well all that he does leads to death of the spirit and body. Yes the death of everything. You cannot believe the lies that wicked and evil people tell you because they are the ones leading your soul to hell.

Right now the world is so paranoid that we live in paranoia – fear. You have to stop living in fear and remember THE DEVIL OR EVIL IS A THEIF. EVIL STEALS THE IDENTITY OF GOD and use it against you.

Everything that is good evil tries to destroy by trying to blend in but evil cannot blend in. Now we have people believing in secret societies and getting paranoid.

Come on people evil is real. Secret societies yes are real and we have made them powerful on earth but these societies are not powerful when it comes to death. Death is pure evil and not even Satan himself can over throw death.

Death is all powerful and truss mi Satan fears death because he knows he is going to die in the spiritual realm.

All that he has done to deceive and kill humanity he too is going to die. Don't get me wrong because the snake is not done yet. His belly is not full. Remember how small he was in the beginning well he's not small anymore he is huge and no one on the face of this planet can stop him because he has the power and he does use it.

We as humans have given power to this man of old – he's not new and will never be new he just knows how to use his power wisely. Don't think for a moment that this snake does not have his allies. He does and when the time is right they will join forces and devour humanity. One can stop this snake but "SHE HAVE TO LIVE CLEAN" I do not know who she is but if she is not clean humanity will not be saved. I have seen the one to defeat the devil but I have yet to see the one to defeat the snake. I've separated the two because in my eyes and from what I see the two are different but yet they are one in the same. I do not know how to explain this for you to comprehend but it is unexplainable in simple terms.

I want to explain secret societies here but I fully can't so I am going to touch on it.

Do not stress over secret societies like I've said and although they are powerful in the living they will have no power in death. Evil uses them and in the end they too will become enslaved by evil. Evil has them in it's fold and trust me infinitely on this evil will do to them like it did to Eve. She died no that's not a good example because she stayed true to evil. No keep it because she died and she will die again in the end. As for humanity anyone that follows evil they will eventually die and I know this is a poor explanation but I am hoping that you will get it.

Death is the key because death is all powerful when it comes to life – taking life. But God is all powerful when it comes to life and death. True life cannot die and death have to bow down to God because God has the key to death. I know revelations said the angel of God has the key to hell and death but without God this angel would not exist nor would he have the key. Hell is the prison for sin and death and hell is the final death for evil and wicked people including spirits and yes death himself.

I am off track and I am sorry because this is where the triangle comes in. Know that the triangle is not a trinity and will infinitely never be a trinity but we as humans associate it with the trinity. In my homeland Rasta's use the inverted and upright triangle. I use to get upset when people that are not suppose to use the triangle use it but now it does not bother me because good and evil use it and all it tells me is that evil must bow down to God. An evil person that uses the triangle is acknowledging God and saying to me that evil bows to God meaning concede to God which is life. Yes they are admitting defeat because none of them know what the triangle represents.

The triangle is like the Ying and Yang it represents life in its entirety. It represents good and evil as well as pure evil just like the Ying and Yang and all represent God and how this universe and life was created. The triangle as we see it is one half of human life.

When you look at the pyramid and the triangle they tell you and show you what humanity has lost in terms of life, the universe, galaxies and stars.

The pyramid or triangle represent life and to say the pyramid is a triangle is incorrect on my part because the pyramid is not a triangle and no it's not a spaceship but a containment unit for evil just like the Ying and Yang and if you have higher knowledge you will know what I am talking about. Right now I am jumping the gun and I am going to confuse the hell out of you so I will not elaborate further. Just know that the eye in the pyramid is not bad all it is saying is that we must look up because greater knowledge comes from above. The eye is significant because this is the eye that sees it all and know it all and it is not America that has this flag meaning the knowledge of the eye in the triangle. If you were to look at the African flags there's one particular African nation that uses the eye and triangle in its flag so America is definitely not the all seeing nation. Africa is and truth be known parts of America broke from Africa long ago.

The pyramid/triangle has been around before the conception of man. Yes it's an order because we classify it as an order so we will keep this as an order. The triangle has nothing not one thing to do with evil. The people that are under this order are chosen and highly spiritual. They hold the key to life but more importantly they hold the key to death. They are the ones to keep evil at bay and this is complicated given the current issues facing earth – this planet.

And yes for those who think you cannot use this key for evil meaning you can use this key for evil and once you do you lose this gift. There are many ways to lose it trust me on this. When you lose it you can never get it back. You have to be true to this gift and only use it for good.

Strayed again

The five pointed star with the female goat and for those that do not know the goat is female and not male and no no Satanist or whomever can dispute this. This is infinitely true because the goat represent fertility and stubbornness so if you don't know now you know. True sin or evil is not male but female because it was a female that give birth to sin – evil. Yes she's Eve people. Eve is the mother of sin and not the mother of civilization - good. Some say the goat fish hence the fish is used for evil or in evil. Remember your so called Jesus fed a multitude of people with one fish. Get it now. Put it together and know the true death of evil in the spiritual realm is water. You must go through water before you get to spiritual fire which is your final torment – death. Water is what evil fears in the spiritual realm hence we destroy and pollute it in the physical. But no matter the destruction of it in the physical, evil cannot and will never destroy it in the spiritual because in truth evil fear all that is good. Evil cannot comprehend good. They can only comprehend evil and do all that is evil. Yes this is why evil and wicked people tell you to baptize but it matters not because when you baptize yourself you are baptizing in death – spiritual death and this is why I tell you to repent. Repentance is the key and you must ask God forgiveness. Ask for forgiveness of sin.

Like I said no one wants to die but yet we live to die. We destroy ourselves without thinking of the consequences then cry to God for help. God cannot go against our decisions of life and death. Many of us die because we made the choice to die like Eve and no matter how we know this and read about this we still continue to die – follow death.

Evil is telling you what it is and what it is all about so why choose evil.

Life cannot tell us about life because we have it but yet refuse to maintain and sustain it in a good and blessed way.

Evil is saying come to me and die I will give you everlasting torment and eventual death. Why would you want this and want this for your children and future generations to come? Come on now tell me. You are going to die there is no ands ifs or buts about this. There is no sugar coating it. Death is real and we see it every day. This is the same death in life and in the spiritual so why want this for you once the spirit has escaped its fleshy prison. Come on now. Truly love yourself and live for life not death.

Strayed again but If you say I am wrong in regards to the female goat I will slap you myself, yes I'm being violent but hey oblige me. You can say no because I so do not advocate violence too barbaric and sinful but in this case I can slap you not hard because I hate pain. Now look at the female gene that's all I got to say. Evil is the same in both worlds okay so now you know.

Look at the snakes on the stick yes we say it represents medicine but the snakes represent two males meaning for every female in the spirit world there are two males. This you cannot dispute either. You are getting the full truth. Why the hell did you Satanist use a goat damn I am offended. Goats are not ugly damn they are passive and stubborn yes but not ugly. You should have used a woman or just use the snake. Why a goat and don't tell me nothing

A LITTLE TALK WITH GOD

about sacrifice oh yeah Abraham right got it the ram and his sacrifice unto Satan – Sin.

Damn people you all make Satan look so hideous and you say you know him please none of you know Satan. Satan himself should be offended at his depiction. Shit them pictures be ugly as sin well worse than sin. The man ain't ugly. Satan is extremely handsome. No one on the face of this planet is as handsome and debonair as him. Like I've said if you were to put all the earth's handsomest males together none would come close to the beauty of this man. He is that cute, a hottie hot hot hot hottie because you haven't seen male beauty until you see this man. So to depict Satan in this way is an insult to him. No baby God isn't going to sin me for telling you the truth. I am not defending Satan because he is cunning and vile but you need to know the truth. Satan is not a beast creature he is quite handsome and even in his state of decay he is still handsome. Yes I will harp on his beauty because if you see him you too will harp on his beauty. I cannot lie I have to tell you the truth and no trust me infinitely that he's not more gorgeous than God My Boo and Lovey so don't get it twisted.

Satan cannot compare to God's beauty. God's beauty is infinitely bright, a true light that transcends all the universes and the scope of our minds. God is it in my book people so don't even go there.

Off track again so people lose that ugly pictorial depiction of Satan because that's not him. Satan is an actual man a damn handsome man that has 666 with a line above and below the 666 on his side and not on his head. This is Satan's true markings so for all of you that use 666 without the lines you are infinitely wrong. You are so not serving or worshiping Satan you are worshiping some other man or thing. Well the goat thing and that goat thing is so not Satan. So who are you all worshiping? No come on for real how can you say you are worshiping Satan when you don't have the proper sign? This is bullshit now come on. If you are going to worship the man and depict his sign do it right. Shit you're not true Satanist you're all just wannabees. Yes you can hate me but get it right. You say you are true and faithful to him well do it right and stop making an ass of yourself.

Yes Satan is a man but he's not the one you should be worried about because in the spiritual world all evil does not return to man all evil return to woman. Do you not represent her in your pentagram? Do you not represent her on your countries flags? The five pointed star represent the female and the six pointed star represent the male but in fact the six pointed star present the union of male and female so the male population does not have a flag in the truest of sense. You hang fellows that's all I got to say hence hanging the taking of life. So to you the Satanists you are not representing Satan the male but Satan the female. Now you know evil in its pure form and that is who you represent when you use the five pointed star you represent female not male.

We worry so much about physical evil but no one worries about spiritual evil. Spiritual evil is what we should be worried about because it is harder to break. Spiritual evil bounds and like I said it is that deadly. Like I said you pray for death and if you make it out alive then you are blessed saved.

Stop buying into physical wickedness all the time. I am not downplaying physical wickedness because people do use black magic white magic voodoo obeah the dead to harm you yes but physical evil is peanuts compared to spiritual evil. Spiritual evil bounds and good luck in trying to break it because it is that hard to break. You could turn east west north or south this evil is next to impossible to break, take it from me.

Spiritual evil does not require a human source to do its dirty deeds infinitely know this.

I am going to do something different. Below are some prayers I have written and I thought I would share them with you because they mean a lot to me and it is my way of connecting and talking to God when I have quit and free time.

PRAYERS

Father rescue me from sin

Rescue my children from sin and never let them walk in the ways of the wicked – evil

Let them see your way God and forgive me for not asking you for them initially meaning ask you for good upright and just children

God you do not change here on earth but good is changed in the spiritual realm

God I am asking you to forgive me because I did not know to ask you for perfect and upright children and now the clutches of sin has them

Sin has shaped their thoughts

Their lives

Will has become fully grown

Father I repent of this sin because I truly did not know

Forgive me because I truly do not want any of my children to leave your side and walk in the ways of sin

Show me clearly what to do to correct this wrong

I know the choice has been made but you are the healer and the fixer – the knower

You are the only one that I can come for help in repairing the damage that I have done

Father it hurts me to see the choice that I have made and I know it hurts you too

You are hurting

A LITTLE TALK WITH GOD

All I can do is pray

Pray for the future and the future of my grandchildren and continuing generations

Father my grand children are not yet here

Please I am asking you with all my love, true love to let them walk upright and just with you as well as in your sight. God they must be infinitely good and walk in the goodness and integrity of you

Father and God let them talk with you at all times

Let them cleave to you and run to you at all times with their pains and ills – sorrows and happiness - goodness

Let them infinitely never leave you for sin and death – evil

Let them have nothing to do with evil or sin

God everything that they do they must do it truthfully, honestly, peacefully and with pure and true love - goodness

Please let this be for more than a thousand generations but for all eternity – lifetimes to come

Father no matter how evil comes there way never ever let them turn from you and never ever infinitely never ever let them fall for the tricks of sin – evil.

God if this prayer is pleasing or just in thy sight and if there is no wrong or fault in what I am asking you please let thy good will be done and grant me all the goodness that I have asked of thee

Let thy good will be done in earth, in heaven and in your abode

Father I can't take sin and evil anymore

A LITTLE TALK WITH GOD

There is too much hurt and pain and I need to be happy

Need to be free of evil and sin

Father I know you truly love me

Please do this for me

Please take hold of my life in a good and blessed way

Take hold of my children's life in a good and blessed way

All those I truly love and hold dear to me

My family, children, you, the angels, my peeps and true loved ones, my guides please take care of our lives in a good and blessed way

Please let us cleave to you and truly come home to you

Prepare a clean place for us

God truly prepare a good place for us so that we can live in peace and harmony with you and only you

God this place that you prepare for us must be void of all sin and evil

No more tears Father

No more

No more hate, pain and suffering

No more

It's time for evil to end

It's time for wickedness to end

A LITTLE TALK WITH GOD

Please be there for your children. Return to us and abide with us all so that we can live harmonious with peace as well as with you

Father I truly love you and don't want to leave you

You have to know this

You have to know that I truly love you and will not willingly hurt you or leave you. Yes I know I test your faith and loyalty but God who do I run to in good and bad times? Who do I hold in the highest of esteem? Who do I cling to and look to for everything and I mean everything? You are the one so no matter my bad days and sometimes hurtful words and naughty ways I will never infinitely never give up on you because you are truly loved by me. I truly and infinitely love thee.

Father please hear me and harken unto my words – prayer

Rescue me

Rescue your people

Rescue my children

Rescue My Peeps and True Loved Ones

Rescue those that will now truthfully and truly follow you for all eternity

All my love

True love

Michelle

A LITTLE TALK WITH GOD

Eternal Father the wages of sin is death
Evil lurks everywhere
Clear my pathway in the spiritual and physical God

As I humble myself to you, bless me with thy true and perfect love
Bless me with thy true and perfect thanksgiving
Bless me so that I may walk in your perfect, pure and true footsteps forevermore
Bless me so that I may uphold your integrity - truth
Bless me so that no evil anywhere befall me or my family

God sanctify me with your true love
Make me pure and whole again
Take away all manner of sin from me and my family
Father God guide me perfectly to you
Never let me stray from you or your path of truth
Hold me forever in your loving arms

Father as I write to you
I humble myself unto thee
I seek perfect favour
Perfect love
Perfect prosperity
Perfect and righteous everything from you
All that is good, truthful, right, just and pure I need from thee not just for me and my family but for the family you have given me as well – your good children
Father, hold me dear and perfect to thy heart
Be my saving grace
Be my true love
Be my ALL forevermore

Michelle

A LITTLE TALK WITH GOD

Eternal Father, separate me from the spiritual and physical heathens that will try to destroy me

Free me from the spiritual and physical evils that befalls me

Free me from the spiritual and physical evils that want as well as try to do me harm

Eternal Father, seal me with thy truth and never let me leave it – your truth

Seal me with thy true love

Never lie to me but comfort me

Educate me so that I can comfort and educate others about you honestly and truthfully

Father prepare a perfect, pure and loving place for me with you

Prepare a perfect, pure and loving place with you for my children, family, peeps and true loved ones

God prepare a perfect, pure and loving place with you for your people – all of us

God not just in the physical and spiritual but in your abode as well

Let all that we do be based on true love, truth, honesty peace and not war or hate neither jealousy

Eternal Father, truly help me to truthfully help others

Let me never fail you or turn from you

Heal me now my love

Heal me

A LITTLE TALK WITH GOD

Heal me perfectly and let no sickness ever befall me or my family again

Eternal Father you are whom I look to for everything in life and beyond. Do not fail me but be the goodness that I need.

God and Eternal Father there is so much at stake for me but it is you that I trust infinitely to deliver me out of the hands and pits of our enemies.

God my enemies are not just my enemies they are yours as well because truth lies not in evil – death but truth lies infinitely in you because you are truth – life.

Eternal Father and God I cannot stress the importance of you in my life – you are infinitely important in my life and I cannot let you go. I refuse to because you know my devotion to you and how I am cling to you. Yes I am like a thorn in your side – a good thorn thou well I hope.

Yes I have my faults but you look beyond these faults and have seen the goodness of thoughts as well as the heart and for this I infinitely love you and thank you.

Father, Eternal Father, you are My Love, My Truth, My All and as I cleave to you for everything know that I truly and infinitely love you. You are my rock and protector and for all the goodness you have given me and bestowed upon me I infinitely truly thank you.

Michelle

A LITTLE TALK WITH GOD

Eternal Father grace me with your presence of truth – true love and honesty

Grace me with your mercy

As I listen to Redemption Song by Bob Marley I cry out to you

My pain is real

The hurt is there

And my heart cries out to Africa

Sudan – all the countries in the Motherland including the land you made me in – the land that my mother gave birth to me in

Father, please open up the eyes of African's and let them see your way – the truth of you

How much more God

How much more shall die

How much more of your people must die and live in pain before they wake up and see that the Babylonian Way and Pagan Way is not your way. Will never be your way.

How much more should feel pain for all of Africa to wake up

We are the ones to kill ourselves while the world stand aside and look – applaud our shame and disgrace then point fingers and demean us by calling us every negative name in the book

God we are not willing to change because we have forgotten the truth.

We put aside the beauties of life and took up the impurities of sin - deceit

God what does it take for us to learn, see and hear what this man is saying?

Open our eyes to the truth Eternal Father because I cannot cry anymore. I cannot mourn anymore. I cannot feel pain anymore for a nation of people that will not listen to the truth. A nation of people that would rather live in sin and die in sin rather than accept you – eternal life.

The war is escalating in the spiritual realm

I see it time and time again and I can do nothing to stop it

Father as is brews it escalates here on earth and it his happening

I do not have the power to save the world only you do. She that is clean is the only one to save humanity and I truly do not know who she is because I have yet to see her face. But as for me God I am truthfully asking you to save humanity by giving them the full truth. Please stop the lies and let your people free themselves truthfully and truly come home to you in a good and pleasing way.

You have the power and I am asking you in love true love to save Sudan for collapse – war. God please hear me as I reach out and extend my hand to you for help with the Motherland. God your people came from there. My ancestors came from there and I cannot turn my back on our ancestral homeland. Yes you gave me a beautiful home but my people have and has destroyed your name and the kingdom you have given them. We helped the devil to destroy you and your land. This has been our legacy throughout the ages. We continuously aid the devil in his conquest to bring you shame and disgrace. We put others over you and it is disgraceful and shameful because everything you have given us as a people – nation we destroy and pollute – turn from you. We have shown you time and time again that we do not respect or cherish what you have given us. We do not hold on to what you have given us nor do we hold our heads up in high esteem. We do not take care of what you have given us but as soon as troubles come wi run to you fi help and for you to bail us out of our messes. But yet none of us can do right and good by you. God this isn't fair and I want to walk away from my people but my spirit compels me to stay and help. My spirit compels me to try and wake them up in hopes that they will repent and turn back to you and the truth you have given them - us. God even with all this I fear for them because I know hell is full with our people and the more hell gets the happier death is. God we have to see the errors of our ways and the road we travel on. I've seen mine and I do things that are wrong at times and I truly and infinitely need to correct this because the road I am on today is wrong and I don't want or need to be on it anymore. God I can't no matter the heart because at the end of the day you are whom I need. You are my life and lifeline and I do not want or need to disrespect you or bring you shame in anyway because of someone else. So for this wrong I am truly asking you to forgive me and help me truthfully and honestly to get back on the right track to you and move infinitely away from this evil. God what is the value of my good when this person seeks and do, does wrong. Am I not as guilty as this person so what good am I to you and me. The heart is clean yes but if the other person's heart is not clean then I am dirty and I refuse to take on another man's sin and let it burden and weigh me down – cast me in hell with him. God there is goodness in you and I will not fight with another man for his wrongs – deceit. I rather walk away with my integrity than to continue in sin because I know the value of our integrity come on now.

A LITTLE TALK WITH GOD

God you know if North and South separate Sudan is screwed

You know nothing will stop outside nations from raping the South of their God given right - blessings

You know many more people will die for OIL

The world can stop the genocide but they stand aside and watch because they want the oil but none knows that oil will not save them. God you have to honesty open these people's eyes and save them not just for me but for them and future generations to come. God you cannot let oil be their great divide because as it is evil has divided them already. Evil lurks in the dark to kill and conquer them and you cannot let this happen. God you are not the god of death but the God of Truth hence I come to you with truth and ask for true and honest and yes good help for these people.

None of them knows that the oil wells are drying up and that renewable energy is the only thing that can save them

None of them knows that the man is whispering to his people

He tried that shit with me said he's speaking Hebrew but he was speaking Urdu

But you shielded me from his lies and false tongue

You made it so that I could not understand and that the language became an abomination unto me

You must now shield your people

Open their eyes to the truth

Let them hear Redemption Song and hear what Bob Marley had to say. I know there is no book to fulfill and everything meaning everyone can change. Redeem them Father, let them repent like the people of Nineveh. Do not cause them to be enslaved again by the Amorites because you did tell them in the days of old that the iniquities of the Amorites is not yet full and it is so today. God you know the Amorites and their wicked ways. God the Amorites – Babylonians is not finished but I am asking you in truth and true love to finish it. Squash it because I know the powers of you in the spiritual realm. You can squash this by giving the command. I know evil can be conquered with your words so please hear me and squash all evil in their tracks so they cannot hurt humanity or anyone anymore forevermore.

God we can free ourselves, we can change the course of history, we of ourselves can destroy sin, we can send evil packing but we need you. We need the command – your true words to do so.

I know wickeder is yet to come. They all think that whoever has the world oil has all the power but that is so wrong.

The oil will not save them because shortly diseases not known to man will kill them soon. They are not thinking about the cannibalism epidemic that will take center stage on earth shortly given our global climate changes. This comet that is coming is going to destroy them. Starvation will ravish the land, no money or riches will save them.

None can save each other because there is no Noah's Ark to save them in this day and time it will be gone given the next 19 or so years. This time frame will decrease if man does not change their dirty ways this I infinitely know.

Father it was foretold in Genesis all the way to Revelations because when the death angels come and three are here there will be nothing that can save them or will save them because they choose not to listen.

Father you cannot separate Sudan, this man in America knows this. These are his people but he stands aside and look, waiting for the Holy War, Jihad. Many more of his people are going to die and many of my people are going to die and you cannot give him the victory over us because you gave no one religion of men to give to men - humanity.

Your laws are exact and none of your messengers can interfere with the Ying and Yang – Life and Death – the laws of the universe. This I know because I interfered in the destruction of my people in the spiritual realm and no matter how the angels tried – the angels of death tried I blocked them. I know the truth now and I refuse to stand in their way again when it comes to my people because their sins have gone too far. I know their death and destruction and time as we say is longer than rope and they will reap the fruits of their wickedness – sorrow real soon.

This is life God not war. You know evil must kill. Evil must kill every last member of your fold in order to have this domain but what he evil does not know is that you will never leave your people unprotected. You will save them even if it takes thousands and thousands of years. God I know the more we kill is the further in time you get from us and this is why it takes so long for you to answer us but I say unto you Screw Jihad and never infinitely never ever let any of them in because of their wickedness. Yes I know none will ever get into Paradise with the killing and the pitting of one religion against the other.

God it hurts me to see this. Knowing the lot of them is hell bound. This man knows this. He knows certain things and instead of using it for good he uses it for evil now they are poised ready to build a mosque near ground Zero mocking the dead and mocking you. They are saying to you and the world see what I can do? I have your dead. They are my martyrs and now I build a shrine in the honour of my god because we had victory over your own the children of God – your so called Jewish Nations.

Everywhere they go they set up shop in their own cunning little way. Their way of saying I have defeated you. Look at what we can do? Whatever we want to do we do it and no one sees it or can stop us. Religion is king and God to them because they have the backative of all evil everywhere. Evil is a united front hence religion is at the top of its game – this earthly domain. They have forgotten their dead, their loved ones and for those who know of this and are high rank and the ranks your time will soon come and hell will hath no fury when it comes to you. The beatings, the piss to drink and feces to eat day in and day out will be your stay because I know the special place that is reserved in hell for the lots of you. God I know the truth. I know the truth of Islam and this is what you were protecting us from. You were protecting us from physical and spiritual death – religion. God your children, your people are not to follow Christianity and Islam I know this now and fully comprehend what you were showing me.

Psalms One is a testament because we are not to sit or eat with them. You showed me this with the Jewish man.

We are to leave out of the fold of wicked and deceitful people.

We are to protect our children from religion all facet of religion because religion is a lie. It is death all around. It deceives and brings us all of us unto our deaths. Religion I know is idol worship, the worship of man Satan. Religion is a death trap and a death sentence and none of us know it.

You cannot murder your own and say it is someone else.

You cannot do things in the name of national security and then wage war. War will not save them and it is because of their dirty deeds, religious misdeeds that destruction continues to ravish earth and the people of earth.

We cannot live dirty and expect our prayers to you will become clean.

We cannot pollute the earth and expect good to come of it

We cannot constantly kill others and think we are going to have a place in your domain

We cannot kill the earth with all manner of chemicals and dirty things and think that the earth will continue to maintain and sustain us for all eternity

We cannot continue to kill and think that natural disasters will not come – death will not take at will – our will - sins

We cannot do evil and expect to be rewarded with goodness for our sins

We cannot live to die and think when the spirit leaves the flesh we are going to live – continue on with our journey unto better and good life

We cannot hate and continue to hate and think we are going to see you

We cannot lie and think we are going to address you – speak with you when we are dead

We cannot continue to believe and think sin is going to get us and audience with you in the end because you judgeth no one nor do you have anything to do with sin.

You are life and not death therefore what is death belongs to death and what is life belongs to you meaning all good life belongs to you and only you.

God please do not let Sudan follow in the way of the wicked because the pitting is there, the spy satellites has been set, these are the nets, the traps, the games of war. People in the South and North will die at the hands of man. God it is not right for another man to go in and try to pit land against land, people against people. What right do they have? The world cannot see the trap God and yes they don't want to see it but you need to expose them and let North and South learn. Egypt stand as a testament and none of my people are learning. None are listening because they don't want to hear. They want to stay ignorant and let others disrespect them and you, your creations.

God none, none, none, none must walk on the way of evil again because I know the truth of North and South, good and evil, God and Nod. How much more tears must I shed for people that know the truth, had the truth but turned from it for what, sin and death. We are killing each other, we are allowing evil to do this to us and none knows that this is just a ploy on deaths part. Sin and death is not faithful to anyone. His job is to kill and he does not care how he does it or who he kills as long as blood is on his hands, he has made human sacrifices onto his god which is the god of death. They are assassins, cold blooded murders that have no respect for life and the life you have given humanity. Sin will never do better. He cannot change and will never change because blood is on his hands. He is blood – red- death runs the world our earthly land - domain.

God the oil will not save them because soon the lava comes and it will ravish the land with fire. God they do not know that the lava is almost halfway there. It is a quarter of the way now but when it rises half way woe be unto humanity because all volcanoes will erupt and play their trumpets at will. Man will see and learn, cry and wail, the mountains will flee and then man will know that you are the true and living god and they should have listened to your call, cry – plea. Too late will be echoed globally, too late will become the cry of humanity, too late will be the food they eat marching unto hell. They will not see your abode because of ignorance, vanity – greed – free will. God they need to prepare for this comet, store up food, plant crops on the land so that when other nations are starving and dying they will have plenty to carry them through. Father, do not wait until it is too late. Please open their eyes please and let them see the real and true truth and walk away from the devil's table, the devil's religions and infinitely kick the devil out of their domain. God without them the devil will become powerless, a victim of his will – his evil deeds and schemes. The devil will die because death would have him and he will not be able to hurt the nations – your nations – your children no more.

God when the comet comes how will they survive? How will they clothe themselves? How will they feed their people? The comet is coming with devastation and radiation in it. It is coming with DEATH, THE DEATH OF HUMANITY WRITTEN ON IT.

They also need to prepare for this great famine that is coming and coming soon if they do not start developing Renewable Energy. God you cannot let them be like the children of Noah they will die you know this and I infinitely know this. You know the water levels are going to become so scarce that water becomes a commodity. People will not be able to buy it and yes many will die.

Snow is hardly falling in some regions. Snow that melt off in the spring to cool the earth down and provide abundance of water to drink.

God how can we be so ignorant not to see this?

- SODOM AND GOMORRAH

- THE TIME OF NOAH – UTNAFISHTIM as he is called in other languages
- EGYPT
- THE GARDEN OF EDEN
- NOD

We know the evils and destruction of these lands but yet we fail to learn from it. This is the final warning and the final call and if they don't wake up none can blame you this time around. You did foretell and warn. You did show but all believe ONE MAN IS GOING TO SAVE THEM when they know otherwise. Death cannot save man only LIFE can and they know this but refuse to live by the truth. How can a dead man save a man in the living? Come on now.

IF HE COULD WHY THE HELL IS THE COMET COMING?

WHY THE HELL IS THE WAR BREWING AND ESCALATING IN THE SPIRITUAL WORLD?

WHY ARE PEOPLE IN THE SPIRITUAL PREPARED FOR BATTLE?

A BATTLE THAT MUST AND WILL COME TO EARTH

A BATTLE NOT EVEN I CAN STOP BECAUSE IT HAS STARTED

A BATTLE THAT WILL LEAVE THE LAND DESOLATE

MANY WILL DIE

THERE WILL BE NO PLACE TO RUN AND HIDE

THEY WILL DIE

Sin and death knows this

The devil as they call him knows this

THEY DON'T KNOW THAT THE DEVIL HAVE TO GO TO THE CLERGY IN ORDER TO START A WAR. THE DEVIL MUST GET PERMISSION FROM THEIR GOD WHO RESIDES IN THE CHURCH IN ORDER TO GO TO WAR. WE KNOW THE CHURCH WILL NOT REFUSE HIM BECAUSE PERMISSION IS GRANTED ALL THE TIME.

THE DEVIL, THIS MAN SITS AT THE HEAD OF THE CHURCH AND WAR IS HIS AGENDA, NOT SAVING SOULS, NOTHING ELSE BUT WAR. THIS IS HIS HELL BECAUSE HE CANNOT LIVE IN PEACE AND ALTHOUGH THEY SAY PEACE BE UNTO YOU THERE IS NO PEACE IN THEIR HEARTS ONLY WAR.

PEACE IS WAR. I KNOW THIS. YOUR CHILDREN KNOW THIS. WE CANNOT FIGHT HIM ON HIS LEVEL WE WILL NOT WIN. WE HAVE TO CONTROL WILL. THIS IS HIS WEAPON AND TOOL. WILL.

FATHER, MAN CANNOT CONTINUE THIS WAY. MANY GENERATIONS EXISTED BEFORE THEM. THEY LIVED IN PEACE AND NOW THEY ARE TRAVELLING ON. THEY ARE WITH YOU BECAUSE YOU CREATED THEM AND SHIELDED THEM FROM THOSE THAT WERE FORMED, THOSE THAT CAME THROUGH THE EGG AND THE SPERM. THOSE THAT HAVE ALL THE QUALITIES AND FEATURES OF EARTH, DUST THIS PLANET WE CALL HOME.

FATHER, YOU CANNOT LET YOUR CHILDREN GO DOWN WITH THOSE OF SIN. YOU HAVE TO RESCUE THEM AND PROVIDE FOR THEM A BETTER HOME.

I CAN SAY I WILL NOT ALLOW YOU TO DO THIS BUT I CANNOT SAY THAT BECAUSE I AM SO NOT YOU. IT DOES HURT TO SEE WHAT IS GOING ON AND NO ONE, NO GOVERNMENT IS DOING ANYTHING TO STOP IT.

IF MAN DOES NOT INVEST IN RENEWABLE ENERGY WHAT ARE THEY GOING TO DO WHEN THE METEOR OR COMET COMES?

What are they going to do when the rivers dry up?

What are they going to do when the snow stops, the rain stops

- **Father STARVATION**
- **Hunger**
- **Famine**
- **Lack of good drinking water**
- **Countries left in ruin**
- **Economic ruin**
- **Political ruin**
- **Dead bodies will litter the streets**
- **Death will walk amongst the living, smiling, claiming**
- **The devil will be smiling because we as humans have given him the tools to win and he will win in his domain**
- **He will be laughing because he has more meat to eat**

- *His kingdom will be filled with slaves*
- *Those that bowed down to him*
- *He will make them work night and day to satisfy him*
- *Please him*
- *Many will cry out for death but death will never come*
- *They have chosen Hell as their home*
- *Everyday they will be fighting and cannot die*
- *Everyday they will engage in perverse sex*
- *Disease will fill their loins, their body*
- *Aches and pain will be their home*
- *No relief in sight*
- *No doctor's for a cure*
- *No hospitals to run to with the sick*
- *Now they will know that you are truly not there*
- *Now they will know that what you told them was the truth and they were the ones to not listen just as Eve did not listen*
- *Now they will know what Satan as they call him meant when he told Eve she will not surely die because in his home there is no death just hard labour, suffering and pain for a time then you will eventually die. Now you will know true pain because all that the spirit tried to show you via*

the flesh you did not take heed. You refuse to know that spiritual pain is greater and far more deadly than physical pain.

- *Now they will know the full truth and the full comprehension of the Garden and what happened to Man*

- *They will want to run to your abode but none will be able to cross over*

- *The time extension you have given man will now be truly over – gone*

- *No more Redemption Songs will be Sung*

- *Bob Marley gave them all but they refused to hear - listen*

- *I have given them books BUT THEY WILL NOT TAKE HEED. Just as they did in the past they will continue to do now while hoping the saviour they want will come. Each want a saviour to be like them, dress like them, commune like them, sin like them but yet know not that we cannot live like them when we've accepted your call. Accepted your true offerings to teach them.*

- *Marcus Garvey taught them how to conduct themselves economically and positively but they refused his teachings – his lessons*

- *Many died for them causing those that died to die in vain*

- *No more is foretold of except for the one that must live clean. If she does not live clean no one will save them. No one can save them from what is to come and what must be because of their wickedness – the disgrace and shame they leave on earth.*

- *The Comforter came, did your work, told what needed to be told and they would have rejected her, rejected your words once again, laughed as they did in the days of old because their hearts were that wicked, destructive and evil - vile.*

- *Now they are laughing, crying, saying if I had only listened*

- *Their false prophets will now be with them*

- *They are saying why*

- *Why the lies*

- *But it wasn't lies, it was the truth because they believed it to be the truth*

- *Believed in religion and all it had to offer*

- *Believed the halves and quarters*

- *Rejecting the whole*

- *Rejecting you*

- *All wanted you to come from them*

- *They never knew that you were with them all the time – all along*

- *All they had to do was turn within - listen*

- *Turn to the true love within them and listen*

- *Turn back to the true love of you*

- ***The true love of you***

Aah Father, they still don't know the beauty of you

Redemption Song has no merit, scope or meaning to them because they know not what redemption song is

Redemption Song cannot be comprehended by them so they go on killing each other based on religion, skin colour, financial gain, economic premises, greed, sexual gratification, self preservation, self worth, Vanity - sin.

My Love, they don't know all that the devil, this man offers is death because he is the one to die, has died, been crucified but they cannot resurrect him. No it's not Jesus and this is why they bow down to the dead in hopes that the dead can and will hear them. They hope and pray that their dead will get them into Paradise but their dead can't. They hope and pray that their dead will help them but their dead cannot do a thing because they are not strong enough, have no power in the spiritual world. That is why they cause havoc in the physical because the physical is filthy and dirty as them, sinful as them – vile like them.

We know this and this is why they did what they did to Eve. But even with doing that they could not and will never get in unless they come and become fully clean. Even with intermarrying with the children of the Garden, your children they could not get in because we know and still know that any children born through this state will not be accepted because the child will take on their trait and become like them sinful. Intermarrying with sin only brought forth a different race with a different hair type and even with the different hair type they are still the children of sin. Lies still reside on their lips, evil still owns them, have them in its home. Evil still teach them because they live to kill – know not the true meaning of peace – peace be unto you. They still deceive; no love is in their hearts because all their desires are of evil hence they commit evil – do evil - kill.

Cain showed us this and even though he had the mark of his father he still helped his people to stray, leave the fold, take on a new home. He could have changed his fate but he did not, he became his father's son, he murdered his brother therefore continuing his father's dream and desires. He continued his father's will and that is to murder, kill, conform, convert and deceive every child of God and carry them to hell with him. So far he is doing a good job but the one thing that he does not know is that the children of God can petition the dead, petition you God for justice, fair justice. The children of God can go into hell and take what does not belong to Sin and death which is your people out of hell. These are the people that were unfairly killed, your people that death is holding prisoner and using as a ransom. He does not know you cannot hold God hostage and his time, the time he pleaded and begged for he got but the time is almost up and that which is rightfully Gods will be taken from him and he must live the rest of eternity grovelling, begging for mercy at the feet of you God but no mercy will be given because he must die and will die at his own hands. This is his murderous fate.

Every life that he has taken he will have to pay with his own life

Every rape he has committed he will be raped

Every lie that he has told will come back to crucify and haunt him.

Everything that he has done in the name of sin and evil will come back to him.

I know you God and you will shield your people from his cries because none will hear him beg or plead for him because he knew what he was doing. He knew what he did was wrong. He disobeyed you God. He wanted what he could not have, could never have because goodness and true love he does not have and will never infinitely never have. All that is within him is love – evil and death. ***True Love will never turn from God's true people – God's children because that goodness, pure and true love is God himself and he it truth - ALL.***

God I don't know what else to do. Please do not let me cry anymore for nations of people that refuse to listen, refuse to accept the truth.

They don't know that your true people cannot lie to them and you would never infinitely never ever send dirty and unclean people to educate and teach them. The people that you send have to be clean, must be clean meaning change from their sinful ways, repent of their sins and walk in your truth and righteousness. They must face hell on earth because they are tested by physical and spiritual evil just like Job to see how faithful and true they are to you.

God they must walk in the valley of the death in the spiritual and physical world.

They have to and they must learn about time

They must know about the physical and spiritual more importantly how the spiritual world affects the physical world.

God we know everyone can see you once they start walking in the right light but see you how that is the key - question?

God they don't know that the messengers that you have given them cannot deceive them

Many has come and deceived but they were infinitely not of you because they use books of lies and deceit to educate and teach. You have never given us any forms of books to teach or educate. When the right time comes, I know this for a fact we will no longer write books but you will put the right and truthful words in our mouths for us to educate and teach the right and proper way. This I know to be infinitely true and exact. You never gave us books. I have seen your book it is called Holy Bible and it is very small. This book hath nothing to do with man's book of sin called the holy bible because all that sin do is try to mimic you and say he is you. Man does not know that if you gave someone a book to teach humanity that book cannot destroy lives.

That book cannot lie or contain errors or contradictions, typos yes but contradictions infinitely no because your degree of knowledge varies and you are not dealing with one race of people you are dealing with all God's children and their knowledge vary in regards to their beliefs hence when you are teaching you cannot teach one way in the beginning. It is when everyone is on the right accord meaning same level you must teach one way because all is on the same and right accord. None of God's children must be left behind. If one is left behind it is not due to you it is due to him or her because they did not want to listen or take heed.

Onwards I go.

That book cannot deceive

It cannot preach and teach hate

It cannot preach and teach superiority

It cannot teach you how to sin and tell lies

It cannot condemn anyone because everyone would be on the same accord meaning unified and living in peace. They would be void of hatred – prejudice because they would not see skin colour but see true love, the infinite love of truth within earth and the universe - God.

It's not to say your spirit will not stir racially it will but you have to contain this force because it is extremely powerful

– strong. This force oh Nelly is harsh. Trust me if you think my words is harsh wait until you encounter this force because if you are not strong you will fall at the wayside trust me on this. Truss mi only God can tell.

For me this force is generational – ancient. You will protect your ancestors and defend them because you are attached to them. It's hard to explain and put it in human perspective but trust me that fight – zeal is there to defend your ancestors just as you would defend God and the people God has given you. Some people use violence which is wrong but for me its words. Trust me words are my weapon – power over evil and wicked people. This ancient or generational bond is pure – true love. That connection of truth and true love is so great that you want to keep it at all times. This connection is your history people and you have to cherish it and truly love it because we all came from truth despite the way we feel about others. I truly love my ancestral roots hence I infinitely love and cherish God and the ancestral family he has given me.

Onwards I go.

Everything that is good and clean God's messengers would know and do because God would be beside each one teaching and showing them his abundance of truth – true love and life.

Eternal Father and God these people – clergy told us as well as taught us to believe in lies and if you were to ask all of them will tell you yes they believe. None of them know. None of them have the knowledge of you.

All of them believe one man is going to save them because this is what he told them and therefore the clergy teach this. None of them want to know the truth. None of them want to know you. According to them this man is going to speak for them, speak on their behalf and they believe him but none knows that no one can speak on their behalf.

They should know this by now because the dead cry out in the grave. The dead do speak to the living for them to know the truth and none is listening. Everyone have to give an account for their sins. No one can beg for them in the grave I know this God and you know this. A dirty person cannot petition you for anything. **_Tell me something God a man that hath sin can he petition you for the righteous or for righteousness?_**

Can he petition you for anything?

A sinful person cannot petition you because they cannot speak to you or come into your abode. They can't get to the foothills of the mountain so how can they petition on the behalf of anyone. God when we do things that is wrong in the physical do we get away with it?

Are we not punished so why do we think it is any different in the spiritual world?

God can a righteous man petition you for the guilty without he himself being guilty?

God he knew no one could save these people so he devised more lies for humanity to believe in? He caused humanity to bow down to him and worship him now the entire world believes that you are him and that you died for them.

Tell me God can a man kill life?

Can any spirit kill life - spirit?

More importantly can a man be you?

Can a man kill you? Come on now. Really Lovey this is not joke can a man kill you?

Have you become that lowly that a man can put you on a cross and drive a nail in your hands and kill you?

What is man saying?

What are they trying to tell me and you? Are they trying to say they have your life in their hands and they can do with it as they please?

Are they saying they own you and you are a slave and that you must do their will – what they want you to do?

Come on now Lovey who are we to do this to you and put doubt and shame on you. Who are we to say we are greater than you? We can't even bathe right – wash ourselves properly but yet we want to stand before you in filth and give you filth. Come on now.

Who the hell is man to talk or speak on your behalf?

We are dirt, dirty because we made our skin dirty.

Do we not stink and smell bad when we do not bathe? So who are we to say we are clean? Come on now. Please. God I am no different but I try to walk right, talk right, pray right and do right – yes all that is good and right in thy sight. I cannot change me to please anyone I have to be me and if that is not good enough then its humanities problem and not mine. As long as you infinitely love me and protect me I am infinitely good to go.

No God why should I change me to please man – a mere man or woman that is dirt – dust of dust come on now. You require good hearts – good people not vain and superficial people. Beauty hath nothing to do with physical appearance because the flesh is comprised of worms, worms that eat our flesh when we die so what is the flesh of man but filth – the toilet of nastiness – evil and sin. You require goodness, good deeds. It is your goodness that makes you clean and holy not the flesh but the spirit. Your goodness makes you young and pure at heart and this is what you look at the goodness of man – humanity and nothing else.

When we sin we are ugly – sin ugly hence I know sin cannot be clean it can only decay, rot – stink worse than pooh – shit.

Now they baptize in the name of the father son and holy ghost. They follow a trinity and say three in one. God how can there be three in one. How can you be three in one? Plain out they know not the true truth of you and for this many have a home in hell waiting for them because in this man's house there are many mansions if it was not so he would not have said so. Ah Allelujah what a weeping and a moaning when they get to the grave. It will be then that they will find out that baptism belongs to the devil and this is his way of marrying them to him. Through baptism they are bound to evil as well as married to evil. God the righteous knows that you do not baptise anyone and if we are baptised in the physical we are to repent of this and truthfully ask you for forgiveness because baptism is wrong.

Many of us do not know God and I did not know until recently when I put the pieces together. You showed me certain things and I could not figure it out but now I know the truth and I am free.

The righteous also know the significance of your ring. This is our true bound to you because this ring is our wedding band. It is not gold but shiny and it has nothing to do with the Star of David because this ring is round like a wedding band. White Gold or even silver best describes this ring. It is that beautiful. This is our bond and marriage to you. This is our protection your devotion and truth to us that your circle can never be broken by man or anything. The only way this bond can be broken is if we divorce you like Eve did. We have to turn from you and give you up for this bond to be broken and who wants that knowing the pain and ills that face them – us in hell.

God no one can petition you on the behalf of sin. We can pray for others yes but we cannot petition you because you have nothing to do with sin like I've said time and time again.

God if that person is sinful, do everything for sin, die in sin can he or she become clean? He or she cannot when they are in the grave. They made their choice and this is the choice they have to live with until their eventual death.

Can a man make sin become clean without he or she becoming dirty? Each individual have to change their dirty ways.

This man knew he couldn't save them

He had to do the will of him that commissioned him

If they knew you they would know that you would never sent false teachers and prophets or messengers to deceive and lie to them come on now. You are clean why would you send a dirty person to them to make them more dirty? Come on now.

If they knew you they would know that you would never send false teachers and prophets to rob them of their beauty come on now.

Their truth which is their soul

None of them know that you would never give them religion to deceive them – religions of sin – Pagans, the Babylonians- the people of Nod. You know and I infinitely know that religion is Satan's or Evil's ploy – joy. He Satan as we call him gave his people religion to deceive humanity. This is his game because he knew religion would keep the people believing in him, doing all that is evil while thinking they are going to see you God and go to heaven with you when he Satan knew and know that they are going to go to hell with him and burn. Humanity does not know that this was one of the master plans to keep humanity dirty while death takes them to hell – to his home. It worked and it is still working because humanity believe in him hence they call him Jesus. The Greeks call him Zeus and the Israelites call him Mutuyahu.

None of them know you do not reside in temples, mosques and synagogues

None of them know that you truly reside in them

None of them know that truth cannot lie; it is not capable of lying or telling quarter or half truths

Right now you are watching

You have left each and every man to his or her own desires

You will not intervene or interfere unless they come clean and do that which is clean and not dirty or filthy

They must want and need change before you can come in

They must strive for this show you this

Their homes, heart, mind and soul must be clean before you can come in

If they don't ask for help you will not give it

They don't know all they have to do is turn from evil and all will be good

They don't know that they can live in peace if they tried

They don't know if they reject sin, this man, evil, their lives will be at peace and good things will start to happen to them and their lives will start to become prosperous – blessed.

They don't know that energy is colourless

It is free

It is happy

They don't know that we can break down time

They don't know that they can make time motionless

They don't know that energy does not need air all it needs is space to move and grow – clean water to move about freely.

Evolve

They don't know that man can live without food and water in their pure state

They don't know because they can't truly feel

They can no longer see

They don't know that this earth, this planet they are fighting for is nothing without them because the planet this planet we call earth feels. It has life. It is life and it too grows and will eventually die because of them unless they change their filthy ways.

They don't know that life exists beyond the threshold of their eyes – time

Beyond the threshold of space the space they know

They don't know that planets, universes and worlds more beautiful than this life exist and what they call planets are not planets but stars. This solar system humanity cannot find nor will they find because no dirt lives there only clean.

They do not know that beautiful life forms that do not have anything to do with humanity exist.

They cannot see this because they are stuck here

Stuck in a physical shell that traps them on this planet

Traps them in this dormant and dying universe this universe that riddled in filth because of their sins

They cannot see that this isn't life but death

They cannot see that they made this planet the planet of the dead – the living dead

They cannot see that death cannot move forward it have to die and this is why it makes their lives so miserable on earth because it is miserable. It hath not life beyond the grave.

They cannot see nor do they know that death have to keep resurfacing through birth and nothing else

They do not know if we continue to give birth to sin it will never stop until all human life and spiritual life is destroyed

Father knowledge is vast but there is no knowledge on earth. They made this planet their home but it isn't. Now they have found out the hard way that death is not there only recourse to get home, a lot of them will never get home but die along the way.

Yes as sad as it is. This was the fate that we chose and now it will be too late for man. Many will now be singing TOO LATE because the comet will have found its mark and it will not stray off course, it will definitely kill them unless they make a positive change for the better.

Michelle

A LITTLE TALK WITH GOD

My Peeps and True Loved Ones I strayed with that prayer but all needed to be said because I see what is happening in the world and helpless to do anything to save it. All I can do is write and hope that all that I write will open your eyes to the truth, God's truth.

There are many preachers and deacons, many clergymen and women professing to know. Many teaching from the bible but I have no bible, meaning I do not fully quote from the bible because God does not need bibles and books of men to tell about him. These people cannot tell the truth about God because they know not the truth of God. No book that tells a person to rob and kill is of God. It is of men. Written by men to mislead deceive and tell lies. God can never go back on his word and you need to know this. God will never tell someone to go kill another person – take his life. He would never ever infinitely never ever do this because he is life and not death and you meaning each and every one of you must know this. God cannot kill it is not within him to take life. He's life why would he want to take life. It does not make any sense. God cannot commit suicide come on now. It is life for life and not life for death with God.

Yes we can all talk about Paradise and Hell but none can show you what they look like. None can tell you what life is truly going to be like once we have accepted this Man – death.

All I can say is if you don't trust God or truly love him continue to do what you are doing. Continue to turn a blind eye to what is going on. Continue to go to church and worship in dirty houses. Yes I can call them dirty houses because none of you respect God. You still trample on God when you wear your dirty shoes in churches, mosques whatever you deem holy. Places you said and say belongs to God.

No matter if you condemn me. This I know for sure and that is heaven and hell is side by side and no one can cross over into each other's land. In hell you will have no resting place. All that I have mentioned above you will find and do in hell. The choice is yours. You don't have to believe me. You need to know. Once you know you can continue on because your faith is now sealed and there is no one, nothing that you do will unseal your faith because you of yourself made that choice.

You cannot blame the devil because he is doing his job.

He is going to be paid for what he's doing and his payment is death the death of his spirit.

Just as how you go to work and get paid for your services the devil is getting paid. He's happy doing what he's doing because at the end of the day he knows when punishment is being handed down and being dished out he's not alone. Billions will be with him. All the oil that you are murdering for, all the genocide that you are committing, you are going to taste the same thing in hell and don't think it will be easy, it will be infinitely worse because spiritual fire is infinitely hotter than physical fire.

All you black people that turn down other peoples children, use obeah, voodoo, black magic; all that you do don't think you will not go unpunished. You will be punished because you know what you were doing was not right. You know and knew this is wrong but yet for a little bit of wine and a piece of meat you sell your souls to the devil and think you will not have hell to pay. Trust me infinitely on this you will have hell to pay because you will become more than Satan's bitches. You will become more than his slave. If Satan says eat the feces of hell you have to eat it you cannot refuse. Many of you are saying you would rather die before you eat feces ah guess what you are in hell you are going to die and you have to eat the feces you have no say because this was what you signed up for in the living.

A LITTLE TALK WITH GOD

You signed death's contract so what he says you must do. Satan cannot kill you in hell because Satan and death hath no authority here. Woman, the mother of sin has all the command. If she says eat the boils on my ass you have to do it because guess what all sin goes back to her not man. This is evil in its purest form. Satan has to bow down to her. He must submit to her because she is the true death – the death of life – sinful life. So know, infinitely know that Satan cannot kill your wretched or evil spirit because he hath no authority to do so. Death does not listen to him it must listen to her. So to say you would rather die don't make me laugh. You will not die right away because evil hath 24000 years to torment you and make you suffer in spiritual torment, spiritual fire before you eventually die which is six days if you if you divide by the square meaning use the four sides of the square which is 4. Yes four is the birth of evil but 6 is its death – timeline. No not nine like some will have to believe. You now know the truth so use the truth to talk to God – the true and living God and make the right decision and accept life for infinite generations to come. Though Satan hath the mark of the beast you say his daughters are the ones to carry on tradition because each will have 6 days to torment and punish you at will. So good luck in hell because what you get is what you deserve. Oh for you wife beaters – abusive husbands, dead beat dads trust me there will be no joy in the morning for any of you. Oh Allelujah weeping cometh but joy, relief will not come. You are in a woman's domain now because just as how Satan cries like a bitch for what he did to Eve because she is the final 4 meaning hath the final 6 I feel sorry for y'all. No for real people because my belly is hurting me a little right now and I am getting sick to the stomach as to what is going to happen to y'all. May God have mercy on your souls and I truly mean this because nothing you do on earth will save you from this judgment literally. A woman beater, neglectful father, a child abuser, a vile and disgusting child rapist and murderer weeping come but no joy cometh in the morning because your pain will be infinitely severe. If any of you think God is going to dirty himself and send his people to save you truly think again because unnu done. Unnu done yu hear mi. Unnu done – more fiya – fiya blaze fi unnu because not even the sun and all the lava of this earth hot so.

All a unnu whey a brandish di devil and have tattoo unnu done. Chicken nah go save unnu cause unnu done. Yu hear mi unnu done cause sey chicken a go stop bake and fry. No more blood jus spiritual fiya fi unnu.

All unnu obeah worker – workers of iniquity unnu done cause nothing is going to save unnu. Every memba a fi unnu family done because sey a no fiya fi one but fiya fi all.

No no no no buts here. Times have change because we did not take heed. We forgot and forget that our sins don't just affect us it affects family members as well hence I pray to God in a clean manner to not let my sins affect my children and if I have any good on my record let those good deeds help my family, including those that have passed on as well as the good and true family God has given me. So iniquity people unnu done cause wey no ketch you a go ketch yu pickney and if it no ketch yu pickney it a ketch yu cousin – someone in yu family. Sin no joke and play. Sin serious so wey yu no noa olda dan you. All unnu murderer wey a tek life like game meaning life is a game to unnu, unnu done. Woooooo fiyaaaaaaaa because sey unnu mek people buy unnu fi sport and now hell full a black people. A sary fi unnu but mi no sary fi unnu because sey unnu willing disrespect life – God so truss mi fi unnu punishment wussara dan dat of Satan – Sin. Unnu tek life – a part of God. God gi unnu life an unnu tun every inkling of goodness and his good land inna duppy town. Unnu willingly soil unnu han and rub unnu han with evil and fi dis unnu a go more dan sary because sey unnu youth them a go pay just like unnu. Unnu no think of what unnu a do? Unnu no care about life so since unnu want death a death of the worse kind unnu a go get. Remember the 12 gates of hell. Four to the East, four to the West, four to the North and four to the South yes people these gates are represented by the 12 tribes of sin – well the children of sin anyways. A no God's gate dem a hells gate and these gates donate the severity of your punishment as to evils you do and commit on earth. Hot a claps to backside when unnu go throw those gates because in my father's house there are many mansions. Know the truth – well you know now -----woooooooe mi belly, mi belly, mi belly. Hell hath no fury like a woman's scorn.

Oh yea for all of you that was promised a spot in hell – well a place of importance let me just burst your bubble now and tell you there are no places of importance in hell. So if Satan told you you will sit at his table in hell forget that. No one can sit at Satan's table because he hath none. Death is at the head of the table not Satan so know that. Satan is a bitch nigga in hell come on now. Death is King because death rules supreme and trust me death gets a chuckle when you run and hide. No for real. No one can hide from death because death knows where you are at all times baby and this is the beauty of death and the power of death. For real. Truss mi yu caane talk to death, no clergy can talk to death or even see death so all that you believe in is for naught because life requires life not death. Life requires and need God death requires nothing because he knows in time you must die and will die because his boo – his honey which is sin made it so.

What right do you have to turn another man's child back?

What right do you or anyone have to take a life senselessly?

Life is important and it is valued by God, cherished by God; none of you know the beauty of life. It is so beautiful that you don't want to lose it. You cherish it because life is a blessing, blessed by God. Go back to Genesis and see when God created man he blessed them and said they were good.

Those that are formed had this but we were the ones that chose to leave. Those that were created never left the fold. They still exist but guess what we cannot see them anymore. We say they are angels, guides but they live amongst us well not anymore because we have polluted the land and caused so much bloodshed upon the land that they had to leave. They had to reside someplace else in a land of true peace and not war.

None of this you can comprehend because it is beyond the scope of your mind, the scope of your reasoning and beliefs. All of you are looking for things that are supernatural and not natural. All of you are looking for one to save you. You have to save yourself. You of yourself know that no one can save you. Can another man tell you of your sins? No this is not the right question because a person that has the true gift of God can tell you about your sins as well as about you. Yes from the time of conception to the time when you are going to die so no to ask that question is not right.

You of yourself know that a lot of the stories told to you are not true but yet you go down in hell believing them.

You take your children to hell with you, causing them to believe these false stories. You kill others that do not conform to you and your beliefs and then turn around and say you are going to live in heaven with God. You are doing the will of God. Was not one of God's commandments "Thou shalt not kill". So why are we killing and going against God? **_Rest assured you will go to paradise but that Paradise will be HELL because God does not condone what you are doing. Nor is he pleased with what the lot of you are doing._** He told John to show you this and John did this in Revelations to the best of his knowledge because he wrote it down. Now the time has come for the seal to be broken and the lot of you are whoring like there is no tomorrow believing in people that don't know the truth or can tell you the truth.

You are all whoring like the harlot of old.

All lurking in the dark to kill

All lurking waiting for a bone that is cast onto dogs

You all have God stop looking around and look to true love, that which is in you. Once you have this you can do no wrong. Sin will die. It must die, have to die. You know this so why keep on deceiving yourself.

Why keep on believing in garbage?

No one can tell you how to clean up yourself. No amount of baptism by dirty and filthy people can clean you.

No water baptism, no holy water, no voodoo water, no communion, no consecration water or whatever can make you holy. Drinking wine and calling it communion, saying this is blood of my blood, flesh or my flesh is just disgusting and unholy - nasty. Tell me have we gone so far into cannibalism that we have to start eating human fresh and drinking their blood. We eat the carcass of animals as it is already isn't that enough? Now we are eating human flesh and drinking blood then turn around and say the people that practice cannibalism is nasty and we do the same thing. Go figure. We indulge in cannibalism so much that this practice in world wide – wide spread.

We are drinking blood and eating flesh where are we going to go with this kind of nastiness?

Tell me where are we going to go?

Women pass blood every twenty eight days and trust me sometimes it's painful as hell so why the hell would we want to drink someone else's blood, drink their pain?

Are we that stupid and ignorant?

Talk to any woman and they will tell you after so many years of seeing their menses we wants it to be gone. It is a pain in the ass but we know our bodies are the true keeper of time meaning we tell time as to the months and seasons in the physical realm and after that time is finished allotted we move on. We are not the true or the keepers of spiritual time hence we say in the physical we are passing time. Overstand now? Get it if you can't figure it out and use your own common sense it was given to you. He wanted the key to time – Life but God buried in all of us. Every woman on the face of this planet have the key to time which changes every twenty eight days to receive and create new life. By him procreating with Eve did not change anything because Evil stayed true to evil XX were as Life stayed true to Life XY. We are in sync or aligned with the planets this he does not know. This is why you say Mother Earth, The Cradle of Life and the Womb. Hence Wo-man yes everything is in the womb.

Life is a given but it has a time limit, it has a key and it cannot be unlocked by one it must be unlocked by two. One must give and the other must receive. This is the way it was and the way it will forever be the physical. Once you get to the spiritual realm and beyond this changes and then we can truly talk about spiritual birth the goodness of life beyond what we know to be spiritual realm. Right now all we know about is life and death the spiritual and the physical but the beauty of life far exceeds what you know. You need to know about the two before you can go on to the third.

A LITTLE TALK WITH GOD

God cannot be one; he cannot be alone so when anyone comes to you with one tell them get lost because you know there must always be two.

A sperm and an egg

XY

XX

XX cannot be two you say

Look

X = 10 in some lands

X = 1 in another land

10 + 10 = 20

2+0= 2

1+1 = 2 if you are using the one plus one analogy

Mother and Father

Get it now. So no Never One but TWO and the male sperm proves this to you.

I repeat never One but TWO

Ah go ahead and blast me pastors because you can't faze me anymore nor can you comprehend the scope of this. People will know the truth and they will learn it because it is destined to be this way. Your churches, false praise and worship will be tumbled down and your churches, mosques, shrines, synagogues will be left desolate and trust me not even drangcrow otherwise known as scavengers will want the carcass of your dead because it will become abominable to them.

They will walk away from it; none will want it, not even your dead that you bow down to will want it because disgrace and shame will now be upon their faces.

Yes like I said you can do all to me, condemn me but trust me the more you condemn is the more God is going to prove.

You cannot give the people blood of deceit to drink anymore

You cannot baptise with water because water is no longer pure, you have defiled it. None of you know that water baptism means nothing on earth but it is deadly in the spiritual realm. Once you are evil meaning you are evil in the physical realm you must be baptised in the spiritual world. You must be baptised in sin because you died in sin and this is where water baptism comes into play. This is your marriage to sin. You are literally baptised in water in the spiritual realm if you are sinful. This is your pain and suffering because water is the first to touch you and not fire. Spiritual fire is the final death.

None of you know that God does not baptise but Satan or sin does. Baptism does not make you holy it just make you more sinful and more of an abomination unto the true and living God.

You have polluted it so water baptism is no longer accepted by God it has become a condemnation unto him

Those that you baptise are not clean but filthy and their souls will go to hell with you

Your slate is not wiped clean, it is still there and you have to give an account for your sins

My sins that I have committed I have to answer for it because I did sin against God. All I can do is pray in a clean and truthful way for forgiveness and hope that whatever good that I do outweighs my sins. Yes I can pray for God to wipe my sins away but he cannot. What is on record stays on record and the only way to expunge your sins is by the goodness that you do.

God cannot go against his laws for man, not even me. I must live a good and clean life.

I have to do good and ensure that my goodness outweighs my faults – sins.

I too converted and I have to give an account for that

I've begged God for forgiveness and hope that he truly forgives me because I truly did not know. You do not know as well but now you know so you too can repent by asking God to truly forgive you and make you whole again.

I too hope that at least one GOOD that I do God finds favour in it and blot out some of my sins on judgement day

I cannot commit murder, deceive, rob, rape and steal and think that I will not be held accountable. It is a foolish person that thinks this way.

Adultery is a sin, been there done that, does that mean I am not guilty of this?

Does this mean when I get baptised this sin is wiped away? The answer to this question is no your sins are not wiped away and like I've told you above baptism have nothing to do with God but have everything to do with death, sin and the devil – evil.

I am still guilty of sin because it is written down and even though God forgives us for our sins it is still on our record. Know that the way God forgives is by the goodness that we do. One good done in truth and true kindness wipe out a multitude of sins. This is your forgiveness know this and do not just believe. Sin cannot cancel out sin only goodness the good you do in the physical world can cancel out sin.

I did wrong

Some of you do the same and think you will not be held accountable for it because Jesus will petition for you. Go back and read Blind Obsession Rebuttal – The Truth is Now or Never and you will see that you must be accountable for your sins.

Everyone must be punished whether you are punished on earth or in the spiritual realm you will be punished and trust me infinitely it is better to be punished in the physical than to be punished in the spiritual.

Spiritual punishment is far worse because death is the final punishment and trust me it is severe. More severe than the punishment you get on earth. You will go to hell and if the lot of you think that we are living in hell on earth, and the fighting that is going on is awful think again. This is peanuts compared to what hell is all about.

I've told you I have been through it. I know what spiritual and physical hell is all about. You know something is wrong but you can't get out.

You want to die but can't

You pray but your prayers are not being answered

You know you are in hell but can't get out because it is not your time you have to go through it

You think you're cursed

People look at you differently

They can't help you

Nothing you do will be able to help you because you have to go through it. You are literally bound and chained in hell because this is how it has to be. If you come out alive and sane then you would have past your test. You would have been one of the lucky ones because you made it.

<u>I know what I am talking about hence I tell you because no matter how evil your enemies are you of yourself would not wish this faith upon them. You of yourself will pray goodness for them.</u>

When you get to this stage of testing, spiritual testing you of yourself will want to die, this is how hard and deadly this stage is. It does not mean that you are evil, or God is punishing you. God is teaching you showing you so that you do all the good that you can as well teach others honestly and truthfully.

I never want to end up there again and that is why I pray for my children and unborn grandchildren. I see the follies of this world; I see what life has become. Humans do not value it therefore we kill at will. **Hell is not pretty. It is not peaceful nor is it pure. If you are crying now wait until you get there because you will die and nothing that you do will save you. Death is constant. It is slow and painful. The flesh does not feel pain the spirit or the energy within you does. The flesh is just a conductor for the spirit and hath no power. The energy or spirit inside of you hath the power. Your spirit is like electricity and that electric current feels pain. Everything that hath life feels pain yes emotions but as humans we see things one way. We cannot see the full picture. Everything must be inside the box. It has to be the way you see it and if you can't see it it does not exist and this is wrong. Life exists even when you can't see it. The air we breathe is life itself but we can't see it but we can feel it. Don't think for a minute that this air cannot die. It can die and this is done through** *the pollutants and filth we put in it. So know that the pain you feel on earth is nothing compared to the pain you are going to feel in hell. If someone was to punch you you would feel pain. If you are in a car accident you feel pain. We cry out when we feel pain and say it is not fair why is God letting this happen to me? This isn't pain my love trust me infinitely on this. Spiritual pain is far worse. Like I've said when you feel spiritual pain you want to die and can't die. It is that severe and harsh. Prayers mean nothing in the spiritual world because it cannot save you you have to go through it. God will not help you you have to face it until the time is up and you are released from it. I cannot stress the importance of living a good and clean life. Spiritual hell is not pretty. Yes the devil looks pretty and his offerings are pretty but take the makeup off and you will see the ugliness of hell. Like I've said sin is like makeup. Let's put it this way. Take a look at some of the most beautiful women and men in the world. Now take the makeup off, get rid of the photo shop, get rid of the cosmetic surgeries and you will see their true beauty. Some are not so beautiful and pretty are they? This is hell at least the best analogy I can give you and even with me giving you this analogy some men are saying if this is hell then I want to go there because it's not so bad. Well it is bad. It is that worse. Remember Spawn well your skin not skin spirit will become like his once it is burnt. Not pretty now is it. And yes this is how it was shown to me and I am relating it back to you. Sin is butt ugly – ooh Nelly don't get me started honey.*

<u>I cannot save you and don't even look at God to save you once you are in hell because you chose your own faith. You continued to trust and believe in sin. Know this; infinitely know this God will not save you because you made the choice to continue to follow sin. God has shown you time and time again what sin</u>

is all about and you are not listening to him. He's given you a mandate to live by and you have refused him. Now he's given you renewable energy to live by and if you refuse him and continue to live in sin then you will die just like the people of Noah's time. You have a choice now it's up to you. The final mandate for man is 2032 and if we don't clean up ourselves to the best of our ability by then then humanity can kiss themselves and this world goodbye. God is showing that you can do this. The smallest amount of good change affect sin and destruction. You all know this but refuse to do that which is right.

If you are doing all that is good meaning trying to live by God's integrity then you have nothing to worry about.

You are not hurting anyone

You are trying to live a clean life

Doing all the good that you can

You have your checklist with you check them off

I keep my house and body clean

I don't cheat on my wife

I don't cheat on my husband

I don't covet my neighbour's house

I don't want what they have I am happy with my own

I am happy with what God has given me and I am going to cherish it and not give it away falsely

I am going to hold on to what God has given to me because it is well given and it is blessed by him

I don't sit with vain and deceitful people in church

Made my body God's temple and I am purifying it with good and clean thoughts

Pleasure I enjoy with my wife

Pleasure I enjoy with my husband

I do not force my beliefs on others because I have none

I KNOW GOD NOW

I AM LIVING FOR GOD

WALKING IN HIS INTEGRITY

I am trying not to cheat on my taxes

I am trying to do all in my life honestly

I don't scream at my wife when things go wrong

I ask God for help and I know he will give me the answer even if it is in a song, or something I read, or watch on television

I do not abuse my wife but respect her because true respect is from God and if I abuse her or my children I am abusing God as well as disrespecting God.

I do not abuse my husband but respect him because true respect is from God and if I abuse him or my children I am abusing God as well as disrespecting God.

I am building positively with my wife and children

I am building positively with my husband and children

I do not have to live a lavish lifestyle to know that truly God loves me and is truly taking care of me.

Everything that I do I will do out of true love and passion

A LITTLE TALK WITH GOD

I will give out of true love, the true love of God

I help my neighbour because I know she is in need even if it is just a bag of milk that I buy I will buy it for her because I know she truly needs it and I will not want or expect anything in return for my goodness because I know this is what God would truly do and this is what he needs me to do. I know by me doing this I am blessed and highly favoured by God.

I will scale back on the unnecessary things that I buy

I will scale back on my overindulgence in alcohol and groceries so that the food that I buy do not go bad therefore I will not waste as much nor let the food that I buy go bad – spoil and I have to throw it out.

I will save for the future, for my kids and grandkids

I will give more if I can but I will not give all because if I give all then I will be sinning and I will go hungry and have nothing to show for it and this is not what God wants nor is it what he needs. The future is there and I have to save and prepare for it one day at a time.

When I go on vacation I will bring pencils, erasers, pens even if it is just a bottle of Aspirin for the needy and ensure the hotel that I stay give it to them (the needy). If these hotels do not give my offerings - gifts to the needy they will lose it all this I know. God will take away from their prosperity if they cheat and withhold all that I have given them for the poor. And yes you can give these items to one school one year then another school and or hospital the next. As long as the needy get the help if good faith and goodness then God will be pleased.

Summer time I will try to buy my neighbours children ice cream if I can even if it is just once because I know this is good

I will help out at the recreation center by tutoring kids if I can and this I know is good

My work sponsor a child in Africa and Russia and I contribute a dollar each pay to the sponsorship fund I know that is good because I am truly helping some with their life and future in a good way and this God infinitely loves and cherishes so yes I am in God's good book. I will also ensure that the children of Africa and Russia benefits from this because God don't like scammers and I refuse to give scammers my hard earned money. If you say you are helping others truly help because God infinitely loves truth not lies and I am blessed and highly favoured by God when I do all in truth - honesty.

I don't go to a church that is dirty anymore and I know this is infinitely good because I am showing God true respect and true love

I don't go drinking all the time with my buddies anymore. I am spending more quality time with my wife and children and this is infinitely good because God loves a true and truly loving and caring family, a family that respect each other and do things together.

We go out more even if it's just for a walk and this I know is good for the mind body and spirit as well as good for my health and health issues.

I do a lot more good things and yes I know God is pleased with this hence I am stress free in many ways.

I don't do all the bad things I use to do well at least I am making an effort not to and I know that must account for something and this is good

I don't walk with evil people anymore and this is a plus and a bonus and this I know is infinitely good

I visit my parents more

A LITTLE TALK WITH GOD

I visit my grandmother more

I visit my grandfather more

I don't push my children to do the things that I like or play the sports that I like. I let them choose what sport they want to play – the sports that they like.

I don't force them to do things that make them unhappy

I talk to them and boy that is not an easy feet because they have a minds of their own

No no I can't believe I am helping my wife with the laundry

Doing the dishes too

But that's good though because it is a lot easier on her.

We spend more time talking, walking, cuddling man this is scary but it is good. Stress level is down too. Wow this is great thank you God you truly know what I need.

Who would have thought me do all these things but hey it's not hurting anyone and all that I do does not create confusion or chaos in my life.

God sees that I am trying and therefore he cannot sin me for this because I am trying to be and do good. God cannot turn his back on me now, he has to come and live with me. I have God now and it feels great. It is wonderful because I do not desire the delicates of this world anymore.

My life is good, home is good and hell no my next door neighbour can't come to me with no damn gossip or the door will be in their face. Well no I kinda like the gossip but I have to stop.

Now my Peeps and True Loved Ones you know and you are beginning to get and have the truth.

Can you hold God accountable?

Accountable for what?

It's like what you said. I am trying why not help, come back now, come into my life and stay. I know it will be hard because sometimes I will beat up on him when I am angry and when things do not go my way but I am human and I am sure he would rather me beat up on him than go out there and get myself into trouble.

True but are you living by his integrity and doing what HE GOD tells you to do?

I am trying to.

Then yes you can.

Oh pastors, imams and priests shut the hell up. Close your damned mouth.

<u>If you are doing all you can meaning all the good that you can and you have truly asked God for help and he does not help you then yes you can hold him accountable because he will be guilty of not truly helping you when you needed help. This you can tell him on the day of judgement, even now. When I say judgment I am speaking about death – in the grave. If you tell him God I don't want to sin no more, truly help me to live by your integrity and truth and you are living by truth, meaning you've stop cheating on your taxes, telling lies, hurting others including your wife and husband as well as your kids and God does not hear you then yes you can hold him accountable because you are coming to him with truth and he's not hearing you. You are going to God clean and with honesty, you are not fake and you intend to keep being clean truthful and honest for the rest of your life and God does not help you you can hold him accountable. And</u>

no for some of you you can't just say God I am going to be clean and honest today and I am going to hold you accountable for everything that goes wrong in my life from now on. Never going to happen trust me. This is something you work at and it does take time.

In so doing if you keep on trying and God turns his back on you then you are not to blame because you went to him in truth and he refused you and this is wrong on his part.

With all this said it is not to say that people won't hurt you or try to hurt you but if you are not in their way they cannot hurt you. If you are living for God they cannot hurt you because God will close you off from them. You will not desire to be amongst them. You will be in God's world and they will be in theirs.

The one thing though and hopefully in time God will segregate his people from the wicked meaning good companies will rise so that his people can work for these companies. In so doing we don't have to cry and worry about our souls anymore because these companies will hold God near and in high esteem. They will do things honestly to ensure their existence in the future and no people I am not casting stones.

All we can do is to pray for this and once God sees enough of us praying in a clean and good manner for the same thing, the goodness and betterment of humanity he will return. If he doesn't then yes we can hold him accountable because he does not live by his true word and integrity. If God cannot live by his word and integrity he cannot sin you because you asked and you keep asking plus you are doing everything to please God and not just yourself.

Know that God cannot go against his word. As humans we go against our word and we are not faithful or true to God.

Know that even though you pray to God for a clean and honest home obstacles do come in the way meaning negative forces still come in. You can keep your home clean but sin do creep in. Remember your children have friends and their standards and values are not yours. They will disrespect your home and make it unclean so you have to know the friends that your children keep because what they do at your house they cannot do it in theirs. You have to speak to your children on the friends that they keep. I am not casting stones in regards to anyone's children or child I am speaking from experience. Truss mi sometimes its not your children that cause you pain or even cause your home to be unclean but others and I am going to leave it at that because I know. Oh God do I know. If only God could show and tell you but mi noa.

Good values are blessed but bad values are as sin – death.

But what if you are wrong?

What if all that you have said is wrong and it makes not difference?

What if when we are called to be judged on that final day and we say well God Michelle said I was to stop beating my wife and I listened

She said give five dollars and I listened and gave

She said to do more with the family and I listened and did more with my family

She said not to sit with filthy and deceitful people and I listened and stopped. I do not sit with filthy and deceitful people anymore

She said not to fornicate and commit adultery and I listened and stopped fornicating and committing adultery

She said to pray inwardly and I listened. I started to pray silently and talked to God truthfully in a clean and good way

All she said I listened and tried my best to do all that is good and pleasing in your eyes.

WHAT IF GOD SAID I WAS WRONG?

Know that God judges no one and this I learnt because God has nothing to do with wicked and sinful people. God deal in good not evil. Evil judge and cast stones but God can never ever, infinitely never ever judge. His laws are right and just and they can never judge because right is right and wrong is wrong. Right can never judge wrong but wrong judges right. Meaning wicked people and spirit judge. In the grave God cannot judge you only evil can judge you meaning judge the wicked because good people are not in hell only wicked people. This has nothing to do with heaven because heaven is just a resting place for good. This is why you have heaven and hell, God and Nod, good and evil. Hopefully I've explained it right.

Now if God said Joe I am holding you guilty for listening to Michelle and doing what Michelle said not what others say but what Michelle said:

THEN FOR ALL THAT YOU HAVE DONE IN GOODNESS AND TRUTH, PURE TRUTH BECAUSE YOU TRULY LOVED GOD AND WANTED WHAT'S

BEST FOR HIM AND YOU AS WELL AS YOUR FAMILY NO EVIL YOU TRIED TO DO. YOU DID YOUR BEST IN EVERYTHING THAT IS GOOD AND WITH ALL THAT YOU HAVE DONE AND GOD SAID YOU ARE GUILTY I WILL TELL GOD AND I AM TELLING GOD NOT TO HOLD YOU GUILTY OR BLAME YOU BUT HOLD ME GUILTY BECAUSE I MISLED YOU. YOU ARE NOT TO BLAME.

I WILL TAKE FULL RESPONSIBILTY FOR THIS BECAUSE I WAS WRONG. I MISLED YOU AND FOR THIS I AM INFINATELY GUILTY OF SIN AND DESERVE TO BE PUNISHED AND NOT YOU.

God cannot say he does not know this because I have told God this already. He has given you to me so therefore I have to teach right and do right in the sight of God and man. One of my responsibility is to make sure that you have right and exact knowledge not lies.

I cannot live by man's standards I have to live by God and my life I must and infinitely try to live clean. I cannot be an example for God if I constantly live dirty no come on now.

I will make mistakes and my past is there to prove this. I am still making mistakes but the beauty of making mistakes is learning from them so that you can teach and educate others not to do them. So don't think me holy or have preconceived notions about me. Know me and what I am capable of this is all I ask because my mouth can get foul.

Make no mistake about me. I will take full responsibility for deceiving you if God said I was wrong. I will not back down and I refuse to back down from this because I know the value and preciousness of life. If I am guilty of sin know that God is guilty of sin also because it is he who is showing me things and educating me not man. He gave me guides and if the guides are wrong then God is wrong also.

WHAT NO WAY

YES WAY

Know that God does not judge anyone. We say judge because of lack of better words. Your deeds are written down and if you refuse to listen to God and follow his rules then you will die. Death is the punishment for sin you know this.

I CANNOT TEACH YOU OF TRUE LOVE, THE TRUE LOVE OF GOD AND IT IS A SIN. NO THAT IS NOT FAIR TO YOU AND I WILL BE THE ONE RAPING YOU OF YOUR SOUL AND YOUR DIGNITY. I WILL BE THE ONE RAPING YOU OF YOUR CHANCE TO BE WITH GOD AND THAT IS SO NOT FAIR SO NOT FAIR TO YOU. I WAS THE ONE TO TAKE AWAY YOUR GLORY, ROB YOU OF YOUR GLORY AND THAT IS A SIN.

COME ON NOT EVEN JESUS SAID THAT

I AM NOT JESUS NOR AM I A PROPHET I AM SIMPLY MICHELLE ONE THAT TRULY LOVE GOD AND YOU. I DO NOT CLAIM TO BE NOR WILL I CLAIM TO BE. IF I AM WRONG I HAVE TO OWN UP TO IT. I HAVE TO TAKE RESPONSIBILITY FOR IT. I CANNOT BLAME SOMEONE ELSE FOR MY WRONG. THAT IS SIMPLY NOT RIGHT.

I refuse to tell anyone I am Jesus or a prophet because I know Jesus does not exist but evil does death does. If you were to look at the story of Jesus and put it in proper perspective you would know that the pictures of Jesus represent death. It is death that man is following to their graves because God himself hath children and not one child alone.

No one can say they are the only child of God. I know God and I infinitely know that God would never give his children over to death come on now.

God would literally make his children die for death's children. A really who unnu? God mek im pickney ded fi wicked people? God no love im pickney den. Wicked a wicked and God don't deal with wicked and sinful people come on now.

Like I've said what belongs to death belongs to death and God has nor does he have anything to do with death come on now.

God cleeeeeeeeeeaaaaaaaan come on now.

No even I would let my children be a sacrificial lamb for wicked and evil people. Wicked people no better so why the hell would I sacrifice myself or my children or anyone for them. Mek dem tan dey. A who dem. Dem noa wey dem du. After dem dun tun yu dung, mi fi feel compassion or even feel sary fi dem. Hell no honey I love God too much to go walk on sins bandwagon. Truss mi mi ass too pretty – beautiful for sin to kiss cause mi no waane ketch germs.

A God alone so if I am wrong and I teach you wrong then your punishment I must bare because I did teach wrong. Like I said God knows this and my decree is on file with God and it's in this book so I can't say I did not say that because I did write it in this book and all God would have to do is open this book and quote me word for word. Yes you too.

Baby Love your soul is precious so use it wisely. Know that no one can be sinned for goodness. Goodness is a blessing and it is not wrong but you have to know who you give to because it is not all you must give to.

Never give your wealth to a wicked and sinful person because if you do you will lose it all and you will never recover your true blessings so know who to give. And yes I am speaking from experience.

When you are not sure who to give to no if you feel a way in giving someone then tell God he will make a way for you so that you do not give away your true blessings this I know first hand.

For me I tell God of the Good that I need to do once my books start to sell because I am depending on God to help me let his good blessing that he has bestowed upon me reach his true people. His roots not people who are leaves and branches but his true roots. People that will infinitely stay true to him as well as teach their children to be roots of God and for God for infinite generations.

I DO THINGS THAT IS STILL WRONG TODAY. GOD KNOWS IT AND TRUST ME WE WILL HAVE IT OUT BECAUSE NOTHING IS THE SAME WITHOUT GOD AND HIS TRUE LOVE SO IF TRULY LOVING GOD IS A SIN, WANTING AND NEEDING TO DO RIGHT BY HIM IS A SIN, WANTING AND NEEDING HIM TO LOVE ME INFINATELY IS A SIN THEN I AM GUILTY OF SIN AND I AM GUILTY OF MISLEADING YOU AND THIS I AM TRULY SORRY FOR AND ACCEPT YOUR PUNISHMENT BECAUSE I DID YOU WRONG. YOU SHOULD NOT HAVE TO BE PUNISHED BECAUSE OF MY SIN.

I am the one to cause you guilt so why should you be punished. I misled you. I deprived you of your soul. I deprived you of God. You listened to me. I am the guilty one and not you. So yes if I am wrong and you find out on that day that I have misled you and caused you to sin more, caused you to go against God then God cannot hold you guilty but me. I am the one he should hold guilty and let you go free because I did you wrong. I will bare the punishment and take FULL RESPONSIBILITY FOR THIS.

I go on record before God, his angels and his children to say I take full responsibility for your sins if I have misguided and misled you in anyway. If I knowingly taught falsely I am guilty of sin and he God should not hold you guilty because I misled you. I was the one to give you false information. I was the one doing the misguiding and not you and for this I am infinitely guilty and accept punishment - GUILT.

But this does not mean you should misuse my words to commit sin, do wrong. This does not mean you should use my words to spread hate, tell lies, rape or kill anyone. Infinitely know I will not under any circumstances accept responsibility for this because you all know better. This does not mean you should go out there and kill, rape, rob and steal. Anything that you do that is sinful like rape as mentioned above or kill let's put it this way if you go against God then you are on your own. . TRUTH DOES NOT HURT AND YOU SHOULD NOT HURT. WALK IN GOD'S INTEGRITY AND IF YOU SEE ME DOING WRONG DO NOT HIDE IT. If you do wrong I will not be held accountable for that. So don't even go there because God knows the heart. Continue to do good. Yes at times you will fall but pick yourself up and ask for forgiveness. Get back on board because I am with you in all that you do. Yes if you fall I am with you just like God is so no more hate and lies and sinful deeds okay and don't you dare cross your fingers because I know some of you.

IF I AM WRONG SAY NA HA GIRLFRIEND YOU ARE WRONG

TELL ME WHEN I AM WRONG BECAUSE IF YOU DON'T YOU WILL BE AS GUILTY AS ME AND YOU WILL BE PUNISHED. AND PLEASE PEOPLE DON'T

BE BRUTAL. DON'T WANT YOU TO KILL ME. I AM SENSITIVE.

You will stand up for us I mean if God said you did wrong that was not right?

"YES"

You quoted yes.

"YES"

You mean it?

"INFINITELY YES YOU HAVE MY WORD AND GOD'S WORD ON THIS"

But

"No buts, I've already told God this and it is written down so I can't go back on my word. There's no givesy backsy here. Like I said true love does not hurt baby. All I want and need is for you to live the best life you can live for you and God because God is the truth and he never fails and will never fail."

But what if you are wrong?

"GOD IS NEVER WRONG HE IS ALWAYS BE RIGHT. IF I AM WRONG TRUST ME GOD WILL TELL YOU"

But

Stop the buts will you I've been through enough in my life and I know what pain is all about and God is RIGHT, no one can tell me that he is wrong. The truth can never be wrong it can only be right – infinitely right.

I KNOW GOD IS RIGHT AND THE ABUNDANCE OF LOVE THAT HE HAS YOU CAN HAVE IT IF YOU JUST KNOW AND TRY. YOU NEED TO TRUST GOD.

What good am I if I mislead you?

What good am I if I take your soul?

Is that true love?

Tell me come on tell me is that true love?

Anyone that truly loves you never ever want to see you hurt, never ever want to cause you pain and suffering. If that person does then that is not true love he or she never truly loved you. That person is not true. I am not perfect I'm just like you. I make mistakes too and I am learning just like you.

True love does not hide nor is it stingy

I know what evil can do and with all that I said above in accepting guilt many will come after me. Many will use my name and even write books in my name to say otherwise so you have to be on your p's and q's. Remember the devil and his people will do all that they can for me to fail and for this I am leaving them to God. All that they do God will undo and God will show you these people that are trying to hurt me trust me infinitely on this. God knows my loyalty and over time you will too. It's not about me my peeps and true loved ones it's about God. Anyone that wants to see my hurt and demise is not of God. They are of the devil and do the work of the devil you know this. Like I've told you God will never give you dirty people to tell you about him. When God choose a person to deliver his message they are well chosen you should know this. Yes the devil and evil people make lies look like the truth and it is up to you to question God. If it does not feel right in your body and mind then it is not right for you. ***If you feel that I am telling you something that is wrong then I am not right for you and God the True and Living God is not right for you.*** We've all been taught to follow sin I am no different but now I know the full truth based on what was given to me and I am living by this truth. Certain things I cannot clarify clearly but the one that is to come she will clarify things better but she must live clean. Who she is I do not know and maybe one day God will show me her clearly so that I can tell you exactly what she looks like and what land she will come out of. You all know now how lies can become truthful and how man use lies to manipulate and deceive. Once you are on the pathway of truth God will show you all the lies because lies are that powerful and deceiving. It is hurtful. Tell me something when we do wrongs do we not deny it. Go back to the beginning in the bible Adam and Eve and even Cain when they did wrong did they own up to it? Did they not blame someone else? When we do wrong some of us run and hide because we do not want to get caught? Everyone denies the truth. Evil and sin must deny the truth. They must kill the truth and when they do they hide and say I did not do it. When they go infront of a judge they plead not guilty. It is no different with God. We do wrongs and we go before God and plead not guilty when we know we are guilty.

God cannot hold you accountable for the truth. Trust me infinitely when I tell you God can never ever infinitely never ever hold you accountable for the truth because you did not do anything wrong but he sure as hell can hold you accountable for your sins – your wrongs – lies.

Look around you. Look at the good and the bad, the Ying and the Yang who contains it?

If God did not have an abundance of love, true love and patience would he make the sun shine on the good and the bad?

Would he not leave us to die?

Remember I told you the comet/meteor is coming this is real it is not fiction

If God did not truly love you would he be warning you of what's to come?

You have to prepare for this, what's to come. The shortage of water and food, the new diseases that will infect the land, the cannibalism that will sky rocket out of control, this snake that is rising to devour the people

You cannot be like the children of old. They did not listen and see what happened to them, they followed death to his home and death has them still

If God truly loves you why would he see you suffer?

Why would he want to see you in pain?

Why would he let others hurt you?

We are the ones to believe in death.

We told God we accept death and this is why he has left us alone to face death.

We are the ones to believe people that tell us we have to die to see God. Instead of questioning them we accept their lies. We die to see death we do not die to see the True and Living God. I've told you there are two gods the god of Death and the god of Life and for those familiar with Greek Myth Zeus and Hades. God is Life and you do not have to die to see him. When you see nature and the beauty of nature each and every day you see God because nature is true life. It is serene and peaceful. Nature does not wage war with anyone or anything. Don't even think of natural disasters because this is not nature. Nature nurtures us, provide good food for us, clean and pure drinking water, shelter but we are the ones – humans are the ones to destroy nature. I've told you these disasters have nothing to do with God it hath to do with our sins. We more we sin the more the earth dies and the more we die. Our final death is this comet that is coming.

A LITTLE TALK WITH GOD

Like I said humanities mandate is 2032. This date is not just for America it is for the globe and if we do not take heed the earth will continue to shift to align with the comet that is to come. There are no ands ifs or buts about this. There are no scare tactics here. Noah did warn but the time of Noah is now. I know many have come and gone, foretold and nothing has happened but I am not them. I refuse to be like them because I know the pain and heartache of trying to decipher disaster dreams. You see them but you cannot interpret them sometimes and this is because we are not to interfere with death. We can because I did. Jamaica and Haiti were to be destroyed – wiped off the face of this planet but because of interference on my part there destruction was stayed. I know the death of Jamaica right now but I will not sound the alarm. I am allowing the old mothers to do so because hell is full of Jamaicans – yes my people and trust me many will weep and mourn because none of them know that for each senseless murder, for each sin the earth mourns and set itself up on a collision course with death. When earth cannot take it anymore destruction comes and this destruction that is coming man will not survive because the death of humanity will be written on this comet – wormwood. We can change this but it is up to each individual. Good must separate from evil because evil must take his children. God is the only ark you need because I infinitely know that God will deliver his people from this final destruction. Yes you can say I do not know what I am talking about and this is fine. You can call me crazy but none of you can or will hold me accountable because if you are reading this book or hearing about it I would have done my job. The Job which God, the True and Living God required of me and like I've said the decision you make today will be up to you.

Like I've said we die to see death. When the spirit leaves our body are we not dead? Meaning is the flesh not dead so why want that. Why want to die? The True and Living

God never prescribed death for anyone so why want death? Why let others tell us we have to die to see God when we all know that this is wrong? Come on now. God never told us we had to die and please don't come with the Jesus crap because you know that this story is false - wrong. Come on now. When do the lies stop? Choose Life and live because if you chose death you will die. It's that simple.

Know this God is not letting disaster happen to us we are letting disaster happen to us because we know the wages of sin is death so if death comes in the form of tsunamis, earthquakes, storms, cyclones then we cannot complain because it is our sins that are causing them. The less we sin the more earth will tone down and bring about balance and true harmony. We know better so we have to do better come on now. If a place is not clean God will not reside in it. If you tell God to go he will go and not return. Ours sins are our way of saying God I do not want or need you in my life. If your body is not clean God will let you know by making you smell yourself. We need to clean the outer and inner and cleaning the inner is not an easy feet. It is hard to do because we don't know what organs need cleaning. Ask your doctor about internal cleansing and if it's okay start cleaning the inner. Twice per year is fine but make sure you clean it. If you can't clean it twice per year (the inner) drink more water, maybe a glass more per day if you only drink two. Make healthier choices in your diet but clean yourself up and let God come in.

Segregate yourself from wicked and evil people and you will see how calm and beautiful your life becomes.

FORGET IT JOE, DO NOT QUIT YOUR JOB. QUIT IT AND I WILL BE SO MAD AT YOU. INSTEAD OF EATING LUNCH WITH THESE PEOPLE GO INTO YOUR CAR LISTEN TO THE RADIO ON YOUR LUNCH HOUR, SKETCH, READ A BOOK ANY BOOK OF INTEREST

A LITTLE TALK WITH GOD

AND NO I WILL NOT PROMOTE MINE HERE. WATCH YOUR FAVORITE SHOW ON YOUR PSP, LISTEN TO MUSIC ON I TUNES, BUY THEM IF YOU CAN AFFORD THEM, AND YES EVEN READ THE BIBLE IF THAT SUITS YOUR FANCY BUT I WILL NOT ADVISE IT. I REFUSE TO BECAUSE I KNOW THE HATRED WITHIN THE BIBLE AND THE LIES IT TELLS ON GOD.

MEDITATE ON GOD, HAVE LUNCH WITH GOD TOO. GO FOR A WALK, TELL GOD TO WALK WITH YOU IF YOU WANT HIM TO, SMILE AND TELL GOD JOKES IN YOUR MIND, SIT IN THE PARK, WATCH PEOPLE PLAY BALL IN THE PARK BUT SEGREGATE YOURSELF FROM THOSE THAT ARE CAUSING YOU HARM AND PAIN.

GOD DEFINITELY DON'T LIKE WHEN YOU SIT WITH WICKED PEOPLE BECAUSE GUESS WHAT THESE PEOPLE ARE NOT FOR GOD NOR ARE THEY FOR YOU. IF YOU ARE FOR GOD TRUST ME THEY WILL DO EVERYTHING IN THEIR POWER TO THROW YOU OFF.

THEY WILL TELL YOU ABOUT THEIR LOVE LIFE, WHO THEY ARE SLEEPING WITH FROM WHOM THEY ARE NOT SLEEPING WITH. THEY WILL TELL YOU ABOUT THAT PERSON'S LOVE LIFE, EVERYTHING THAT IS WRONG WITH SOMEONE'S LIFE THEY WILL TELL YOU BUT YET THEY WILL NOT BE ABLE TO SEE WHAT IS WRONG IN THEIR OWN LIFE.

GET ME JOE.

Yes mam

Good now if your wife likes lingerie and you can afford to buy her some sexy sexy sexy ones go window shopping.

No I don't have my line yet. Would love to have one though. Hopefully when I do I can entice you to come and buy some for her.

Ha-ha you are promoting your line, not fair plus you are enticing me, see that is so hypocritical of you and so not fair.

Got me and I love you. Truly hug me and kiss me.

NO

Why

You are enticing me and I am so going to tell my wife

Hey kiss her for me because now she will love you even more because you cannot be fooled. You are on your way to knowing God and not letting anyone fool you when it comes to you and God as well as true love.

Confusing but I don't want to entice you. If I do get a lingerie line scope it out and see if it is your fancy. You're not be obligated to buy any. You know how much I love lingerie and shoes. I better stop there because I am so going overboard right Joe.

Yes you are.

Do you get what I am showing you now?

Yes

I have not finished my prayers yet have I?

No

Free download on LULU. I will put them into book format and you can download off LULU for free but to date LULU does not have free down loads in book format. This is sad for me because I so need to upload some free stuff for you guys and it is damned frustrating not being able to. I detest e-books but if I have to I have to and yes I am wining.

You have not given us any free books as yet?

No but one day I will and trust me you will enjoy well I hope because nothing changes with me you all know this.

Hopefully one day I will get to travel the globe and we can meet face to face and talk about what you dislike about what I am telling you. I know I also have to clarify things that are confusing so make notes and highlight what needs clarification. I'll do my best to walk with my books okay. I have a couple short stories and that I will put under this banner and by the grace of God will make some of those free to you too but please don't tell LULU.

Our secret

No because there are no secrets with God and that is just plain out false on your part and you have just promoted your other line.

Come on Joe see with me? I am batting my eyes and pouting my lips. Pleassssse!!!!

No because you are asking me to lie for you and that is wrong, it is a sin.

Hey I am doing a good job and this is what I truly love. No matter how I come at you especially you Joe you do not cave in and this is what God need. When the devil and his agents come at you with things like I have done you will be strong enough to say no and carry on. Do not cave in because you are showing God that you are his root and not one of the leaves and branches that is blown away by the wind.

True love always my friend, true love always.

Wait

Yes Joe

You know you have just opened up yourself for evil and wicked people to hurt you. You know they are going to come at you now more than ever for you to fall and for you to reside in hell with them.

True but you know what Joe I infinitely trust God to protect me and shield me from these people. Also, I am not worried about evil and what evil do because the more they do to hurt me is the more God will hold them accountable and protect me. They will have to answer to God for what they are doing because **THEY KNOW WHAT THEY ARE DOING IS WRONG.**

God will not make me fall at their hands. I know this because all that I do in God for God can never fail.

All that you do for God that is good cannot fail

Everything I do and yes all that I do I do in God for God.

Don't think that because the devil and his people are there they won't be held accountable. They will you know this. Everything that they have done they have to pay for it and account for it. THEY WILL BE HELD ACCOUNTABLE AND TRUST ME THE PRICE THEY PAY WILL NOT BE PRETTY BECAUSE THEIR PRICE IS DEATH.

You don't willing hurt someone because they don't conform to you. You don't take what is not given to you, you don't mislead and misuse. If God tell you do something do it clean, truthfully and honestly and not in a dirty manner.

A LITTLE TALK WITH GOD

People can say you are misleading.

They can but tell me what have I told you that were wrong?

You get down on religion. In a way are you not telling us not to believe?

I will never tell you to believe anything I will tell you to KNOW because knowledge is one of the keys to God.

Once you know God no one can come to you with belief meaning no one can convert you to their evil doctrine or doctrines.

God is infinitely not a doctrine he is life and you have to know this. It's either you are for life or you are for death.

Let me tell you something once you get off the track of life the climb back up the mountain is hard. Some don't make it back up the mountain hence Moses showed you and to a certain extent Martin Luther King Jr. told you. I've told you about the three (3) races on the mountain but it is up to you to get there. It is up to you how you get there. I cannot put you there you have to get there yourself – on your own.

Look at a mountain can many of us climb it?

Some try and fail. The mountain is the best way to describe the climb to God because 99.9999999 percent of us fail to reach the top of the mountain – the top with God.

This too is what God has been trying to show us over the centuries and we cannot comprehend. We can't learn nor can we listen. If God say stay with me don't go don't go because you cannot see the future – your life in time but God can hence he tries with us but we constantly fail him.

Let no one tell you that it is easy to get to the top because it is not trust me infinitely on this. If you are on the top of the mountain with God let no one take you off because the day you come off it is the same day you will regret it. Eve found out the hard way so please do not be like Eve and follow sin to your death because when you die you will never ever infinitely never ever see God or have life again.

God is important but trust me evil will infinitely never ever make it easy for you to stay on track – the track of God. Evil will throw everything at you for you to fail hence it is imperative for God's children to separate themselves from evil and evilous domains. If we as God's children continue to live amongst evil people and marry them our lives will forever be stressed and sinful. We will forever live in stress hence Psalms One (1) tells you how to live. We must conduct ourselves in this like manner because if you do not walk in the council and councils of the ungodly they cannot hurt you and you will infinitely be at peace. You have to be true to you and God. You have to be good to you. Like I said I cannot tell you what relationship you must have with God because this is between you and God. If you want to have a talkative relationship with God do it. It is your relationship and I cannot tell you it is wrong because like I said I tell God everything and I mean everything. Trust me if God could speak to me face to face I would have him pick out the clothing I'm to wear including my underwear. No for real because I don't even think God knows the extent of how much I cherish and truly love him. This feeling that I have for him is insane meaning it's like I'm going to go insane for him. Like I want to burst out and light up earth with this bright light for all to see. This love is so hard to explain but if I could show the world what I am talking about I would. It's like a solar eclipse then but there would be no darkness and the entire world would see this eclipse at the same time and yes everyone would go aah including wicked people. I guess this is the best way I can explain it. I do not take God for granted hence I tell him everything. I tell him of my needs, my hopes, my truth, my everything. This is truth – true honesty. The scope of your love – true love and truth is determined by you and not others hence I cannot say the way you love – truly love God is wrong. This is your truth and not mine because my truth is not your truth well no I'm wrong your truth is my truth because God is my truth and he is yours too.

I am not telling you not to go to church but go to a church that is clean and a church that put GOD first. The praise should be about God and not man and profits (prophets).

Did Revelations not say there are 7 churches and God has a bone to pick with all 7 of them?

You are telling me you can hold God accountable that is just wrong. That is blasphemy and I don't agree with you on that.

Why?

No one can hold God accountable; he's the creator that created us all; he created everything so no, he cannot be held accountable.

How did he create us all?

Remember we were formed those that he created were good and he blessed them. Adam was formed came through sperm and an egg.

Ya Ya but I still stay you cannot hold God accountable.

Why not? If you tell him you want to cleave to him, live a clean life with him, segregate yourself from wicked people, repent of your sins, you are trying to live a clean life and he has done nothing to help you then why can't you hold him accountable?

We are the ones to make the choice?

Did you or did your parents choose for you?

The school you go to

The religion that you praise and worship in

The people you associate with how many parents have chosen for us?

How many parents teach their children to hate based on colour, religion and sex?

How many parents will kill you for Jesus?

How many parents tell you that Jesus is God?

Jesus is coming back to save them and you

How many parents teach you and tell you that Jesus who is God died for their sins but yet we are still sinning?

How many parents take you to church and sing the song Moses Moses take off your shoes because the place you are standing on is holy ground but yet still have their shoes on in church on holy ground?

How many parents teach us to trust and believe in the trinity when we know there is no such thing as Trinity, god the father, god the son and god the Holy Ghost?

How many parents still teach that God favours the Jews over everyone else but yet God still cause it to shine on the good and the bad, so tell me how is that favouritism?

Shall I go on?

There are many factors and no we cannot blame God for this, yes we can blame Adam and Eve but we can't because **each and every one of us have the ability to change the course of our destiny. Each and every one of us have a right to choose. We all have a choice and**

whether we chose good or evil it is up to each one of us.

But how does this relate to holding God accountable?

It doesn't, but know that you can hold God accountable. What you cannot do is hold him accountable for evil and the evils of this planet. Yes sometimes I blame him when I am angry but I infinitely know better. If we had stayed with God on the mountain and refused sin none of this meaning evil would not have infested the land and caused it to be dirty. We are the ones to make the land, this planet and our lives unclean – dirty because we accepted sin. Infinitely know that sin cannot go on God's mountain. Yes I quarrel with God and say he is to blame in some way but this is me and the relationship I have with God and you cannot do what I do without truly knowing God. You have to know God and have a personal relationship with God in order to unleash on him like I do and this you will learn in time. We cannot, infinitely cannot hold God accountable for the sins and wrongs that we do. Like I said we made that choice and he did tell Eve not to eat the fruits of sin and she did not listen. She did partake of sin therefore causing sin. Even if were to look at it from another angle and say Adam was not Satan. Say we take the bible at its word not I cannot go there because this is infinitely wrong and it is a sin if I do that because I know better.

Plain out she did not listen and it is costing humanity until this day. It's almost 24000 years since the birth of sin and we are still not listening.

I said you can hold God accountable and how you hold God accountable is if you are trying to walk in his integrity and issues and problem continue. You have done all to block all facets of evil from coming into your life, you've prayed and prayed, asked God for help and no help comes then you can hold him accountable because God is truly not there – listening to you. You are trying your best to live a clean and good life and he God is not listening to you then yes you can hold him accountable.

I cannot add generational curse to this because here generational curse does not apply. This is between you and God – your truth with God.

Just like that I can hold God accountable?

No give God time because spiritual time and physical time are not the same. God will show you what to do but sometimes we cannot comprehend. Remember this is not God's domain. He does not reside on earth because it is filthy, polluted with evil. Blood has ravished the land. We as humans have become filthy as well so it will take time to filter out the negative, or penetrate the negative forces that surrounds us. Do not expect the unexpected meaning know how God gives you your answer. We don't always get answers in dreams. We get it in a song, a movie or a stranger giving you encouragement. Sometimes I would grapple with God and get mad at him. I tell him he does not care nor does he live by his word. Trust me infinitely on this my daughter would come into my room and say mommy listen to this and she would play me a song. She would even try to sing it and I would listen to the song and that song would give me the answer as to what I needed. I got songs like Step Aside by Tamela Mann, Still with You by Eric Benet; Love is calling by Duane Stephenson.

What do you mean?

Presently we have prayers that we use to connect to God, we also have dreams. Remember there is spiritual and physical wickedness and wickedness is greater. It is harder for physical and spiritual good to go through or get connected with God because evil is doing everything in its power not to make your true and good prayers and thoughts go through to God. Evil is also making it hard for God to get through to you. Sometimes the answer is confusing meaning God is giving you the right answer but when that answer is coming down to you it has to go through negative channels to get to you.

I don't understand.

You have approximately seven billion people on the face of the planet. Think of the miles and miles of negative energy that you as a person have to go through just to get to God. Your prayers have to pass through these avenues as well just to get to God and the same is said for God when he is sending back answers. Look up do you not see a blue sky in the day and a black or dark sky in the night. Both are negative energy so your dream and or answer have to go through this before getting to God and the same is said for God when he is replying to you.

Comprehend?

Sort of

The journey is far and this is the same thing with dreams. When your body is in a state of rest, meaning not so much negative forces are affecting you you dream. See things; communicate with your guides and God. Goodness has to go through this negative channel because we made it so. We have given evil the power to dominate and confuse our lives. It was never like this. Remember evil could not get in but we gave evil an opening and he is using it. He is also using the back door because he found another way in so we have to close off all access to evil when sending and receiving messages.

Is this the same process as above?

Yes it is. Some things are immediate and some take years to manifest – meaning when God gives you the answer it can take years to come true.

Everything is spaced out like you said?

Yes but this isn't God's fault it is the fault of man

So then you can't hold God accountable and you have just proven this

You can.

Alright say God's chosen people are a billion in number in the physical.

All of you are praying for peace

Wanting to be segregated from evil

Want a place to live for God in peace and harmony

You want no evil to enter

You trust God to infinitely do this for you and he does not then yes on the day of judgement as we humans call it and even now you can tell him if he does not do this, bring back peace true peace to your life, come back and help you so that all of you do not leave his fold, you ask him to take all evil from around you both spiritual and physical then yes you can hold him accountable because you infinitely mean what you say. You are trying your best to work for this and if God does not do this then you can hold him accountable because he is not listening to you he is listening to the evil people of this world and he himself would not have wanted peace. He does not live by his word and integrity, he would be a liar and he cannot hold you accountable for your sins because he too is sinful. And no, no evil can hold God accountable. Infinitely know this because I know evil will try but it cannot work because there are no loopholes with God. God does not deal with evil or in evil - stink. Remember you are going to God with truth, peace and true love, he cannot refuse you and if he did something is wrong. If you and decent and good people are going to him for a common cause, you are trying and he's neglecting you then something is wrong and on that fateful day when you stand before the Judges (not God because God judges no one and yes this is why your book of sin mentions judges) and they say Joe you did this and this, you have the right to say judge I am guilty of that but remember on this day I asked God, pleaded and cried to God to take sin from me, help me not to sin and I tried but he God did not help me, sin kept coming and no matter how I resisted it kept coming. I know you test, the devil tempted but I told you not to test or tempt me any more because it is painful and I do not like it. It caused me grief and pain but evil never led up so I am not to blame you have to take that one because I was truthful to you and told you I could not bare anymore. My burdens were too great and you can't say I did not tell you because all is recorded. I told you and I can't speak for others but myself. I told you I needed a place where people aren't killing themselves, a place where there is total peace and true love. I told you I needed and wanted you God, no one else but you God to be the head of my life, my home, my relationship, my family and not man. I need you to make right and perfect decisions for me, I needed you to be the center of my life and all that I do you must approve it. Remember I told you and it is you to fail me not me fail you so you cannot hold me guilty because I did tell you this and tried my best to be humble and live clean so you are the one to hold yourself guilty because you did not live by your integrity nor live by your true word and true and pure love.

Just as you can hold God accountable, God can hold you infinitely accountable as well. Trust me infinitely on this God can and will hold you accountable for your wrongs – sins.

If God is taking you out of your sins – messes and you keep going back into them he can and will hold you accountable because you are not living by your word nor are you walking in his integrity.

Before I continue because I know some of you are going to come at me with Job but the book of Job is incorrect. Even though I've quoted it know that this book is incorrect because God cannot talk directly with sin. Like I've said life and death is infinitely not on the same accord because death hath to do with sin and God does not partake in sin.

Go back to Greek Mythology now put the book of Job together. Think of Hades and Zeus the two brothers of death. One dressed in white and the other in black – yes ding ding ding ding ding the Ying and Yang. One is spiritual death and the other physical death. Get it now? Good if you say yes because now you are learning.

So when this book say God asked Satan have you considered my servant Job and God told Satan to do all to Job but do not take his life this is a lie. Know that this is taken for the original books of Greek Mythology. God the True and Living God cannot tell sin to punish anyone. This is an infinite lie being told on God.

God infinitely does not punish. Sin punishes because the wages of sin is death but life is truth everlasting.

If you are living a clean and good life why would God punish you? What sense would that make for God to just come and punish you for the goodness that you do? Come on now.

In every way evil is looking for a loophole to get into God's good book and it cannot work. Nothing that evil try will work because good is good and evil is evil. Evil must lie and continue to tell lies to cover up each lie he has told just to keep you believing and satisfied. Eventually you will find out the truth. Some of us will stay with evil because we like the lies, the pain and

hurt and none of us can blame God for this you can only blame yourself because you stayed. You wanted the lies and abuse – the put down.

Lies are not a part of God so you cannot go to God with lies because you will be rejected – turned away.

If God said Duane or Simon I need you to sing me songs and you sing songs that mislead and tell people to do wrong trust me God will not hold you accountable. You will be held accountable and be guilty of sin and the punishment for this is death and there is no ands ifs or buts about this. You will be guilty as charged.

But God never told me how to sing. No he did not but if you know God you should know that you must sing the truth and be truthful because God is truthful not sinful.

If God say Ruth stay in your job stay in your job because he is making a better way for you. If you leave the job God will hold you accountable because you did not trust him to work things out perfectly for you.

If you Billy say, God on this day I am going to take baby steps towards you and one day you go back on your word because some say Billy try this way it is faster to get to God and you followed that person. Billy, woooo Nelly will you ever be held infinitely accountable because you broke your word to God – with God because you listened to someone when you shouldn't. So stay true to your baby steps. God cannot hold you accountable for taking baby steps because you are truthful to him hence after 25 years you are still taking baby steps. If any form of religion come and offer you a better way, a faster way to get to God run dem and tell them to kiss your ass because your baby steps is your word to God and no one not even me have or has that right to come and take you off your track and causing you to sin. Your word is your word and you have to live by your word until you see God. "Well come here let me tell you about God."

No, infinitely no because I am doing just fine with the decision I have made with God. I am taking baby steps and God does not mind so don't come take me off track."

"But there is a better way and God told me to tell you of this way."

"Let me tell you something Mister Preacher Man – Woman God would infinitely never tell you to tell me of a better way to him because I told him I would make baby steps to him and if God wanted to relay this to me he God would tell me and because I know he would never go against our pact of truth and true love – the decision we made I know you are lying to me so flee from me you viper of sin. Never come to my door again because I rebuke in the name of God the True and Living God."

"My child this is not God's way."

"No it's our way – God's way and my way so kiss my ass and flee you demon of the underworld. Tell Satan and his vipers of deceit I will never leave my God to join him so know your place and do not step on God's ground anymore because you are not welcomed here and you have to adhere to the laws of God – the laws of life and death. I do not choose death I chose life and it is by life that I live not death. You cannot break the laws of sin hence I rebuke you and refuse you." With all that said evil – this preacher – teacher must flee and he or she can never come back to your door again. Evil must adhere to your wishes and if evil tries again woooo Nelly I will not feel sorry for evil because evil would have broken the code and all evil on that day that they broke the code must eternally die not just in the physical but in the spiritual. Evil would have broken the laws of death – the Ying and Yang which is the laws of creation – the laws of the universe. No no do not go there and say well what about sin. You sinned because you committed the act not sin. Sin got you to sin and this is what sin must do. If you refuse sin and broke the laws of creation in any way all sin must die on that day. There is a huge difference in getting you to break the law and sin breaking the law. You can hold sin guilty but guilty of what?

Causing us pain and suffering.

Lying to you

All sorts of thing yes but can we truly blame sin for this?

Did sin commit the act?

Was it not you that committed the act?

If you've rejected sin and the pull to do evil is more than you can control then yes you can hold sin accountable because the pull is great hence I tell you separate from evil. If you do not try to separate from evil, God will hold you accountable because you know to separate from all evil yes wicked and deceitful people.

No don't even go there because all I have to say is Psalms One. You cannot listen to others tell you their way or religion is better because no way is better in regards to getting to God. We know religion leads to death so religion can infinitely be the better way unto the True and Living God. It is the way onto death hence many of us have died for religion – death. Whatever good steps you take unto the true and living God keep those steps for lifetimes to come and teach your children these good ways also so that when evil try to seduce them they can never be rocked. Dedicate your children unto the good care and upbringing of God and evil will infinitely never touch them (your children) because they are under the protection of God. The key word is good. You have to tell God good care because God deal only in goodness. If you say God I dedicate my child in your care God will not listen to you and evil will take this statement as his cue to come in and because of this you not saying good care you cannot hold God accountable if anything goes wrong with your child or you. Everything that you ask of God you must, infinitely must tell God they must be good and right – just. If you want and need a man you must infinitely ask God for a good man. One that does not cheat or is abusive, or is lazy and stubborn – hard headed. You must ask for progressive men that are truthful and honest. Do you see where I am going? If you ask God for a man you will get a crebby crebby and you cannot blame God for this crebby crebby man because a no God sen im a di devil because sey you did not tell God you wanted and needed a good man. So from the word GOOD is not in your asking God cannot give you a good man – your asking.

If you tell God you are never going to step foot in church again you had better live by your word because God will hold you accountable if you go back into a church. You are going on your word and you are not truthful. You lied.

But my daughter is getting married in a church I have to be there. My mother has died and I have to be at the funeral. The service for her is being held in a church.

You will still be held accountable for this. So before you tell God you are never going to step foot in a church tell God I don't want to ever go back to church but you know I am going to have to. I have children that will want to get married in a church. I have my mother that wants a priest to speak over her body and for this I have to be there because it is important to me. On occasions that I need to be there please forgive me. By you telling God this beforehand he cannot hold you accountable because you went to him with the truth as well as with your true feelings.

Sometimes God will open positive doors for you if he knows this is going to hurt you. Maybe your daughter eloped and the family throws her a party in a hall with family and friends. Maybe you mother decides before she dies she wants her funeral service to be held outside rather than in a church. Your daughter may want to be married outside instead of in a church. Maybe your mother do not want a clergy to preside over her body she wants you to do it outside. She knows you are clean and your prayers are clean and God listens to you. If this is the case don't use the bible but talk to God to make her journey light meaning not filled with pitfalls. Ask God to truly forgive her of her sins and give her rest. Tell God to shield and protect her in the grave and make one of her goodness blot out many of her sins. Remember it is a foolish man that said his mother never did anything for her. If she showed you true love and tried with you she did do something for you.

Also know if you have your doctor's office, dentist office, school, or whatever uses the parking lot of a church for additional parking and you park your car in the churches parking lot God can hold you accountable for sin because you went back into church. The parking lot belongs to the church hence it is a part of the church. Yes I learnt this the hard way well not the hard way God just educated me on this and man I did not want to concede. I argued with God in my way but God won out in the end. No people I cannot argue with God and win because despite my stubborn ways at times the truth will always be the truth so please know this as well.

Remember evil cannot get into God's abode or in heaven. Only a clean person can go to God. So for an evil person to do as I said above, God will not look upon them nor will he listen to them. Trust me God will have a frown on his face. Infinitely trust me on this. There are many forms of goodness and you have to know them.

If you are for God stay being for God because the day you fall trust me the climb will be harsh and painful. Some of us don't get back up and that's why we wonder why we cannot prosper nor have anything. Yes I know I've stated this above.

Do you comprehend now?

Yes

Good

So we have to give up evil and not just say this.

We have to work at it. We have to live in truth with God.

We have to trust God to work things out in time

We have to have faith and courage, try to live like JUST – RIGHT.

Is it easy?

Never will be. As long as there are negative people around, in earth and above the earth it will never be easy for good people. Remember it is not evil that is keeping the planet earth in orbit it is the good people and the good that they do on a daily basis. Trust me if all the good people were to stop the good that they are doing and take a break trust me this planet would be in shambles. No war is not shambles by sin true shambles would be the earth moving out of alignment and you feeling the movement as it aligns truly with the meteor that is on its way to earth. That is true shambles.

Know that wicked people will try to throw you off the true path of God not just in the physical but in the spiritual as well.

If you tell God that you don't want to do something he will help you. God has never denied anyone or anything his true love. Keep your word to God. Always always be truthful to God. Never lie to him because lies hurt him and he does cry.

Trust me he does. Just as your spirit in the spirit world cries he does cry.

God lives by his integrity and his truth; it is man that does not live by God's integrity and truth.

Trust me it is not easy to live by God's integrity and truth. It is hard because trust me evil forces will try to knock you off in the spiritual and physical.

Something happened to me and I told God I would never go back to that place again. (I don't want to get into the story) I told God if he ever made me go back to this place I would never forgive him because I am going to keep my word to him. So far I have kept my word but it does not mean that it is easy for me. People I dream about this place me going back there in my dream and trust me I get angry with God sometimes but I refuse to go back and I am still holding steadfast. I refuse to be rocked or moved in this way. I love God infinitely and I will not do things to hurt him willingly. So don't think it is just physical wickedness you have to contend with. You have to contend with spiritual wickedness as well.

I've told him that I never want to hurt others, everything that I do let it be done out of true love – goodness and truth, not for a reward but because this is what I truly love to do. I've been told to go back by someone in the physical world and my answer was no. I gave God my word of truth and told God I would never go back and I aim on keeping my word. I need what is best for God and if what's best for him is me not walking in the council of the ungodly nor standing in the ways of sinners then I am going to do it. No one can tell me to go against God or do this because this is what God wants but yet he or she is going against God. Hell no. I don't care who you are I will not go against God for you. My word is my word and I have to live by my word until the day I die. God has asked me to write a book and I will write until the day I die or until he tells me not to write anymore and just go and speak to people. Yes we can write but you also have to show the goodness of God and trust me God will show it to you.

Whenever you make a vow, a promise to God, do your best not to break it. Like I said it is not easy and people will come to throw you off even rock you but never go against God for them. If you cannot take your burdens no more ask God to release you from your decree and not hold it against you. It does not mean you do not truly love God it means you cannot handle the thwarting of evil. God does not want or need to see you in pain hence he is forgiving. He knows what you can and cannot handle. I've told you can be angry at God meaning take your anger and frustration to God and take it out on him. If you feel like punching God's lights out in your anger tell him you feel like punching his lights out because he doesn't understand or get you. If you feel like saying, "what part of no fucking evil do you not understand? I don't want any evil to come near me or interfere with me and my children and you are allowing evil to reach me, interfere in my abode. What do you not get? What part of evil do you not understand?" This is your feelings, how you feel. God cannot sin you for your feelings because these feelings are the way you truly feel. With these feelings it does not give you the right to go out there and hurt anyone. This tirade is between you and God. Not your clergy but God and no, no one can tell you not to get mad at God. Its better you go to God with your troubles and besides at times God get a chuckle out of it and your mind will kick in and say are you finished yet. Well this is God. If the mind say to hurt the person then you infinitely know that this is not God but the devil – your evil twin which is the evilness of the mind – heart. In book two I will show you and trust me this is how I am with God. I cannot be fake with God because he is my everything; he's my all and I have to be real and true to God.

I cannot say I truly love God and as soon as I am out of sight meaning as soon as God rescue's me I go back to living in sin.

What kind of life is that?

Why should I be hypocritical?

And no it doesn't mean I will not cuss you to the ground or roast you as the younger generation will say. I will if you rub me the wrong way and try to turn me from God and trust me the Jamaican bad words will come out, even the ones you never think existed will come out because I will not just cuss you I will cuss everything of you including your mother, your family, your kids, your race, your country and your ancestors. I will go so far back in your bloodline that you will hold your head down in shame so know what you are doing when it comes to me and the seeds – good seeds – good people God has given me.

I know there are wicked and jealous people out there that loves to see you on your face.

These are the same people that eat and drink with you

The same people that want it all but do nothing in goodness to have their own

These are the same people that are saying why her or him?

Why not me?

They don't see themselves. It's not why you and why not me. If you have a good heart, clean hands then yes God will see you. He will elect you to do his work, whatever he needs you to do he will tell you to but because your heart and hands are not clean God will not use you. You cannot begrudge someone or try to hurt anyone and think God will use you do his work.

You don't represent God with this attitude because you are a worker of iniquity. You belong to the devil and it is the devil you work for not God.

God deal with clean people not dirty and unclean people. Yes you will go through sin and do sin in the past but when you come clean and truthful to God and show God that you are his root you will be more than amazed at how God uplift you and your life.

I may write the words and God will make you edit the mistakes and in so doing we are both working for God.

We are doing his bidding and we are doing it honestly and truthfully. Yes you can show me were I've made my mistakes so that I can correct my books and make them right. And no I do not need or want dirty people to correct my books only God's true and rightful people. Yes people I am extremely picky when it comes to my work for God. If you are not for God then don't have nothing - anything to do with me or God. What God has given to me and his children – people no wicked or crebby crebby must enter or come in. I refuse all wickedness and wicked people including the spiritual wicked. Evil know what they are doing and none is going to use the words God has given me to screw God. Wicked people can eternally and infinitely fuck the hell of and go to hell and burn. No God enough is enough because it was evil that deceived not you and look at the world today. Look at the fighting and backbiting. Look at the hatred and lies that continues to be spread. Everyone lying and saying they know you when they know not you. How can a man or woman say they know you and trample you down? Come on now. You are

LIFE not death so how can a dead man say they know you when they are dead? They can only know death because death is their God hence they die. They cannot live come on now.

There is no I am going to do a better job with God. It simply cannot work. Yes I tell God I need a special place in his heart, want him to infinitely love me more than everyone else but do you think God is going to love me more than you? NO.

I know he loved Solomon dearly (this according to your bible) but in the end look what Solomon did to him.

Look at us today. We say we love God but look at what we are doing to him. We sold God out to the highest bidder and that's sin and death.

All that is good God has given to us and we destroy it then turn around and cast stones – lots when we know that we of ourselves are the guilty and sinful ones. Come on now.

I would be honoured if I had a special place in God's heart. Trust me I would love it infinitely. Hey I don't know if that is possible. I know God truly loves me and he is inside of me and my aim is to please him with all that I do and it is not fair for others to come and knock me off. Like God I am not concerned with evil. I am concerned with his good and righteous people those that he God has given to me as well as need to journey home with him. These are the people I need to secure for God and in doing so, securing them I am securing a place for them in God's abode. I cannot secure a place for wicked and evil people because a lot of them know the truth and refuse it. They kill the truth with their words and books of lies and I refuse to be like any of them. I infinitely do not need your soul or spirit. God has given me mine hence I am alive and you are alive because he has given you life and he God is sustaining and maintaining your life – our life. I cannot use your soul or spirit in the grave because it is not all that is in the grave that will move on to higher and better life – cleaner life. I will not lie to you and I refuse to lie to you. I will not do it for evil either and will infinitely never lie for evil. I don't want to end up in hell and death cannot offer me anything because I know how death comes – how death takes human life – all evil life. I know the death of spirit – how evil spirits – soul dies and death knows this so death cannot fool me. It can come at me yes in the spiritual because the pull is great there hence I know who resides in hell. I do not live for death but live for life. I know the strength and pull of death including the stench hence I do not tarry around death I tarry around life because life does not stink but death stinks because sin reeks of death. Yes sin is that stink and filthy hence our physical body stinks smell when we do not clean it - bathe.

Some of us are saying no it does not and all I have to say is smell your armpits, your ding dong, your breath and hairy motel.

It would be nice if everything was perfect but it isn't perfect because there is evil in the way.

You have to know about evil and what evil can do. You have to live your life accordingly. Mistakes happen in life like I've said but you have to know when to pick yourself up and say Father, My Love, I have sinned, I know I did you wrong and I take full responsibility for this please forgive me.

It's not hard to do. It is simple but we make it hard, think it is hard. You will fall but you have to get up, rise up. We have to own up to our wrongs.

We chastise our children, beat them when they do wrong but yet when we do wrong we don't want to be chastised. We don't want to own up to our wrongs. Tell me if we don't own up to our wrongs how can our children learn right – own up to theirs?

How will they be able to own up to their wrongs?

Will they not continue down the wrong pathway as us? So can they be blamed?

Is it not you as a parent, a teacher, a preacher, an imam, a bishop to be blamed?

Are you not the ones to teach wrong?

You of yourself know something is wrong but yet you are telling others to commit wrongs. You are committing a sin so how can this be of God.

Why tell Sister Jenifer she is wrong to commit adultery but yet you are married and you are sleeping with Sister Angie?

How is that right?

Are you not committing adultery?

Are you not committing sin?

If your congregation is giving you tides and offering why fatten your pocket and leave Sister Beverly hungry?

You know things are hard with her why not stretch forth a helping hand and truly help her and not want the money back nor have her work off her debt in your eyes by doing this this and this for the church or even you in your household. Come on now. Sister Beverly is hungry your job as a child of God is to help her come on now. Help. She's the first to come in on Sunday's and clean the church. Set it up for people to come and listen to you lie to them, deceive them and then turn around and rob them by passing around your collection plates not God's collection plates because God requires no collection plates nor does he use them. You are a thief plain out because the tides no not tides the blessings of God that these people willingly give is for the poor and needy. This is their poor offering unto God to feed the poor and needy and all of you rob the poor and needy. Oh what a weeping and a moaning.......fill in the rest because your destruction cometh like a thief in the night. Thief a go rob unnu cause thief no like fi si thief carry long bag an thief screw or have screw face when thief rob dem dis mi noa. Unnu a thief and fiya fi unnu. Wooooooooooo Nelly unnu a go ball. Ratid fi si unnu. Unnu a dick aroune with the name of God anna rob people a dem soul. Wooooooooooo fiya Laade Ooh Fiyaaaaaaaaaaaaaaaaaaa. Hell full now mi God because mi cup a ovaflow. Fiyaaaaaaaaaaa fi di wicked heathens dem. Fiyaaaaaaaaaaaa fi di evil duppy dem. Fiyaaaaaaaaa fi di obeah man dem. Fiyaaaaaaaaaaaa fi di obeah oman dem. Fiyaaaaaaaaaaa fi di preacha dem. Fiyaaaaaaaaa fi di back bita dem. Fiyaaaaaaaaaa fi di murdera dem. Eternal and everlasting fiyaaaaaaaaaaaaaaaa hotta fiyaaaaaa more fiyaaaaaaaaaaa fi di sperm dona an egg dona dem. Pickney no fi sell an man fi mine dem pickney. Fiyaaaaaaaaaaaa, eternal and everlasting fiyaaaaaaaa, hotta hotta fiyaaaaa fi di pedaphile and child molesters dem. Fiyaaaaaaaaa God more fiya fi all di wicked and evil dem. I too have sinned God but I am trying to correct me and my dirty ways. I cannot and infinitely cannot change my past but I know, infinitely know that I can change my future in a good and blessed way hence I am trying to cleave to you so that all that I do is good, blessed and highly favoured by you.

Many young men and women are left mother and fatherless how many of you have picked up the cup of God and become surrogate mothers and fathers to these children? No come on now. Step up and represent God with your good deeds. Many of these children need food and shoes, clothes to wear but many of you have not charity to be like God in good deeds and you are say you represent and know God. None of you represent or know God because nothing good comes from wicked and evil reptiles that sliver and hide under the coattail of sin – Satan while trying to steal the identity of the True and Living God.

If you are of God you will do good – all the good you can do for the needy.

If you are of God you will be examples for God. You would step up and be surrogate mothers and fathers to these children come on now. Trust me if you take good care of these kids and not abuse them or use them as sex toys because I know some of you will want to do this and trust me your ass will be grass when I am done because if your mother or father is in heaven they will be kicked out, every seed that comes from your bloodline will be kicked out because I give you my word of truth and goodness I will petition God for this and I infinitely know he will grant me this just and right petition. If you are representing God let God hold his up in high esteem and not let God hold his head down in shame and disgrace. What good are you doing for God come on now? I know my past and yes you can dredge it up to try to screw me but rest assured God knows me and my good intentions. No one can change their past but they can change their future as well as the here and now in a good and positive way. So no matter you dredge up my past I will still be holding onto God infinitely because he knows the goodness of my heart and the truth of me – my true and good intentions towards him and the people he has given me to take care of, teach and educate in a good and truthful way.

Tell me something how can we do better if we constantly participate in sin and eat the bread of sorrow?

There is good help and bad help. Help these children in a good and honest way. A way that is truly pleasing to God and you. Forget me, forget you and do God for a change meaning do good by God for God for a change. Come on now. Look at how much good God has done for us and not one of us can truly do good for him for a change. Come on now.

Sister Pam and Sister Angela and Angie too are behind on their rent help them to pay their rent until they can get back on their feet come on now. They pay tides and offerings too. You say your congregation is a part of God well they are a part of the congregation and apart of God so help them because they need it and don't preach on your help or ask for the money back because God does not ask back for anything he has given to anyone because not one of us can repay God for the goodness he has given and bestowed upon us. Forget it no you cannot because none of us can give back the air we breathe, the water we drink, the food that we eat, the sunshine that we use, the moonlight that we use, the hair on our backs and body, the good sex that we have, the children that we have nor can we give back the good children that we have, the money that we make, the fat and skinny bank account we have, the shoes we wear, not even the good parents we were given and yes I can go on and on.

Brother John and Brother Edwin need medical care and not one of you can help with the medical – hospital costs or medi-care costs come on now and you say you are of God and represent God. Come on now you don't represent God the TRUE AND LIVING GOD you represent sin – death the death of life.

Know that when you ignore your people, your community, your country God will not find favour in you. You have to represent all these aspects of life because your people, your community and country is what God gave you. You do not own it because no one can own land on earth because God did not give us the lands of the earth and no matter your land title that you possess you cannot own land on earth. We die and the land is still there – another come and possess it – use it. And no it infinitely does not mean you can walk into another man's country and claim it – possess it. Damn bright.

As humans we want and the more we get is the more we want and the more greedy we become. We don't think of our future or future generations.

We live in the here and now

We also don't care if we leave future generations in debt because that's the future.

We say live for today because the future or tomorrow is not guaranteed.

Well guess what the future is guaranteed for your loved ones if it is not guaranteed for you so why leave them to pay off your debt. They have their own debt that they have will accumulate so tell me how are they going to pay their debt as well as pay off yours?

They cannot and this is why we will forever be in debt to the devil because we have racked up so much debt that none of us can pay it off.

Future generations cannot pay it off.

In a nut shell if we can't pay off our debts how are they going to pay off theirs?

How will we see God if we cannot pay off our debt to the devil – evil?

God cannot pay off our debts – sins because we were the ones to willingly make them as well as accept the offerings of sin when we infinitely know that DEBT is a sin and not of God.

We accepted the debts of sin and now we know or just realizing that no one can repay sin – death not even God because sins pay is always and will infinitely and absolutely be death. It can be nothing else and we all know this. No we are the ones to sin not God so why should God dirty himself for humanity come on now? God has tried and we do not listen so why should he bail us out of our messes. If he God is giving you a way why ignore it and choose the offerings of sin. Eve did and she could not get back in. What say you or me? She got kicked out of God's kingdom people and what happened confusion was all around her (yes this is what your book of sin calls the flaming sword). She was so confused that she did not know where to turn. She went to the east west north and south but could not get back in because she became dirty – unclean. Today we are doing the same. Because we turn to all manner of filth – religion to find God and instead of cleaning ourselves up and living clean for God the goodness of God we make others make us filthier – more unclean.

We have to stop living for self and stop being selfish. Yes we have our needs and they have to be met or be satisfied. Many of us do not care who we hurt to satisfy our needs. I am not saying I am perfect but why hurt others to satisfy you. NONE OF US LIKE TO BE HURT. NONE OF US WANT TO BE HURT BUT YET WE HURT OTHERS. I AM GUILTY OF THIS. I HAVE HURT OTHERS AND IT IS NOW THAT I AM OLDER THAT I CAN SEE THE PAIN THAT I HAVE CAUSED.

We have to try and clean ourselves up and start living the way God need us to live. When God see us trying – truthfully trying then the storms will go away. The storms cannot touch you if you are living clean. The storms cannot harm you because God is now protecting you – shielding you. Your life will be changed for the better – good because goodness is all around you. Yes the goodness of

A LITTLE TALK WITH GOD

God is around you. And no you will not worry about your soul – spirit because your spirit – soul is intact with God.

An no your body will not decay or grow old like some sinful and disrespectful people. Sin is old know this so when we accept sin we grow old and wrinkly like sin and no amount of cosmetic surgery will make you beautiful it just makes you as ugly as sin. No I am not casting stones. Have you seen some of these people who have opted for fake beauty? Many will claim that they are beautiful but they are worse than but ugly. Take a look at some of the photos in the internet. Nothing can ugly so? No come on I am not casting stones but natural beauty is key because the good that you do radiates and shines within you and it is see in you. That is beauty they true beauty of God. No God truly forgive me but I am going to say this but humanity have become as ugly as sin – death. No for real if you were to add up all the ugliness on earth meaning the sins of earth truss mi I don't blame you for not wanting to come back. Earth has become so ugly with sin that it's amazing what we do for sin. God please don't hold my words against me because you know what I am talking about. No one wants the natural look anymore.

We want the fake jelly boobs

The fake nails and ass

The fake vagina and fake penis – cosmetic surgery penis people like the cosmetic fake vaginas

The fake hair and nose

Fake tans and arms

Sinful tattoos – the other mark of death – the mark of the beast. Woooooooo Nelly does Satan ever have you people especially you follow batty black people.

No I only tattoo my skin to show the love of my friend, my homey, my one and only. Great I commend you because you're true to your friend unto death hence you are going to die like your friend in the grave. And if your friend does not have a tattoo and you die and he has one good more than bad on his record. Man do I see death smiling infront of my face because he knows he's got you – yap he's got your back because homey is gone and all that's left is you. No don't cry its reality homeboy.

Death knows me honey and I know death. We're not the same so don't get it twisted. Death has a job to do and his job is death hence his name death. I have a job to do and that job is to write and tell you the truth so that you can live for Life and not live for death. God is your answer. He is the infinite key.

Why not use another name?

Because God is the only true name I know. I cannot use Jah nor can I use Allelujah all the time. I can only you God predominantly and not the other names. Allelujah is the name both good and evil use because God is ALL. He's all around and in everything. Meaning life is in everything.

Like I've said my words are harsh but I do not mean to hurt or spread hate. It is not my intention and if I come off as hateful, spiteful and racist I apologize and ask forgiveness of you and God.

My words should not hurt but comfort – truthfully teach in a good and perfect way. My words should educate and give you knowledge in a good way so that when evil comes to you with its nonsense you cannot be rocked and evil become an abomination onto you. Meaning when evil comes to you you are sick to the stomach hence evil must flee from your door. You won't watch evil programs and when you get brochures from evil you don't look at it you just rip it up and throw it in the garbage. Well this you will automatically do when you are on the right track to God. Once you are steadfast in God I infinitely know you will not desire any form of evil.

Forget about the sex with other people you will not desire sinful things you will desire good things and good sex with your partner and partner alone. Know that one cannot be good and the other evil so know the partner you pick up. If both of you have the same unified goal it should be easy I think. I say I think because I have never had a partner that had the same goals or even similar or like goals as me.

Yes I would love to experience this in the physical one day.

I know God is there with me in every step but in truth I would like to know what this feels like truthfully and in a good and blessed way.

God is my infinite unified goal and no one can take this from me because I am solid in truth with God but as humans there are things you would like to experience in your lifetime with a partner. You know what let me stop because I am going too far.

Yes my Peeps and True Loved Ones I have strayed but now I have to leave you. Stay safe. Don't know when I will be travelling but if ever I come to your town please don't throw pies at me. (Smile)

Hugs and kisses always and remember without true love there is no love and God is true love. He does truly love and care about you. You have to show him you truly love him and want what is best for him.

No more hurting

No more pain

No more lies

A LITTLE TALK WITH GOD

No more evil and evil things

Live for you and live your life in truth.

Truly live for life and not death.

We will talk again, yes in another book a book of prayers which will be available to you on LULU.

I love to say LULU. Love that name.

The true love of God be with you all and may his saving grace forever abide with you all.

True love always

Michelle

Postscript my Peeps I did try to correct the mistakes and I know mistakes have cropped up so please forgive me because you are spending good money. By now you all should know that I do not have a editor to correct my mistakes and I write like I speak. Hopefully over time I will master the art of writing. Yes I will perfect it and be perfect.

Yes I proof read my work but with all the proof reading and buying sample copies from LULU I still find many mistakes.

Michelle

My Peeps and Family I am going to add this one in this book. In all that I am seeing I see nothing but disaster for the United States.

I keep seeing the States burning and this is sad because hard times worse than the hard times they are facing is ahead if they don't change their ways.

This old fight – the fight of the ages I cannot comprehend because I don't know if I can truly explain it so I am going to leave well enough alone.

The West will be faced with a greater economic battle where food shortages will become the norm. We will live like the African Nations the West ruined and I've told you this before.

The West will become the new poor and Africa will become the new Standard – Rich because God has not forgotten about them and if they the African Nations do not reclaim their homelands and clean it of the filth that has tarnished and held it captive for thousands of years then they do will be doomed because the Babylonians will have their way with them and trust me they will become more desolate and hungry because many diseases will be unleashed on them to wipe the African races off the face of the planet. They need to wake up and stop being servants and slaves to everyone because life – true life existed in Africa once upon a time and these nations can no longer hold on to their Pagan ways because did not give them paganism. Paganism is the devil's way and all pagans worship and make sacrifices onto the devil hence they have a white god which is death.

We praise and worship death and this is why we die as well.

Many people will say I am racist from my comment above and that's fine you are entitled to your opinion and this is your opinion not God's. God cannot lie and what is shown to me is what I relate to you because for many of you you deal in the physical but God deal in the spiritual because no flesh can enter the abode of God you have to be in your true form which is energy for which you call the spirit.

No one can see God in his pure state because no man hath the eyes to see air. We breathe it and feel it but we cannot see it.

God is the breath of life hence the good and the bad breathe air each and every day.

Yes we try to destroy it but in truth we cannot destroy God or the air that we breathe we can only destroy our flesh and the food that we consume to keep us going on a daily basis.

Now here we go.

God I see the violence and Jamaica is going to be a war zone yet again.

The young will rise up and blood will flow like river because the people refuse to learn. They continue to disrespect your holy and beautiful name.

God – Eternal Father what will be left of this tiny island now? All I can say is leave them alone and let them learn the hard way because goodness no longer reside in their hearts only evil.

They kill at will because they kill you each and every day.

They've turned paradise into hell hence they own nothing

They sell their own

Rape their own

Kill their own

They kill you God

They rape you

Massacre your land – the land you have given to them

They sold you out and now they have nothing – not even the land – your land – Ja-Mai-Ca.

The battle will be fierce dear God Jamaica will again become a war zone.

God you can prevent it but my mind is saying leave them alone let them kill themselves because they refuse to learn, refuse to respect the good name you have given them.

God how can a man be blessed with your name – the name of creation – the creator and disrespect you like that.

Lovey you gave them a name – your name, an identity that no other nation has or ever had and they are disrespecting your name and you like that come on now. Lovey not even modern day Africa have or has this distinction and honour. My people have it but yet destroy it, disrespect it, disrespect your name – You.

They have given your land over to sin – the devil and now look at them fighting and killing for a place in the devil's kingdom – hell.

Yes this morning my heart grieves but despite my pain I am asking you to truly save them and open their eyes. Lift destruction from them and yes I know I said I would close my mouth and let destruction come upon them but my heart – my true heart cannot turn from them God. I have to beg for them because Jamaica is not the only one that is going to have bloodshed. I see Miami burning God just like

A LITTLE TALK WITH GOD

I saw Texas burning a couple of weeks ago but the fire in Texas was not severe as Miami because all of Miami was burning but I do not know the significance of this because both fires – the Texas and Miami fires I saw actors as if the fires had to do with film – movies – filming hence I do not put much significance on these deadly fires due to the actors I see.

Yes deadly chemicals were involved in the Miami fire – one man having a vial filled with a white substance. God this man was armed and dangerous because he carried death with him – 1 vial that could kill millions.

God these dreams are beyond my scope because although I see Miami being burned it could be Los Angeles and more importantly it could be New York because New York in on the Bay meaning the water around it. The Texas dream do not have to be Texas either and this because that dream came true and it was not Texas that burned but Washington – the fire.

God I have to do a better job of pinpointing the places of destruction but it is so hard given the scope and magnitude of these dreams. For example I thought the tsunami that hit Japan was for China because of the Chinese background and language in the dream.

The 3 caskets I saw in the air represented the Russian plane crashes but I don`t get it because I did see 3 caskets and only 2 disasters occurred to so far. Weird but hey old people always say dreams do not walk straight and I know this now that dreams do not walk straight when it comes to disasters hence I leave disaster dreams alone because they are extremely hard to pinpoint. Yes I know you have to leave well enough alone because of time but God need I remind you of 1313, 2032, and 2132. That`s all I got to say so I am moving on because it`s beyond me – beyond my scope as to why humanity have become so vile and destructive.

God the United States do not see their destruction – their end and no matter how you send messengers to them they refuse to learn and know.

When you go to them the discredit you and even kill you because they believe you are becoming too powerful and this cannot be.

Lovey this has nothing to do with power because a messengers cannot become politicians or heads of states they have to do what you tell them to do and that is deliver the message you have given them to save them.

God it`s beyond me why the devil feels threatened because he knows he cannot hold on to the flesh forever. His people will die and become extinct.

God I see the end and destruction of these people and this does not have to be they can save themselves but they have to want it and stop with the hate nonsense. This is their future and if they refuse it like they did Marcus Garvey and Martin Luther then God they are not worth saving – leave them the hell alone because they are telling me and you that they want to die.

<u>They can no longer let the Babylonians continue to make their hands dirty with their dirty little war games because the Babylonians values not life they value death hence they kill and create strife for death.</u>

They cannot see they are sinking themselves further into debt by fighting a war and wars that were designed to economically destroy them, physically and spiritually destroy them – ruin them.

God the Babylonians have the oil they don`t and I do not understand why anyone would want to fight for what the Babylonians have while putting their future; their children`s future and future generations future in debt.

Have they not learned that no one can defeat Aries – the god of war on his own battlefield because sin knows both domains.

When will humanity learn you cannot fight evil on his own battlefield – his terms. You will never win and cannot win. When you do sin has and have you locked down in the spiritual and no amount of prayer can or will save you in hell – Hades. You will die hence "in my father's house there are any mansions and if it was not so I would not say so." God no one can tell you about your abode because no one that is filthy or unclean can get in. No book of the dead can tell you either because the books of the dead are for the dead. That is their meat, their food, their lies and disgrace, their way of dying – their death.

I can't tell others about the inside of your abode because I am still living in the valley of death – earth.

God please hear me today and open the eyes of your people. Help me to truly stop death because in all that sin does he is doing wrong and it's not fair to deceive nations without them knowing the full truth.

God America is a target so is the whole world and you have to save the world. You have to save my people – rescue them and give sin a taste of his own medicine come on now. Why should sin dominate your people when I infinitely know they can be saved but they have to want to be saved.

Michelle

A LITTLE TALK WITH GOD

God all that is good and true I dedicate and give to you

All that is peaceful and warm I put in your good hands for keep

All that I am – my goodness – my truth I share with you – give you

Michelle

God can a man do wrong and get right? So why do we think this way?

Why do we let others condition us to think his way?

God can the devil – evil do wrong and find peace in you? Shall he not be cast aside like a viper – a leper of sin?

God in all we do we do not think of you. We infinitely do not see you.

Michelle

A LITTLE TALK WITH GOD

Let our love shine

Absent of all pain

Absent of hurt

Let our love be pure

Let it never fade

Cascade into the wind

My darling let my love be with you

Shining in the night

Perfect under the moonlight

Shine brighter than the sun

The stars

My darling

You are the one

The one I truly love

My one and only

My All

My one true love

Michelle

A LITTLE TALK WITH GOD

My love I know life has been hard
The love we share is rare
The times spent with each other priceless
Valued above all others
Valued above all

My Love
My Darling
Let our love be free
True
Filled with truth
Peace and harmony

My Love
Be the wings that I need to fly
Sore where no eagles dear
Where no man dare to go

My Love
You are the truth within me
You are my freedom
The one I need when I need a shoulder to lean on
Cry on

My Darling
You are my All
My Life
The air that I truly breathe
Eternally

Michelle

A LITTLE TALK WITH GOD

My Love be by my side at all times

Never let them make me cry no more

Let not the enemies prevail over me

Conquer me

Let them not take my soul

My true love from you

Let them not take my life

You

My Love free me from the evils of the mind

Free me from the evils that lurks in the dark

The evils that surrounds me

Let them not have dominion over me

Take the enemies from the spiritual and physical realm

Take the enemies out of my future

Take them from all that I know and don't know

Take them truly out of my life – forever more

A LITTLE TALK WITH GOD

My God and True Love let our love reign forever

For eternity

God let our love be true and everlasting

An everlasting bond that can never be broken by man or spirit, angels-anyone

My Darling be free now

Free me now so that I can truly be with you

Live with you

Truly love you

Not just for today but for all eternity

Infinitely

Michelle

A LITTLE TALK WITH GOD

My Darling and Lovey my soul cry out to you
Cry out for your grace and mercy
Your truth
Your honesty
You

My Love you are ALL
The Allelujah in my life
The Allelujah in my soul – spirit

My God you are Allelujah
That which my soul cries out when your spirit touch mine
Soothe me

Allelujah you are all
You are King
The Governor, creator of us all
The creator of heaven and earth
The creator of ALL

Allelujah do not forsake me
Do not turn from me in my hour of need
Do not hide your love from me
As I return to you
I give you my true love
My truth
That which is made from truth
Pure truth
Pure Love
Pure Energy
You

Michelle

A LITTLE TALK WITH GOD

Lovey the hour has come

The time has come for all to be revealed

It is with pure love, truth and good faith that I humbly accept all the goodness that you have bestowed upon me; all the goodness you have given me

Lovey, please do not make me fall from your grace

Let your true and pure love never leave me – fade away

Let your good will be done in your abode, upon earth as well as in my home – my heart

Beneath the earth, under the earth and sea

Let your good will be done in me by me – You

All that is good and pure let it be done in me by me – You

Lovey and True Love

All that you have given me is cherished and truly loved

It is with this true love that I aim to stand by your side

I aim to press on confide in you

I aim to do good by you and in you

You are an amazing God

You are forgiving

Humble

Loving

A LITTLE TALK WITH GOD

Caring

More than merciful

All that I need I found in you

Allelujah my soul cries out for you daily

You are the light, the true light within me

It has been a long road

Treacherous

The climb was hard

Often times laden with tears, fears and sometimes hate

But you rescued me from the demons that surrounded me

You led me to where I needed to be

And for this I truly thank you

It took years but here I am in your care

And I don't ever infinitely never ever want to leave your care or reside out of your abode

Allelujah do not make the nets of the spiritual and physical demons conquer me

Spare me from the lies that the enemies will now cast on me

Spare me from the lies they will now tell on me

A LITTLE TALK WITH GOD

Spare me from the fear they will now inflict on me through their evil plots-diabolical deeds and needs

Rebuke them and reclaim me in your loving arms

Shield me from them because they will now seek to devour me

Seek to conquer me

Take me into your true care

Do not let their lies hurt me nor consume me

Do not let their hate kill me, take my life

Turn back their destruction and hate on them

Turn their murderous ways and plots back on them

Back to them My God

Rebuke them and let me sit with you in paradise – your abode of truth forevermore

The realm that you reside in peace – the realm of true peace and harmony – your eternal and everlasting abode

Father, be my shield and my anchor and never let me live in sin nor let evil take hold of me or my family again.

Michelle

A LITTLE TALK WITH GOD

God, Allelujah blot out all my sins from the book of sin not just in the physical realm but in the spiritual realm as well

Father store up all my good the good that I do in the spiritual and physical in your abode

Store them up so that on that faithful day I can be at rest in peace with you

Store them up-store up all my goodness so that if someone need it they too can have it and cross over to be with you.

God let the choice be of your choosing and not mine

Father let your true love continue to call me

Let it forever draw me back to you

I know fear sometimes rest in my heart and it is you that I am trusting to help me get over this mountain – my fears that is

It is you that I trust to give me a new and truthful start

Father, I need you so much

I don't want to leave you but I want and need to continuously love you

At times my faith is weak but you still stand by me showing me that you care

Father, you are perfect in all that you do and it is with this perfect love that I need to abide in you

It is with this perfect love that I need to hold on to you

I know many has come and gone and for centuries it's been the same old same old

Father I have to abide with you

I can't let you go so please let your true love always lead me home to you

I cannot stray anymore because I see and know the dark side of sin and love

I see and know the pain associated with sin

All I have to do is take a look at the world

Take a look at what is happening to the people of this world

Father, what more can I ask you for?

Earth is just one plain but eternal life is with you

Its life and not death

Life is not fear

Its hope

Its trust

Its honesty

Truth

Material things are not yours because you are not a material being but a spiritual one and this is why our eyes cannot behold you. No one can look at pure energy in the physical state therefore we cannot look upon you – see you

Father, I know we have seen you but not in your pure state. No one can behold you, it is just not possible in the state that we are in and that is why you show us you in the state or form that our eyes can behold – see

Father many have left the fold now

The road is empty now

Man have truly lost their way

We have become children of the living dead

Believing in things that is not of you

Believing in things that are not true

We believe that you will change

But yet not knowing that you cannot change us in the present state we are in

You cannot change us because that will be going against you and your laws

Laws that cannot be broken by you

Laws that cannot be broken by anyone

In the spiritual world changes occur for the good meaning good people so that we can move on to you and behold you in your pure and true state

Father, rest now

Rest now My Darling

Feel at ease in knowing that someone truly loves you

Truly cares about you

A LITTLE TALK WITH GOD

Rest now My Love

My True Love

As I call out your name Allelujah

I give you true love and abide in your name forevermore

Lovey I truly need you

I need life

Truth

Know that I will forever and infinitely need you.

Michelle

A LITTLE TALK WITH GOD

Father abide with me just a little while

Take away heart ache and pain from me

Cherish me

Truly love me

Father, I do not need your love in the physical alone

I need your love in the spiritual as well

I need it everywhere

I've been calling

Been knocking

Answer me

My Love answer me because I do not want or need to fall at man's hands no more

I do not want or need to fall at the devil's hand

I do not want or need to fall by any hands whether physical or spiritual

Uplift me now God

Stretch forth your hands and truly heal me

Heal me from my physical and spiritual pains

Heal me from all that ails me

A LITTLE TALK WITH GOD

Father continue to guide me on your way and open the eyes of others not just in the physical but also in the spiritual

Truly open their eyes not with pain but with your true love

Father, Allelujah as I call out to you

Receive me in your truth and never ever let me fall

Never ever let me go

Allelujah all that I ask grant it with your true love and truth both in the physical and spiritual, also in your abode

I know we are not all genuine and that many times we fail you and for that I ask that you forgive us, forgive me

Michelle

A LITTLE TALK WITH GOD

God I truly need a home office

One with a computer and laser printer

God its hard well becoming hard to write upon my bed

Trust me I need to be more organized

My thoughts need to be more simplified

God I so need a place of my own where I can fully and truly be at peace where there are no distractions – just true peace and tranquility

Lovey you know I need a home office

I truly do

I need more peace

Serenity

Yes my bed is lonely but every minute well not every minute you know what I mean my kids disturb me

God I so truly need a home office where I can truly be with you – connect with you the way it was meant to be

Michelle

A LITTLE TALK WITH GOD

God do not shut me out of your life
Father do not shut me out
Look down upon me and bless me
Fill my heart with praise
Fill it with love – truth
Joy – good cheer

Father you are the one that I cry out to
You are Allelujah
You are ALL
The breath of life
The air we breathe

Father bless me with truth not just in the physical but in the spiritual as well

Shower me with wisdom, knowledge and overstanding not just in the physical but in the spiritual as well

God grant me the wisdom to write about you truthfully

Grant me the knowledge and sight to fully see you and talk to you

Father God and Eternal Father, never let go of me
Never let me fall anywhere not even by the wayside

Father I seek your true love
I seek your true knowledge
Your true overstanding
Your true humility
You

Father, Eternal Father, all that I ask I ask in your abode as well

In the spiritual and physical
Father I cannot do without you

A LITTLE TALK WITH GOD

Cannot go on without you
And although you reside in me
I truly love you
Truly need you
Truly care about you

Michelle

A LITTLE TALK WITH GOD

Eternal Father you are the one that I need

Open my eyes to your abode

Open my eyes to you

Let my eyes behold your beauty

Bask in the tenderness of your love

Eternal Father I know I have done wrong in thy sight

It is with regret and shame that I come to you

Humiliated I stand as I humble myself to you

Please forgive me and forgive me of the wrongs that I have done unto you

Please forgive me of the shame and disgrace I have caused you

Father, accept my humblest apologies and truly forgive me

Michelle

A LITTLE TALK WITH GOD

Take me to your place God

You are my love

My true love

Take me to your place and let me stay with you forevermore

I have seen the evils of this world and don't want to live in it no more

The time has come for all to unfold

Unravel and man will not be able to handle it

They will not survive it

Father I am tired because they will not listen

They don't listen

Refuse to listen

All that you have shown them we are still doing our own thing

Going after wrongs

Doing wrong

I am fed up

Fed up of this system of things

Fed up of man

Fed up of his evil system

The evils of man – humanity

Michelle

A LITTLE TALK WITH GOD

Father can I talk to you

My heart is heavily burdened and anger has taken hold of me

Tell me

Truly tell me what we are fighting for because I need to know

I need to know the truth and I infinitely do not need any more lies

Father we are all guilty of sin

Including me

I am no exception but yet my heart cries out

Feels pain

Knows your burden

Feel it for you

How can we say we love but yet know not what love is

Know not what love means

God how can you see this, see the evils of man and let your people continue to live amongst them (evil)

How can you continue to let us reside with them (evil) in this plain

Father all I want and need is a true home with you

Man can have it all

A LITTLE TALK WITH GOD

Have all the material wealth they desire

It's all about money and greed and I don't want to be apart of this world, this system of things with such a cruel and evil agenda

Father I know things must come to pass

Things have to be before change comes but hurry

For my sake

The sake of my children, and grandchildren, great grandchildren

God hurry and reclaim your kingdom because I can't take this sinful world no more

God look at me

Feel my pain

See my hurt

How could you want this for any man?

How could you want this for your children?

How could you want this for me?

This isn't real

This isn't life

Its death

What I face

A LITTLE TALK WITH GOD

What others face isn't life

Its hell

Please for the sake of love

True love

Hurry up and return

Please help me

You say you love us

This was the message "For God so love us he is worthy to be praised"

This was the message I got written on the building of the school

This is what your children need to learn and know

You truly love us

It is with this truth of love that I petition you to return and save me

Save your children

Your people

Michelle

A LITTLE TALK WITH GOD

God today I am in a questioning mode – mood because my head isn't right

God I have to ask where is your integrity.

Forgive me but do you live by your integrity?
Do you value it?

If you do why is it that a man can knowingly change his sex from male to female and you allow this

God women are knowingly changing their sex to males and in some countries it is lawful to do so

When is enough enough God? When?

Human – humanity value sin over you because you have become wrong in our books and wrong in our sight

God when does the shame and disgrace stop?

Yes we can argue we have a choice to do whatever we want to self – our bodies. We will argue and say it is our right hence we have Will but God no one has a right to change their birth certificate meaning the way they were born – their genes. This is wrong and there is no forgiveness of sin for this.

God I challenge you at times and I know wrong from right.

I know about good and evil but when does it stop

A man cannot change his or their sex to female and say they are female. They are not female they are still a male because their birth and genes say otherwise

A woman cannot change her or their sex to male and say they are male. They are not male they are female because their birth and genes say otherwise

God this is true Sodomy. A man changing his sex to become female is a Sodomite worse than Satan. This is pure and utter evil. This goes against the laws of creation and I know death's sting will be worse for these people.

A female that commits the same act changing her sex to male is a Sodomite and she too is worse than Satan because she is going against the laws of creation and death's sting will be worse for her too.

No law should govern them because they are worse than disgusting – shit.

God no evil that I know is this brazen and bare faced

We – humanity have the balls to go against you and you take it.

We trample on you
We trample you down
We kill you but in all we do we massacre and kill self

God each individual is given a birth and a death certificate and we cannot change it to suit self. Our birth and death are recorded and no one can change it not even you so why do men – humanity think they can change your laws when they don't know how things were created – came into being.

Michelle

A LITTLE TALK WITH GOD

God I don't know but it is beyond me as to why we hurt ourselves and blame you

God when we are in trouble we know you but as soon as we are out of trouble – problems cest la vie

God we are changing our sex and dishonoring you and you take it like it does not matter

We alter our body in the name of fame and vanity and you take it

We kill all that you have given to us and you take it

Humanity kills humanity and you take it

Evil and wicked people have altered our books to include and suit them and you take it

We say books of lies are the truth when we know they are a pack of lies and you take it

Yes I know we live to die and we are going to die if we do not change but God why?

Why do you continue to take our lies?

Why do you continue to let us practice and live in lies?

God my people are the worst. No matter how much you tried to protect us we keep going back into the fire. We keep marrying the fire meaning we keep marrying death

We refuse to listen

We would rather die than to hear the truth
Do right
Live by truth – your laws

No wonder our lands are this way desolate and void of the truth

No wonder they are in disarray because we do not listen. We refuse to learn the truth or hear the truth

We would rather sell you out and kill you just to be accepted by the enemies and their pack of lies

We gave away our rights to accept lies – death and now we wait for a great God to come from the sky

When will they learn that they are gods meaning your children – children of you

No great god is going to come from the sky and save them they know this but yet they believe in the sinful way

We disrespect our skin
We disrespect you
We disrespect our hair
Our spirituality for what a place in hell with sin and death. Come on now God we do not know how this universe came about but yet everyone say they have a right

Have a right to what God?

We don't even know our history but we say we have history

We can't trace our lineage back to the beginning but yet we say we have lineage – heritage

Please we are all bogus.
Liars living as the dead

MICHELLE

God what message are we sending future generations?

God if we cannot respect you how can we respect each other?

Tell me something God can a good parent teach their children wrong?

Come on tell me because today I am upset at you

A good parent cannot give into their child all the time so why are you giving into humanity?

I know I know we are not all good and we did make a choice but God couldn't you do something? God I don't know what I need and want you to do on this day. I'm just tired of the disrespect of you meaning humanity disrespecting you.

God we treat you like shit but yet run to you for everything

We use you for everything including life and never one day do we ever think of you – how you feel

We ride off your coat tail and destroy everything in our wake then turn around and blame you.

God when does it end?

Like the scope of your knowledge is beyond me but humanity have no respect when it comes to you

All we do is claim and believe but yet everything we do is false – wrong

We pick and choose who lives and who dies hence no one values life

Who are we to pick and choose when none of us can create life we can only kill it – destroy it

God today what is the point because I truly don't know why you even bother with all of humanity including me anyway.

MICHELLE

A LITTLE TALK WITH GOD

All I can do is hope and pray
Have faith and trust that God will see me through

The pangs of hell is here
Death draws near but I know God will see me through

For many the truth of God means nothing

Everyone reads but all have and has forgotten Proverbs – the story – and tales of vanity

All man can see is a new testament. Books based on lies because the stories and tales are just stories – fictitious

No one wants to hear the truth that no one can change God's laws not even his children – messengers

God's law is his law and it is he alone that can give exception to it if he so chooses

King Solomon lived a life of prostitution so he told us about it this according to their doctrine – the Christian and Catholic book of lies

Humanity knows not the truth therefore they are not capable of the truth. They cannot tell the truth all they can tell is lies – spread lies

Many tales have been told throughout the ages but yet humanity – man cannot figure it out – life. We know death so we live for death and it is this death that kills us because no one wants to break away from death everyone wants to die

MICHELLE

A LITTLE TALK WITH GOD

I am free God but free how?

There are many sins hence we live to die and I will preach and teach this until my time comes – I die

There is life
There is death

There is hope
There is faith

Life moves on
Life for evil ends – it becomes none – no more

In life there is truth
In death there is only lies – deceit - death

It is a shame that humanity cannot figure out the truth hence we die – live to die

Life cannot lie it can only teach you and tell you the truth

Life is knowledge it cannot be extinct or become extinct.

Life grows and cannot wither but death becomes extinct – will always be no more.

MICHELLE

God why does evil always seek to kill?

Why can't man change their dirty ways?

Why do we teach wrong?
Put you to shame

Why do we believe lies and deny the truth?

God why can't we take responsibility for our own actions?

Why do we have to sin each and every day?

God death knows the truth but yet death lies – deceive. No death cannot change but in reality death can change. It can change its course and decide he too wants to live and follow you – live for life and not death

God beyond the threshold of time everything is different because death cannot change but if given a choice to do you not think death would chose to live? So God why alienate death – make death die?

God Eve made her choice but God how did death make his choice? No God for real we know the choice that humans made and yes death gets in through the back door but God before humanity took shape – form how did death truly come about?

I know the Ying and Yang
Blue and White
Black and White
Positive and Negative but beyond time the threshold of time how did evil truly come about?

I know I've blamed you but something is missing. I am missing something when it comes to the birth of evil – death.
God I know sin – evil – death seeks to destroy life and the two can never co-exist in peace together but the puzzle is not complete. It's incomplete because I am missing parts of the puzzle.

Yes God I too do not know how you came about and that is the greatest mystery of them all.

All is energy yes but the true origins humanity – man including me truly do not know.

MICHELLE

A LITTLE TALK WITH GOD

God be with me today. Solve the issues and problems that plague me

God you hardly talk. No you rarely speak.

You comfort me but yet you are closed mouth when it comes to me

I am the talkative one. I write and talk to you but yet you rarely speak – speak to me

God are you hiding from me?

Yes I know the answers to many things but it would be nice if you did speak once in a while

Yes I know you let songs speak to me for you but Lovey come on now how about you?

You have a voice and I know our tongue is not your tongue – meaning the language you speak is far more superior to ours

God I know your written language but God what language do you really and truly speak?

I know English is not your language nor is it Arabic or Urdu so truly tell me – speak to me in your language – your true tongue.

MICHELLE

No Lovey I don't want or need any secrets between us.

What tongue – language do you truly speak?

Do not shut me out because this is privileged information and yes I am intruding a little bit on your privacy

God no one have or has ever spoken your language before and I want and need to be the first

Lovey I know you communicate with us in the language that we know but I truly want to know your language

I need to speak it and yes write it so that I can communicate with you fully – truthfully

God wouldn't it be nice if we could be on the same communication level – the same page?

Wouldn't it be nice if there were no barriers between us? No barriers hindering us

Lovey all would be different because now we could fully talk to each other and know what each other was truly talking about.

MICHELLE

A LITTLE TALK WITH GOD

Where is my strength today God as my heart fails me

My faith and strength is weak as I feel like giving up because I have done what you asked me to do

My road is wavy
I cannot seem to find the right path. Maybe one day you will allow me to find the right road – the right and true road – path that you need me to be on

It seems my journey I am to go alone but God in all that I do I've asked you to send me the right and true someone to be with me from the get go.

God I know you are with me but sometimes my yearnings get the better of me. I can only come to you and hope. Hope that one day you will truly bless me with the right someone

Maybe it's not meant to be who knows you are the only one that can make it happen – bring me true happiness and although I wish you were human at times I know you cannot be.

You cannot change you to please me. I also know you cannot reside in any place that is dirty – filthy.

Ah well that's life I guess when you are me.

MICHELLE

A LITTLE TALK WITH GOD

God why does my spirit have to be so intimidating?

God couldn't it be friendly – outgoing?

My spirit repels people
It's very anti-social

Why did you have to make me this way?

God I am worse than an introvert
I am boring
I am so not fun but dull – repelling

God who needs this dead and mundane spirit?

I need a spirit that is full of life
Appealing

God please help me to change this boring and mundane spirit

Help me to make it lively – appealing to others
Fun
Fun loving
Good – pure

God take intimidation from my spirit
Help it grow in a positive and good way

MICHELLE

A LITTLE TALK WITH GOD

God why is it that evil empires are still standing? They still have a place on earth to continue on with their wickedness

God why is it that evil and wicked people still dominate, control and destroy the land?

God why can't we find a use for autumns leaves and summers grass to make paper and save our trees?

God why do evil companies continue to design weapons lethal weapons and lethal diseases to kill man – each other?

God why do your people continue to live amongst the wicked – the Pagan and Babylonian dead?

God why is evil so prevalent and hard to get rid of?

Lovey you know how I feel living amongst evil or even beside them

God I don't even want Pagans, Babylonians and wicked people coming near you. No God I truly don't want to see them in your abode because they're wicked and the sight of sin and evil is an abomination unto me. No come on now. Why should I hide my conscience when it comes to sinful and wicked people?

Yes I know God I was once sinful but God I've since learned about the goodness and truth of you.

God I cannot deny the good in you. Now if only you would let me reside on Strawberry Hill, the foothills of your true mountain and let me forever eat, sleep and drink, find true peace and love even with the right someone on your beautiful hill.

Ah how blessed I would be.

A LITTLE TALK WITH GOD

God I need to go to Strawberry Hill.
I yearn there.

My spirit is going to go insane if I do not go there so please open positive and good doors for me to get there real soon.

As for the wicked – evil and wicked companies that design lethal weapons and diseases to kill others – humanity turn their evils back on them infinitely, meaning God return evil back to sender. Life is precious and infinitely beautiful and I infinitely truly love life and no one has the right to destroy it.

God what is there not to truly love when it comes to life? Look at the greenness of your trees, the crispness of the air we breathe, nature – You.

God who are we to destroy at will without caring of the consequences?

Who are we to destroy what you have truly given us?

God these companies are wrong but yet you permit them to exist meaning continue to do evil and destroy humanity – your beautiful kingdom.

Michelle

God there is so much that I do not know.
So much that I need to say but can't because these so much I do not know.

Life is different now because I am stuck in a rut that it seems I can't get out of. But I refuse to let that hold me back and no matter the disappointments I know you are there with me – protecting me.

God I can't let evil get me down I have to press on – move on. Evil must hold back but life must move on – carry on despite the wickedness man and woman do to you.

The global system is run by evil men and woman and I infinitely don't want or need to have anything to do with them.

God you are true and honest and it is you that I need in my life to guide me on the right track – the right way.

God what good am I if I am unjust and unclean?

I've been with nasty mean

I've been with nasty people and all I am left with is shame so why should I walk in the valley of the shadow of death anymore?

Why should I work with evil?

God I can't deal with evil hence I come to you.

You've shown me the mountain but yet I cannot get there. I cannot get to the right one you need me to be on because every way I turn there are obstacles in my way.

God when do these obstacles truly stop so that I can be free?

When does my spiritual bondage stop because spiritual wickedness seeks my death – seek to destroy me and keep me from doing your good and true work?

God evil is so strong now that I want to leave. I need to move out of evils domain because what evil is doing to me is not right.

Why do you allow evil access to me God?

Why do you allow evil to seek my hurt – seek to take my life?

God is my life not precious to you?

Is my life not worthy to be saved?

Is my life not important as yours?

Do you hate me that much to want to see evil totally destroy and devour me?

God I need to ask. You are my life and I am truly depending on you to let evil truly flee from me as well as from around me.

Michelle

A LITTLE TALK WITH GOD

Ah God what is it that we must live this way?

What is it that the good and weak must suffer at the hands of the wicked?

God they give us their infectious diseases to dirty us like them. Infectious diseases created by men to control and ruin nations – people

They give us their infectious diseases to kill us - cause us pain – sorrow

Everything that evil do they do it to destroy and kill. You see this but refuse to lend a helping hand.

I've turned to you but my body – health fails me not because of me but because of wicked, vile and disgusting men. Men that do not care what they do or give you as long as their perverse needs are met.

Men that don't care who they kill with their nastiness of corruption – sexually transmitted diseases – infections

There is nothing pretty about diseases God because diseases are ugly like sin – and infinite sin – murder.

No God evil know the sins of man hence evil continue to infect the land with its corruption of sin – shit. Evil cut your life off and cause you shame and disgrace. They lie and say this race is the cause of this or that disease when they are the ones to create them in laboratories and bring it to other lands. Then they turn around and lie by saying it is these people that are the causes of these disease so that other nations can hate them. Tell me God what part of this is life – good.

What part of this is just and right? So how can humanity say they are going to see you and be with you when shit like this is going on – happening?

No one has a right to destroy anyone because man cannot create life from the air and water on his or her own come on now.

Many of us do not practice promiscuity and we teach our children the same – not to have more than one sexual partner. We try to teach them good values and not to run around but respect themselves and others.

God as wives and husbands, boyfriend and girlfriend, girlfriend and boyfriend we trust our mates not to cheat but respect the home. But this cannot be done because the ones you trust are the ones to disrespect you and disrespect your home. They are the ones to disrespect your sanctuary – body, marital haven – paradise. They are the ones to bring their nastiness and germs home to you so tell me something God when we do this how can we respect you?

How can we respect anyone?

We know having sexual intercourse here there and everywhere is a sin – a grave sin. I learnt this from you God. I learnt having sex with multiple partners is disrespectful to you hence many of us hold our heads down in shame and disgrace.

God why?

I know the beginning of humanity and because we let sin in – accepted sin we must go through this because this is sins way but I don't want or need sins way anymore God. I need your good and clean way.

A LITTLE TALK WITH GOD

It's not fair God for people to maliciously take your life.

What have I done sin for sin to cause my life such pain?

When did true love – truth become a sin God?

Many things humanity do not know and it's not fair – it's unjust. People cannot continue to create diseases to kill each other come on now God. Right is right and wrong is infinitely wrong and you cannot continue to sit on the sidelines and let sin dominate and control us anymore.

I've pleaded with you, begged you and cried to you to ease my pain and the pain of my people – your children but as always you continue to ignore me, pretend like you cannot hear me.

God when will true and justice come?

When will my life be at peace – true peace?

When will I have truth – true truth?

God every day I need you. I can't do this alone anymore man. I can't, I can't, I can't because it's frustrating not having you speak or show me honestly and truthfully what to do.

Yes you are there but what good are you to me silent?

I cannot choose my path of GOOD without you because I don't want or need to fail you and this is why I tell you to make and choose all the right, good, honest and just decisions for me. I need you to make and choose the right, honest, true and good pathways for me.

I am giving you the right to make all the good and honest, true and yes clean decisions for me but you refuse me. I do not comprehend this – the scope of this because I thought you needed roots – good people that are there for you through thick and thin, the good and the bad. God tell me how can your people do better – our people and children do better if you refuse to speak – teach us properly what to do? It's not you can lead a horse to water but you cannot force them to drink it situation. I'm not forcing you nor are you forcing us. If we are truthfully accepting you and doing good then you have to be there for us and speak to us or we will leave. No you cannot say you were not truthful. We were truthful but you kept silent and left us to accept untrue – false doctrines and people – evil.

God I need you to speak to me clearly each and every day so that I can hear you and feel loved – truly loved – needed.

Yes I came from ancestral disobedience but why hold that against me? Why deny me you? Yes I've caused you shame but what about you? Do you not cause me to cry? I can't change my past but I can change my future, me, today – my today. All it takes is forgiveness on your part but that you can't even do because we've hurt you.

We've become dirty with our own sins now we are like pigs in sties wallowing in our own dung–shit – filth of destruction.

All it takes is forgiveness on your part but that you can't even do because we've hurt you and caused you shame and disgrace. We cannot learn because we don't want to learn. We let others tell us nonsense when it comes to you.

I've hurt you bit I am truly sorry for my wrongs and the pain and pains I have cause you. Many things I truly did not know.

God I am trying but I'm failing and I am tired of failing – tired of disappointing you and me.

God why can't you be my true voice?

Speak the truth for me and open the right doors for me.

God if the roads I travel do not suit you then truly tell me – let me know. Truly tell me and be honest with me and give me the right direction to go in so that I can help you and yes help me.

God I can't speak to you anymore because I am hurting and the truth should infinitely not hurt.

Michelle

God we talk about life and death, secret societies – a new world order but God evil has his new world order already. Just look at the lawlessness of society – earth – the new Sodom and Gomorrah.

The new world order is Sodom and Gomorrah – the new lifestyles of men and women on earth.

God nothing has changed hence humanity does not think on a spiritual level. They only think on a physical level – political levels of deception and greed – economic, environmental and genetic manipulation - slaughter.

They only see the flesh but like I said the flesh dies but the spirit moves on to life or death depending on the life you live on earth.

God evil has us in the confines of his wickedness and no matter how we sell our souls evil is still there will always be there because we made it so.

Evil hides and hinders and is secretive in its dealings because those who join the racks of secret societies must offer up sacrifices unto the God of death. They must drink blood and shed blood. They must kill and deceive. Did not Cain show us this God when he took the life – murdered his brother out of jealous - greed? Did Abraham not do the same when he offered up animal sacrifices, human sacrifices (his son) and burnt offerings to the god of Death?

God does humanity not know that animal sacrifices was just a shield – a ploy but human sacrifices is what evil – sin requires because to shed human life is a slap in the face to you – a blatant disrespect in the eyes of you – to you. When evil take a human life evil is showing you they can disrespect you at will and that he evil does not respect you or the life you give.

But with all this humanity will not learn they will continue to kill at will because humanity respects not life they respect death.

God many people who are in bed with evil offer up their mothers as sacrifices.

Many offer up their children to evil – the god of death hence many children die in freak accidents – by the rivers of Babylon. By the rivers of Babylon they offer their children to the gods of death because none can pay back death what he sin has offered them.

Many forgot about the imprints of sin – yes the fine prints.

Many forgot that none can repay sin for anything.

Yes they want a place in the devils kingdom but how many has lost their souls on the way to the devil's land – Mainland of Pain – Hell.

Many do not know that their pain is greatly multiplied and in hell none can be greater than the other because they're all slaves to sin – will be slaves to sin.

There's no place for this person or that person.

There's no special place for this person if they've brought others into the fold of sin – Satan.

Satan can never be loyal to none because true sin is not male but female because she is the one to give birth to sin from her womb and it is she that has to receive sinful and deceitful life in the time of death – physical death – the death of flesh.

God death will walk in hell over and over again and those in hell will not die because sin hath time to devour them in hell for a time. They evil and wicked people and evil spirits will burn meaning the spirit will burn over and over again and they will feel it eternally because we made it so – humanity made it so in the living – on earth.

All have forgotten that hell is not pretty and the money they kill for in the physical they cannot take with them to hell – the spiritual world.

All that fame – the game of greed will unfold because billions right now have made hell their home.

Many parade about glorifying the devil – the dead but fail to realize that hell will be their home – final resting place.

God many think hell is pretty but tell me God how can spiritual fire – the burning of the soul/ spirit be pretty?

God we feel pain on earth but hells pain is infinitely different – hotter. God my people have gone astray because we've sold our souls to the highest bidder – greed.

No one read the fine print that says if you accept death hell will be our home in the afterlife. Hell will be your home when the flesh dies in the physical.

God Satan hath no secret societies because humanity knows about them hence they are not secret anymore.

Ever since the day Eve accepted evil sin was born hence sin became like man – a living soul. Sin gain access to life through Eve hence sin beats you violently worse than a slave each and every day for you to convert and conform to sin. And if you don't conform and convert to sin they kill you, set you up and mark you for death, they dominate and control you financially, religiously and medically. They rape and rob you of your soul for you to conform to them because this is their way of control – dominion over the masses – humanity yes society – the land.

Evil must beat good into submission if good let evil in but if good does not let evil in, evil cannot control nor can evil beat you into submission.

Evil must get permission to come in. If evil does not get permission evil cannot come into your life or home. Evil cannot go against the Ying and Yang – the laws of God – this universe. Yes the laws of creation. The laws of creation – Life and Death is absolute so if evil went against it by not getting permission from you all evil everywhere will automatically die.

Yes this is why evil is the master of the judicial system hence we have Judges on earth and in your book of sin – your book of lies that is called the holy bible.

No one can defeat evil in his judicial system because he wrote the book of judges – yes the book of condemnation – sin.

God humanity does not know that they must infinitely concern themselves with spiritual evil because this evil is more deadly than physical evil.

God I know and you know it is the spirit that feels pain so if we know this why live for sin?

Why join secret societies of sin?

God many can cast spells of evil because the spell of Leviathan is real. Meaning evil spells are real and it's not many that can lift – break these evil spells from people. Evil cannot break the spells of evil only good people can.

God I have to call on you this morning because spiritual death and evil is real.

Spiritual evil is the death of man because many of us are going to die. Many of us have become victims of sin hence many of my people belong to secret societies of sin – evil.

God if we know that evil enslaves and slavery will be your part and parcel in hell why go there – want to go there?

Why sell your soul?

God there is no givesy backsy when it comes to sin and evil so why sell your soul for unleven – unholy bread?

Evil does not deal in the physical par say evil deals in the spiritual because the sins evil have you doing in the physical he cannot have you do in the spiritual. You are evils slave and whatever he requires you to do in the physical you must do it because he knows when you do evil deeds in the physical you must die in the spiritual.

All that evil do and does must come from the spiritual realm hence evil invokes the dead, say they do not want to upset the spirits – gods of the dead. This evil knows is a lie because the dead cannot get upset at the living just like that hence many customs and societies use the dead in their rituals – evil voodoo practices.

No dead can hurt the living just like that. Not even Satan is capable of this because in truth he Satan does not deal in the dead he deals in pure and utter evil – sin. He knows the negative pull of the north hence the north will forever be in conflict with the south. Yes this is where the Blue and White Nile comes in. Dark Blue not light blue represent the north where white represent the south.

Evil and wicked people command their wicked dead but evil can never command the good people that have died and journeyed on. These people cannot be touched by evil because these good people hath nothing to do with death or evil hence they journey on in life and death stays behind – die.

Evil spirits walk on earth with the living and when evil spirits come they come to kill with a head blow. The head blow is the final attempt for wicked and evil spirits to kill you hence the head is significant in the physical and spiritual realm.

Know this is how wicked evil spirits are. They must hit you in the head and from you get this hit by evil your life in the physical is gone because evil killed you – took your life.

God this is a wicked blow – death hence we need to be protected from spiritual evil.

God no matter how much we join secret societies and kill nothing can save you from this spiritual judgment. The judges are there and everything is recorded in writing and they cannot disobey the laws of creation – the laws of life and death. They cannot do it God you and I know this. You and I know what belongs to death must be given to death and no one can interfere with this come judgment day – the day that sin and all evil must give an account for the evils that they do. Once this is done punishment must be delivered and that punishment is death because evil and his people knew infinitely what they were doing was wrong.

God what say man now because all they worship and say is a lie.

Evil has made the triangle evil – made it out to be the trinity. They worship the trinity and say you God is three in one but yet do not know that the upward triangle donate life – the going up of life. No one and no god can be three in one this is mathematically impossible.

From dust earth we came and unto greater life we must go for the flesh but in truth from water we came and unto water we must go. This spiritual water is what evil fairs because this water is the water of truth – God.

Once this water touches evil they must tell the truth they cannot lie.

True life must go back to the source of life but evil life must go back to death – they must go unto spiritual fire to burn.

Good spirits will always guide the good but evil spirits kill – try to kill good life.

No God no one knows the beauty of the triangle hence man – humanity cannot perceive life – truth. Man will always seek to marry – interlock evil with life but man cannot accomplish this because the triangle is strong than man and his evil thoughts.

The triangle is pure hence evil will forever try to destroy – kill the goat and ram and drink its blood saying it is a sacrifice unto the gods – the gods of evil – death.

I know that man cannot destroy the goat nor interlock it with the fish of death. The goat stands supreme because the goat will forever stand at the top of the mountain looking down on man. The goat is the only one that can get atop the mountain hence the goat knows the mountain – holds the mountain supreme.

Yes God evil has his snake according to man and yes as to what I see the snake knows time and is in time but life has his lioness – the she goat – the one to devour evil and eradicate it (evil) from all the plains of the earth and all the plains of the spiritual world – universe.

Michelle

God when are we going to learn that death is not the answer to our problems – sins?

God can a clean man or woman sin? So why do we accept filth – dirt and think it is good?

God right now I am tired of writing about sin and death. I need to write about life – the goodness and truth of life.

God sin has nothing to offer me apart from death so why do I have to write about death so much?

I know I have to teach people the truth so that humanity can learn and make the good choice to live but God why can't I show the truth of your world – abode.

God I've seen hell – been there why can't I see your world – abode?

God it's not fair to hide your abode from me and the world. How can we choose when we cannot see paradise – your abode? You make us see and know hell why can't you make us see and know your truth – your place – the true place you call home?

Don't because I only saw the outside of the crystal city I need to see your true kingdom. I need to behold its beauty even if it's only for a second or two.

Come on God I yearn for you but yet I am here stuck in a place I truly don't want or need to be in.

God I need life – true and honest life.

Why should I continue to live amongst the council of the ungodly?

God I need a good piece of land where I can grow organic fruits and food – trees.

I need a good home where we can call home – live in – be in for years and generations to come. God this place must be infinitely pure and no strife, war, anger, jealousy or sin must enter there. God this will be our place to freely roam and live in truth, honesty, respect, true love, peace and harmony.

God I have to start with the physical because your abode I do not truly know because you haven't let me in to see it. Maybe I'm not clean enough but one day God I will behold the true beauty of you and you had better not disappoint me ahoa. No God despite my perception of thee, please do not disappoint me because you infinitely know my mouth. But for real though when are we going to eradicate all facets of sin and evil – death from the planet earth and the universe?

No God I am being like a spoilt child now – a little brat. I want and need all facets of evil to be infinitely gone from earth, the universe and the spiritual world.

God I am tired of living in stink and dirty. I need clean. I need everything to be infinitely clean and in good and perfect order. So God can you please do something about all the evil that surrounds me, my family and the good seeds you have truly given unto me.

God why can't I have your goodness each and every day? No come on now I need you in a good and blessed way in my life so why should I let evil let me lose out on you – having you in my life as well as having the goodness of you in my life? Come on now no. Why should you let evil dominate and take away from my goodness and good times with you. It's not fair God nor is it just and yes I am getting mad because you are mine, whom I chose to be in my life at all times. Yes I am pouting because you're not giving me what I truly need and want.

Michelle

A LITTLE TALK WITH GOD

God I want to wine and pine like a baby and say whaaa, whaaa, whaaa. No for real and yes I am still pouting because earth is under siege – evils rule.

No God I don't want or need sin and evil in my life or on the planet earth with me. Sin is too controlling, destructive and way to evil for me.

God if you truly love me, yes I am going to go there today and say it. Please don't be mad or upset at me or change – make my words become sinful – a sin. Yes I know it's wrong so you know what I won't say it or go there because I know better and because I know better I have to do better. Just please hurry up and return sin and death back to sender. No God sinful people glorify death – their sins so let their sins the sins of sins return to sinful and wicked people. Why should good people continue to suffer at the hands of the wicked? Come on now God. We need true and honest justice upon earth come on now.

No God I need our earthly space which is all the earth to live in. I need our earthly space to live in true peace and harmony.

I need to enjoy nature with you God.

I infinitely need to enjoy the rivers and springs – brooks

I need to enjoy the beauty of you and sin and evil is taking that from me and I don't like it. It's not fair to you and me nor is it just. It is wrong. Why can't I enjoy you on earth in the true space you have given me? Why should evil and his bands of cohorts take you away from me? What right does evil have to do this? What right does evil have to invade my space and time with you? Why are you God letting this happen? No come on now. Why are you allowing this to happen between me and you?

No, I did not choose filth I chose clean and evil has no right to make my life and my surroundings dirty – unclean. Right is right and fair is fair come on now God. I do not go around and make trouble for sin. I do not invade sins privacy so why are you allowing sin and his people to invade our privacy – space?

To be honest God this is not true love but hatred on your part. No I will not do it to you. I refuse to cause you pain and no one has a right to come into my space – my universe with their nonsense. If evil needs a domain for his people let evil create one and get the hell off our planet. Come on now. No I am bent God because evil has no right to do what he and his people are doing? They are not wanted on this planet God so why are you keeping them here? No you are wrong in keeping evil on this planet? If evil people don't want you in their lives they must infinitely leave and let their degenerate scum bag gods create a planet and universe for them. Fuck them and to hell with them. Evil did not create this planet so evil can get the hell off and take his pieces of crap and scraps with him. Come on now. Who the hell are they to take away and dirty our space come on now? Yes God I am bent because I want and need you infinitely in my life in a good and blessed way and evil is deterring me from having my time – true and good time with you. This is not fair to me and yes I am rebelling. Truly help me to send all evil not matter physical or spiritual infinitely packing. Hell was created for evil and his people God so let evil and his people infinitely go there to live and leave the earth and your universe alone. No God I need and want all evil evicted plain and straight. No givesy backsy I need all facets of evil eradicated yes infinitely gone from our space – this earth and beyond. Truly look into it God and tell me if I am wrong. Why can't I have you when I need you?

Why can't I say Lovey where are you?

And you say right beside you and you take my hand.

No I want and need to go to the river with you and I can't even have that.

I want and need you to marry me with the right someone some day and I can't even have that.

I want and need to play football with you and score touchdowns on you then spike the ball and dance in the end zone and you say you know I let you win right and I would say right Lovey, yea right. Then we would burst out laughing because we had fun and I can't even have that.

I want and need to grow old with you in a good way. Not that you are old or you grow old but you know what I mean. I need to be eternal with you and I can't even have this because of sin.

I can't have anything good with you because of sin and I'm to be happy and forgive sin. No. I refuse to forgive sin because all sin does is hinder, hinder, hinder and because of this I refuse to forgive sin.

No sin should not take you from me or hinder me from getting to you this is simply wrong and I don't care what you say I will infinitely never forgive sin for this because if sin wanted to he would have changed so no forgiveness and living with sin as well as living amongst sins people is not an option. Why should the good people of this earth be the ones to keep sin going and sin destroy and kill us come on now God where is your fairness – just justice – true and honest ways?

Yes I am questioning your integrity because life should infinitely never be this way. No one absolutely no one should hinder me from getting to you not even you and you don't hinder. No I love you too much to have you fleeing from me because of sin. Look at how many trillions of light years you are away from me. God come on now do you truly know the distance? Do you know how far I have to travel and still can't get to you because you are so far ahead in time over time?

I don't need this distance between us so you had better hurry up and return sin to sender infinitely. No I'm not being rude just demanding when it comes to my time and space with you because I refuse infinitely refuse to give you up or give up on you.

Lovey you are life so why should I give you up for naught – death. Death is ugly void of all light – truth and I'm to give up on you. Not in this lifetime or any lifetime for that matter come on now. Death can't give me life – make me live. Death can't make me see you in your truest form so why would I give you up for a god that love to feast and drink blood. Do you know how raw and disgusting blood is but yet we feast in it come on now. Yuk.

What kind of life is that people drinking blood of humans and animals just to get to hell, be in hell all because someone say they must die to see god but know not that the god they die to see is death then they die. Well they cry before they die hence according to them their deceitful and lying demon of a god cried blood or like a river when he saw his death – faith in hell. Yes your book of sin reworded the truth but yet this is what we want for ourselves. God come on now. Yes I have sinned but I know the truth now but tell me no I am not going to go there because you did not give up on me but I am telling you, this time around now that you have given humanity the truth if they refuse you like I've told you before infinitely walk away from man – humanity because they would have rejected you yet again. Give them the hell that they want because they chose hell over you so walk away. Don't look back or have any regrets because humanity does not care about you. They truly care about death hence they sin for death and live for death. Come on now. Learn. Just as how we want you to learn the hard way and when you help us we become so ungrateful that we turn from you and can't say God truly thank you. This is your praise. The true thanks that you get from someone saying God I truly thank you for helping me get over my troubles – problems. No God truly walk away now. Man have kicked you off this planet and have allowed sin to ravish and destroy it now we cry and say why God? Please humanity can royally kiss my MF ass because we are a disgrace and a burden to you. We can't even love you right but you are to bail us out of our messes. God tell me something if you constantly bail ungrateful people out of our messes how will we truly learn? Come on now. Will we not be doing the same thing over and over again?

Yes right

Well there you go this is what we are doing to you. Learn now and smarten up. You cannot give evil a home to kill because this planet was not created by sin or evil.

You cannot continue to let wicked and evil people violate you because we do not know how you came about? We do not know your true origins.

You cannot let wicked and evil kingdoms rise up and dominate your true children because this is infinitely not right or just when it comes to them – your children. We need a good, safe and clean environment to live in and we cannot have this because of sin. This is unjust and cruel on your part.

Your laws did not include the laws of sin because good cannot sin good can only be good. Yes we allowed sin in but for those that refuse and reject sin you cannot continue to let sin surround and dominate them come on now.

Nowhere in the laws of creation does it say man must dominate man, man must subdue the land, control the land. Infinitely nowhere does it state this in your laws but yet man dominate. In the laws and books of sin you are to dominate, subdue, hate and kill because this is written as law in the book of sin. Every sinful human must control and dominate. This is sins way God not yours but yet your remnants – your children live amongst this sinful act – way.

Like I've said God and will ask you again if the head is dirty how can the body be clean? Meaning if we live amongst dirt and filth – sinful and wicked people how can we be clean? How can we see you and be with you?

Because I need and want to see you God – be with you I do not need nor do I want and desire to live and commune amongst sin. This is not fair or right to you and me hence I bother you and bug you about this. I have rights my God given rights to life and death has no right to pollute my space the space you have given me. This is infinitely wrong and like I said it is time you truly do something about this. I am giving you time and if within that 19 years you do not truly do something to help clean up this earth I will hold you accountable for sin infinitely. I cannot charge you for the will of man because man has and have their own will. I also have my own will but my will – true will is you and I infinitely need a true, good, peaceful and honest place with you. I will not speak for man I can only speak for me and this is what I am doing today – speaking for me and yes you. All I do I do in truth for you and if you want to reject me so be it but you have my records as well as this book so you cannot say that I was not faithful and true to you because I am.

No God, man cannot learn and you are not learning. Look at me and how people are to me. I do not commune with them. I cut them off because of what they say to me. I don't like people looking down on me or anyone and I infinitely do not like anyone looking down on you or trampling you down. You have to know when to walk away and yes this is why I am harsh and angry at you sometimes.

God death does not know the true you. Sinful people do not know the true you. Wicked people do not know the true you so why cater to them. Yes everyone deserves a chance like me. You've given me chances and honey I am taking them and clinging on to them but if after this book and my other books man continue to walk the wrong way then do what you need to do in a good way. Secure your true people and let death have his way with the rest. Truly walk away and do not secure deaths people anymore. You have given them (death's people) a chance to redeem themselves and if they refuse to redeem themselves then let it be. Let deaths will be and be done. Truly walk away because now no one can hold you accountable or guilty of sin because you gave humanity a true way out and we rejected you yet again.

God once this is done true will be done, then let true and honest change happen by changing your good people so that they can never – infinitely never sin again. Let this death be the final death of sin and his people. No sin can enter this abode because this abode is true good and filled with good and honest life not sinful life.

God I know you truly love your people and you are for your people so please let the sins of evil and wicked people, let the evils and sins of this wicked system infinitely flee from earth – flee from our domain.

God it is you that I infinitely need and love and not evil so please hurry up and return the blows of sin back to sender – sin. God whether the blows are from wicked and evil people, secret societies, spirits and voodoo people send their blows infinitely back to them. Degree this God so when evil everything come to harm and destroy your good people let the sins and blow fall back on the – the wicked people – wicked spirits – wicked everything.

God you have to truly protect your people in every way everywhere from sin and evil.

No God I infinitely mark all facets of evil's letters in the spiritual and physical return to sender evil infinitely does not live here anymore.

God how can we say we are living for you and participating in everything that is sinful and inhumane.

How can we say we are living for you God and still participating in blood sacrifices – human sacrifices?

When we do these things we are not clean we are dirty and yes we become filthier.

You cannot participate in death and think you are going to get life. Death brings death because we all know the wages of sin is death not life.

God we truly have to do better to secure our future – life.

Michelle

God why is it that humanity cannot learn the truth of life?

God evil has the patent and control to everything but humanity cannot comprehend this.

To keep us in control evil must create diseases to riddle the body so that you go to evil for treatment – a cure but humanity refuse to accept the truth – this truth. Humanity refuse to know that it does not cost sin one penny or even 1 (one) prayer whether clean or good – dirty. It cost you the person – the individual.

God tell me how does it cost sin?

Man create diseases to kill man then say if you want a cure you have to pay me for this cure - medication.

Man design churches – build churches and say if you want God you have to pay me $1/10^{th}$ or 10 percent of your earnings because God say so – meaning it is written in your book – their book of sin and deceit – lies and evil.

Tell me something God can a man or woman anyone pay you for life?

Can a man buy his or her life?

"No"

So why the hell should we pay man collection for sin – their sins – wrongs?

Tell me God can a man or woman buy you?

"No"

So why are we buying you?

Why are we paying tides and offerings – collection to unclean people – churches for you hence buying you?

I know no one can buy you God but we sure as hell can buy sin and evil like I've stated before.

It cost sin nothing but it cost us our souls – lives come on now.

God don't even go there because the wealth that evil and evil secret societies and foundations offer you they want it back and do take it back hence evil does not freely give – it deceives and use you for its own gains – purposes.

Many of those that have reached the top must prostitute and sell themselves like whores to the highest bidder – sin. Evil men and societies use them as bitches – blows for its nasty b—w jobs.

You have to do the will of sin and if sin says go in the air and do me for all humanity – society to see you have to do him or her just to maintain and sustain your life because if you refuse you will go down – be taken down if not killed.

This is the will of sin blood for blood but the blood that sin takes is yours not his.

The money that you get – status that you receive you have to prostitute yourself for it and shit you're not even a trillionaire. You're shit with your dirty millions and if you're lucky and blow the right way you may end up with a couple billions not hundreds of billions or trillions just a mere billion or two. And that's just reserved for the 2 or 3 that really blow the right way.

When you do get those millions you're strung out like a waste chute or caddy hoping to get your next couple millions and when you do get it the drugs come, prostitutes – sorry high end call girls come with the fake ass and fake pussy oh sorry Vagina and Tata's

Everything fake comes including the fake ass entourages that follow you around like crack heads ready for his or her next blow.

Then you have people telling you this one is gay he had to sell his ass to be a part of the gay and lesbian club.

Oh please gaydom has been around from the beginning of time. There's nothing wrong with being gay it's the people that's associated with gaydom is the problem.

They take gaydom to a different level – they are the one to make being gay sinful – hence they become a sin.

Respect who you are. If you're gay you are gay – be gay. Who the hell cares not everyone is going to like you – love you. People find fault of everything in this world – society so Mr. Gay Man – Woman shut the hell up and respect you. Do you and stop hindering people because you're the ones making it bad for yourself. Stop being fucking hypocrites and get the fuck off the true gay wagon if you can't represent and respect yourself in a true and honest way. Shit now man.

Like I said get off the wagon of gaydom because the true and righteous gays can't stand your fake bougy asses anymore. Yes I am speaking for the true gays because they know the goodness and spirituality in them. They know infinitely know that there are gays in the spiritual world. They know that God the True and Living God do not condemn them because the love – true love they have for their partner is true and honest. They don't have to live a lie because they are true – true love.

They the true gays do not whore around like many of the fake gays looking for a new trick. They respect themselves so on the behalf of them the true gays fake gays step the hell off if you cannot truly represent them – yourself in a good, clean and honest way. You have to be true and honest to you.

I am tired of you fakes asses trying to prove a point. There is no point or points to prove, do you. No one has the right to discriminate against you. Sin discriminates not God and if God truly loves you why do you think otherwise?

Why do you let others deprive you of the True and Living God? This is wrong and unfair so do the good that you can do and truly do you in an honest and good way. No one can tell you that you are going to go to hell and burn because those that preach this message is wrong and they are not of God but of Satan – evil.

How can good teach wrong? Come on now. Do your homework. When has life ever killed? When has God ever killed? Come on now.

Remember by their works you shall know them so if a person advocates evil then they are evil not good. Know this and live by this – the truth.

I will not bash gaydom but I sure as hell will bash transgenders because whether you like it or not they the transgenders are the true Sodomites and they are the ones that are unholy – an abomination of sin in the sight of God. And no I will infinitely never ever advocate violence against them because this is simply wrong – eternally sick and sinful and truly not of God.

No one must alter appearance of self via medical procedures and say we are male when we are female. No one must alter appearance of self via medical procedures and say we are female when we are male. We were born male and female. This is wrong and an abomination of sin because what you the individual is saying to God – what you are telling God is that he God made you wrong and he

God is wrong in making you come into this world male and female.

The altering of self hath nothing to do with life but vanity.

The altering of self hath nothing to do with life but has everything to do with sin – evil.

Altering yourself is the true way of sin because whether you know it or not none of us can change our death certificate once it has been issued in the spiritual realm.

Once it has been issued it has been issue – it becomes a decree - law and whether it takes 20 years for you to die you will die. And to be honest with gays and lesbians I would separate myself truly separate from all transgenders because they the transgenders have made Sodom and Gomorrah become real and for this any land that give this act of abomination decree – a home must suffer – die. Your book of sin tells you this so why go against it for filthy and nasty men and woman that hath no respect of person – self and no respect for God. Sodom and Gomorrah must be destroyed with fire and brimstone hence many of your lands are suffering – burning because we've given sin rights – laws to protect them. Once you do this you are telling God its okay, you accept sin and any punishment to do with this act, you accept on the behalf of sin – evil.

Yes you can bash me for this but to be honest I don't care because right is right and wrong is wrong. You cannot pick up filth and say God is going to forgive you for this. You cannot condemn your homeland – land for the nastiness and the abominations of man sins true people.

Yes you can argue your case and say these people are true to themselves this is what they desire and are truthful to it and I will tell you you are a damned liar and murderer because they are killing life. They are not truthful to life or to their life because they are altering self and saying they are male when they are female and male. This is wrong and this is true sin. No one can alter life they can only kill it – kill you and kill all that is around them.

Man has become so sinful and disgusting that we do all the nastiness of sin and think there is forgiveness for some of our sins when there is none.

Any man or woman that has had a sex change via medical procedures or any altering plants or drugs commit sin in the worst kind of way because they are deceiving you like Satan and they are causing you to commit a grave and abominable act – sin and for this you as a person laying with these people will lose your soul because you committed a grave act. It does not matter whether you know or not that the person has had a sex change you will die because you did lay with that person. There is no and ifs or buts about this. This sin is absolute and there is no forgiveness for this because you are saying God is wrong and God is never wrong. God cannot be wrong. We as humans do wrong and commit wrong not God.

Yes we can tell God that he is wrong but prove God wrong. You cannot do it and don't even say he created evil because God did not give birth to evil man did.

Everything in life must have a balance. A negative and a positive but with true live there is not negative only positive and yes this is hard to explain because I cannot fully comprehend this at least not yet anyway. So truly think. I can tell you but I cannot make you. I can give you the truth but you have to need and want the truth. I cannot force anything on anyone because if I did I would be taking life away from God and you and this is simply wrong – sinful and truly sick.

Michelle

A blessed good morning to you God

Did you have a good rest?

I did so truly thank you

God this good morning I come to thee for help. My sons are looking for jobs and I am asking you to please open good and positive doors for them to have a good and rewarding job in a good company. They need the work – jobs.

God truly bless them this morning in a good way so that the jobs they need come to them in a positive and good way.

God they need the help – please truly and honestly help them.

Thank you kindly

Michelle

God today is a good and blessed day let it stay this way for me and my family – blessed and good.

Let no enemies come to my door

Let no foul sent of death linger near

Let the joy and true peace – delight of happiness infinitely stay near so that I can be at true peace forevermore.

Michelle

God in all that you do please hear me and infinitely be with me in a good and blessed way

God you see and know the health issues across the globe with humanity. This morning God I am asking you to give true, right and good cures for all these diseases that man has made

God it's not right nor is it just for man to create – design and make – implement diseases to kill the human body – race. It's not right nor is it just for man to kill and eradicate – wipe out other nations

God the unjust nature of humanity – sin is not right and you cannot continue to let evil men and women kill without a cause. Even if they had a cause they should not kill

God I'm feeling it because I know the nastiness of man. I see it each and every day because I know it. I read about it. God from you know it you see it and yes this is hard to explain because this knowledge is on a different level.

We do evil things to man – spread hate and think this is good. This is not good hence humanity dies.

Michelle

A LITTLE TALK WITH GOD

God I know that you are trillions of miles away but you are still near to me but on this good and beautiful day I ask you to complete me in a good and perfect way.

God you infinitely complete me and I need it to infinitely stay this way so on this day let me infinitely complete you in a good and precious – perfect way; a true and good way. Yes all must be good and pure – honest and true.

Michelle

God do not be ashamed of me because my body fails me

Do not turn from me because I need you to truly complete me in a good and perfect way

I need you to be my good everything

I need you to be there for me when I laugh and cry – feel pain

God I infinitely need all the goodness and blessings of you in my life as well as around me all the time – infinitely

So on this day infinitely complete me in your good and wholesome way

Michelle

God once you've completed me in a good way complete my children and family and the seeds you have given me in a good and wholesome way as well.

God can you truly and honestly do this for me. Also bless the lands that are truly dear to me.

Scotland, Russia, France, Spain, Jamaica, the Motherland – Kenya, Swazieland.

God let your truth reign supreme in these lands and connect the dots so that all evil and hatred leave – flee from these lands indefinitely and infinitely.

Michelle

God I am sorry if I did not ask for protection for all of Africa but I cannot and I truly do not know why but all the lands mentioned above truly protect them for me and drive out all evil from these lands especially in my homeland Jamaica.

I do not know why my spirit gravitates to these lands. Please God take wickedness from the hearts of the people and let them prosper in a good and positive way. Even China not because of the Chinese people but because of the goodness of Eva Lam – the goodness she bestowed on my family. God let her act of kindness towards me and my family be a testament of truth and goodness unto you and because of her her goodness to me bless China because one good act of kindness goes a long way with you.

So on this day, bless these lands and truly thank you for the goodness Eva Lam bestowed upon me and my family.

Michelle

Other books by Michelle Jean

MORE TALK

MY COLLECTIVE THE OTHER SIDE OF ME

MY COLLECTIVE THE DARK SIDE OF ME

BEHIND THE SCARS

BLACKMAN REDEMPTION